D1242322

SOURCES IN WESTERN CIVILIZATION

The High Middle Ages
1000–1300

THE HIGH

Sources in Western Civilization

GENERAL EDITOR, *Herbert H. Rowen*

RUTGERS UNIVERSITY

MIDDLE AGES

1000·1300

EDITED BY

Bryce D. Lyon

THE FREE PRESS
A Division of Macmillan Publishing Co., Inc.
New York

Collier Macmillan Publishers
London

The Free Press
A Division of Macmillan Publishing Co., Inc.
866 Third Avenue, New York, N.Y. 10022

Collier Macmillan Canada, Ltd.

Library of Congress Catalog Card Number: 64-21207

printing number
7   8   9   10

ACKNOWLEDGMENTS

The author wishes to thank the following publishers for their kind permission to use the sources reprinted in this book.

Cambridge University Press: G. G. Coulton, *Life in the Middle Ages,* 2nd ed. (Cambridge, 1930), vol. I; G. G. Coulton, *Social Life in Britain from the Conquest to the Reformation* (Cambridge, 1918).

Columbia University Press: J. B. Ross, *The Murder of Charles the Good Count of Flanders by Galbert of Bruges* (New York, 1960); E. H. McNeal, *The Conquest of Constantinople Translated from the Old French of Robert of Clari* (New York, 1936); Ephraim Emerton, *The Correspondence of Pope Gregory VII. Selected Letters from the Registrum* (New York, 1932); C. C. Mierow, *The Two Cities. A Chronicle of Universal History to the Year 1146 A.D. by Otto, Bishop of Freising* (New York, 1928); E. A. Babcock and A. C. Krey, *A History of Deeds Done Beyond the Sea* (New York, 1943), vol. I.

Doubleday and Company, Inc.: A. C. Pegis, *St. Thomas Aquinas. On the Truth of the Catholic Faith* (Image Books, New York, 1955).

E. P. Dutton and Company: Frank Marzials, *Memoirs of the Crusades by Villehardouin and De Joinville* (London, 1908).

Alfred A. Knopf, Inc.: C. K. Scott Moncrieff, *The Letters of Abelard and Heloise* (New York, 1933); Ewart Lewis, *Medieval Political Ideas* (New York, 1954), vol. I.

Methuen and Company: A. G. Ferrers Howell, *The Lives of S. Francis of Assisi by Brother Thomas of Celano* (London, 1908).

Thomas Nelson and Sons Ltd.: C. R. Cheney and W. H. Semple, *Selected Letters of Pope Innocent III Concerning England (1198–1216)* (Edinburgh, 1953); H. E. Butler, *The Chronicle of Jocelin of Brakelond Concerning the Acts of Samson Abbot of the Monastery of St. Edmund* (Edinburgh, 1949).

Oxford University Press: Henry Bettenson, *Documents of the Christian Church* (London, 1950); D. C. Douglas and G. W. Greenaway, *English Historical Documents, 1042–1189* (New York, 1953).

Princeton University Press: A. C. Krey, *The First Crusade. The Accounts of Eye-Witnesses and Participants* (Princeton, 1921); Erwin Panofsky, *Abbot Suger on the Abbey Church of St.-Denis and Its Treasures* (Princeton, 1946).

George Routledge and Sons Ltd.: C. C. Swinton Bland, *The Autobiography of Guibert Abbot of Nogent-sous-Coucy* (London, 1925).

CONTENTS

SOURCES IN WESTERN CIVILIZATION

The High Middle Ages
1000–1300

INTRODUCTION

I. THE HIGH MIDDLE AGES

TO break the flow of history and to block it off into compartments or periods has traditionally been a device of the historian to assist in the narration and organization of his account. Such a device, if it does not truly reflect the contours of history, perverts our understanding of the historical process, but it can, if intelligently employed, effectively underline historical trends and further the difficult process of establishing meaningful bonds between human accomplishment and chronology. Medievalists have generally broken the Middle Ages down into the Early Middle Ages (500 to 1000), the High Middle Ages (1000 to 1300), and the Late Middle Ages (1300 to 1500). Although to a degree these chronological frontiers are artificial, and historians are constantly attempting to readjust them, it is remarkable how much evidence can be adduced to justify this tripartite division.

If most of the Early Middle Ages in the West was a twilight zone and a sort of no-man's-land when Graeco-Roman civilization was melting away and slowly being replaced by a new western culture that in time would renew its ties with the culture of the ancient world; and if this period was largely characterized by political and institutional decentralization and instability, by profound social and economic retrogression, by alarming ignorance, and by the new Christian religion which dynamically conquered western Europe only to lapse into inertia and decline; such was not the case with the High Middle Ages. These three hundred years were to witness an extraordinary reversal of the course of the previous six centuries; progression, not retrogression, was to be the dominant theme.

Throughout western Europe tough feudal princes began to centralize and expand their authority and to restore orderly government. Some of the more successful went on to establish royal dynasties that presided over the development of large territories from which came the later national states. Abetted by the return of political stability and peace, the economic life of western Europe was gradually able to recover and the condition of the inhabitants to improve. Lands reclaimed from forest and water increased the production of crops required to nourish Europe's growing population. The lot of the peasantry could only benefit from the new developments that changed the agrarian countryside and provided numerous economic opportunities. Everywhere merchants began to be seen on the waterways and routes, buying and selling their wares. Sites of old towns again became inhabited, and hundreds of new towns sprang into existence. These dynamic urban centers provided the setting for trade, industry, and new business and financial practices. The urban population acquired special economic, social, legal, and political privileges that set it apart as a new class — the bourgeois or middle class. Meanwhile the religious life of western Europe responded to the political and economic recovery. Aided by feudal princes motivated by sincere faith, the church underwent a reform that reinvigorated monasticism, established the popes as the recognized spiritual leaders of western Christendom, and led to the series of Christian offensives against the Moslem East. The renewed vigor of the church, with the effective implementation of its doctrine, inaugurated a long and bitter struggle between spiritual and secular authority that detracted somewhat from the political and economic recovery of western Europe. This struggle contributed, however, to the development of political ideas that have become a part of our western thought. Fortunately the new vigor of the church, the expanding economic resources, and the rise of urban centers produced an amazing renaissance that turned back the tide of previous centuries and laid the foundation for a rich culture that was a mélange of the new and the old Graeco-Roman which was gradually rediscovered. By 1300 western Europe had not only pulled itself back up to the level of ancient civilization but had gone beyond it.

After 1300 medieval Europe seemed temporarily to lose momentum. Like the Early Middle Ages, the fourteenth century was a transitional period. Plagued by serious economic, social, political, military, and religious crises, Europe was hit also by a number of physical catastrophes. For a century France and England were locked in an enervating war. France and England, as well as Germany, Italy, and the Low Countries, were also ravaged by civil wars that destroyed stable government. From the East came the threat of invasion by the

Ottoman Turks. Economically, Europe contracted. Its trade declined, causing misery in the towns — a misery increased by the economic readjustment that involved new modes of production and the relocation of important industries. Unemployment, physical suffering, and bitter social and economic tension resulted. Town fought town, and within the towns class fought class. Dissatisfied with his slow progress towards freedom and embittered by the ravages of war, the peasant joined in this discontent and revolted. Unfortunately the church also lost momentum and its respected position. Inevitably weakened by the gradual secularization of western Europe and unable to agree upon a pope, the church was afflicted by a long schism that undermined its unity and enabled strong princes to exert influence over ecclesiastical affairs. Without strong leadership and unity, the church lost its zeal and reverted to practices previously weeded out by reform. These conditions assuredly foretold the Reformation which came in the early sixteenth century. Even scholasticism, the traditional system of medieval thought and education, lost its ability to assimilate and create and yielded to the new humanism of the fourteenth and fifteenth centuries. As if these developments instigated by man were not enough, the forces of nature made their contribution. First there was a succession of severe winters and floods, and then the Black Death descended upon the fourteenth century, temporarily paralyzing normal human activity. The last two centuries of the Middle Ages were a period when all that we regard as typically medieval waned, and there arose instead those new political, economic, cultural, and religious developments that we associate with early modern history.

Whether or not all medievalists can agree that the three centuries between 1000 and 1300 constituted the High Middle Ages, an era that saw many of the finest achievements of the Middle Ages, it is obvious from what has been said that there is formidable evidence to support such a position. Let us now look more closely at the prominent developments and accomplishments of this 300-year period.

2. THE POLITICAL RECONSTRUCTION OF WESTERN EUROPE

When the political authority of the Roman Empire crumbled in the West, the curtain fell on a long era of peace and reopened on a scene of political anarchy that was to last even longer. The Germanic states that took form within the ruins of the Roman Empire were generally incapable of providing strong government. Pillage, anarchy, and murder are the words most used by the chroniclers of the Early Middle Ages. The only strong and orderly states were the Anglo-Saxon kingdom of Alfred the Great and his successors in the tenth century and the immense territorial structure erected by Charlemagne in the late eighth and early ninth centuries. In the ninth century the so-called Carolingian Empire disintegrated as the jealous successors of Charlemagne bathed the land in bloody civil war and as the frontiers gave way before the Moslem attacks from the south, the Magyar push from the east, and the Viking raids from the north. By the tenth century there were more small states and more warfare than there had been five centuries earlier. Western Europe had become a mosaic of petty feudal states that had acquired bit by bit the land and authority of the ephemeral Carolingian Empire.

As dozens of feudal princes fought for power and territorial advantage, it seemed that the political condition of western Europe was beyond repair and that what little remained of culture and learning would be wiped out. But beneath the disorder were forces that were slowly to improve this desperate situation and to provide the means for the political reconstruction of western Europe. The Carolingian Empire had been too large to be held together in an age of primitive agrarian economy and slow communications. Even if there had been many Charlemagnes they could not have developed the administrative machinery required to glue together the heterogeneous territories with their local customs and dialects. Political authority during this age had to be personal and immediate; it was provided by some of the feudal princes in their miniature states where they could dispense government and keep their fingers on unruly subjects. If governed wisely and strongly, the feudal state could become a nucleus of territorial expansion and stable government.

During the tenth and eleventh centuries the political and military system known as feudalism showed how effective it could be in a small territory. Here a powerful feudal prince could force his vassals to honor their feudal obligations implicit in the ceremony of homage and fealty. In return for the fiefs of land, with their manors and peasants, which the lord gave to his vassals for sustenance, he could exact from them knight service, assistance in governing his state, and feudal taxes. To succeed, feudalism had to be personal; where it was, and where intelligent lords effectively used its principles, it proved to be a constructive force responsible for the political rebirth of medieval Europe.

Thanks to Henry the Fowler, the tough duke of Saxony who came to rule over what had been the eastern part of the Carolingian Empire in Germany (919–936), the Magyars were held back by a line of fortresses (*Burgen*) and the political foundations laid for the glorious reign of his successor Otto the Great (936–973). To the south, along the coast of the Mediterranean, local princes were able to prevent the Moslems from acquiring more land in northern Italy and southern France. In the north, the Vikings were able to establish a permanent beachhead only in that part of France thereafter known as Normandy; elsewhere they were forced to withdraw by such stalwart warriors as the counts of Flanders.

Successful in defending western Europe against outside invasion, some feudal lords turned to the expansion of their territories and to the establishment of stable government. There thus developed the county of Flanders, which, with its magnificent location at the lower end of important waterways, was soon to be the center of a thriving trade and industry. Next to it was the duchy of Normandy which the Vikings (Normans) had acquired from a weak Carolingian in 911. Here the Normans rapidly adopted feudal custom, Frankish language and institutions, and Christianity. From here went out the intrepid Norman adventurers to conquer more land and to establish new states. In 1066 Duke William of Normandy conquered Anglo-Saxon England and thereby instituted one of the great medieval states. Early in the eleventh century Norman warriors went to southern Italy, conquered the "boot," and eventually took Sicily from the Moslems. Here it was that Robert Guiscard became Duke of Apulia (1057–1085) and the ally and protector of Pope Gregory VII. Meanwhile his brother Roger completed the conquest of Sicily and smoothed the way for the remarkable Roger II (1101–1154), who united southern Italy and Sicily. Almost next to Normandy there took form along the lower reaches of the Loire river the county of Anjou. The dukes of Aquitaine built a large state in southwestern France, and beside it arose the county of Toulouse. In eastern France, on plateau land crossed by north-south trade routes, the counts of Champagne laboriously pieced together their rich county. In the north–central part of France along the Seine river emerged the county of Paris. Its count, Hugh Capet, was selected king of France by the feudal magnates in 987, and thus came into being the Capetian dynasty that presided over the consolidation of the great French state. Although the first four Capetians were less powerful than their feudal neighbors, they managed to preserve their small county and their crown until eventually they were powerful enough to exercise their royal rights and wield authority over the realm.

Although about the year 1000 perceptive men such as the chronicler Ralph Glaber had good reason to believe that terrestrial conditions were so hopeless as to suggest the imminent end of the world, the upturn in the political fortunes of western Europe during the eleventh century so reversed these conditions that by the early twelfth century there were areas where peace, stability, and strong government were regarded as normal. Unfortunately, eleventh- and twelfth-century Germany did not equal the achievements of Germany under Otto the Great, but there were periods during the reigns of Henry III (1039–1056) and Frederick Barbarossa (1152–1190) when there was real hope for peace and political unity. Except for the Norman kingdom in southern Italy and Sicily the Italian peninsula was never to know unification or peace in the Middle Ages, and there were areas of France where war was an almost daily event.

These political failures were more than offset by the strong feudal states of Flanders, Normandy, Anjou, Champagne, and Toulouse, which were eventually to be overshadowed and brought under the domination of the Capetians, whose political strength constantly increased in the twelfth and thirteenth centuries. It was Louis VI (1108–1137) who ended disorder in the royal domain, forced recognition of his authority, instituted orderly government, and began to extend his power throughout France. Across the Channel the Norman and Angevin successors of William the Conqueror (1066–1087) built a state whose central and local government was the envy of all princes. Although the governments of Sicily and England, with their advanced systems of finance, justice, and record–keeping, outpaced the other states and made better use of the new monetary resources, the rulers of all the more powerful feudal states molded their authority in a similar manner. In the interests of peace they outlawed private warfare among their vassals, strictly controlled the construction of feudal castles, supported the Peace and Truce of God, and exacted severe penalties for disturbing the princely peace of the land. Generally they controlled all high justice and strove to standardize law and procedure by expanding their own system of courts and law, which dispensed quicker and better justice. They labored to install efficient systems of local government staffed by officials whose loyalty was assured by strict surveillance. They placed the church under their special protection, as well as widows, orphans, and foreign merchants. Most so welcomed substantial revenues that they encouraged the exploitation of the soil and did what they could to stimulate trade and industry. To drive out inferior currencies and bad coins, they exercised a monopoly over coinage. None of these things was done easily or without a struggle. Louis VI of France had to fight incessantly to establish his authority over the royal domain. Some princes, such as Count Charles the Good of Flanders (1119–1127), lost their lives because of their attempts to end violence and feuding. But despite setbacks progress was made. From 1066 to 1189 there were only two periods of serious civil war in England. After the death of Charles the Good Flanders was seldom troubled by strife and enjoyed the peace needed for the development of her famous towns, trade, and industry.

Judged by contemporary standards of efficient government and stable political conditions in North America and western Europe, the improvement in the political condition of medieval Europe between 1000 and 1200 may not seem impressive. But judged by medieval standards the progress was almost miraculous; without it there could have been no economic or religious revival, no renaissance of culture, no emergence of western Europe from the landlocked isolation that had been its fate for centuries. Few other centuries have been as important for the political history of western Europe. To combat what may be taught to the contrary it must be emphasized again that these two centuries were dominated by the institutions and mentality of feudalism, and that it was due largely to the effective use of feudal principles that the political progress of the High Middle Ages was achieved.

3. THE ECONOMIC REVIVAL OF EUROPE

Even while the Roman Empire's authority still existed in the West, the third and fourth centuries witnessed a decline in trade and industry in the western provinces so catastrophic that the revenues needed for the army and the organs of government were no longer sufficient. Already western Europe was slipping into an agrarian economy that was to hold the West in its grip down into the thirteenth century. This economic decline, which was a major cause of the Empire's fall, was aggravated by the Germanic invasions; but as long as the Mediterranean remained a boulevard for trade in the lands between Constantinople and the Strait of Gibraltar a certain amount of trade and industry survived in the West. During the seventh and eighth centuries, however, when the Moslems conquered three sides of the Mediterranean and virtually converted it into a Moslem lake, economic relations between East and West were severed; western Europe became landlocked, retreated inland, and came to live almost exclusively from an agrarian economy dominated by the large estate, the manor or seigniory, controlled by aristocratic lords and tilled by peasants bound to the soil. Whereas the Roman Empire had owed its political and economic strength to unity provided by the linking force of the Mediterranean Sea, the Carolingian Empire was deprived of this advantage and was forced to derive its living from the land.

The results of this economic decline in the West were disastrous. As trade and industry dried up, so too did the middle class of merchants, artisans, and professional people. And as the middle class disappeared, so too did the towns in which it had lived. Except for some along the Mediterranean coast, the Roman *civitates* became deserted. In Roman towns where a bishop or local official chose to have his headquarters, there were, to be sure, a few inhabitants, but their occupations were war and administration, not trade and industry. When no longer nourished by trade and industry the great urban civilization of Rome disintegrated. Thereafter almost all of Europe's population lived in the countryside which was dotted with manors. A few fortunate men lived as lords, but the great majority lived as peasants in humble social, economic, and legal conditions. Despite some efforts to stimulate the economy of his Empire, Charlemagne was unsuccessful, and the Europe of 1000 was essentially like that of 800.

The impoverished evidence of the eleventh century may not be able to tell us much, but we do learn that the eleventh century was the first to see positive signs of economic recovery since the end of the Roman Empire in the West. Some signs of this economic revival were an increased population, the clearing of land for more cultivation, the appearance of merchants who derived their living from trade, and the return of Europe back into the Mediterranean. At first these signs were perceptible at only a few spots. In the south they became evident first at Venice; because of its maritime location at the head of the Adriatic and its economic relations maintained with Constantinople even during the seventh and eighth centuries, it had always derived its living from trade. By the eleventh century Venice had become the most important commercial center of southern Europe. It provisioned Constantinople with raw materials and brought back the luxury goods of the East for distribution in the West. It cleared the Adriatic of pirates and slowly established trade relations with the Moslems. This activity became contagious and spread into Lombardy and Tuscany, where there developed such famous towns as Milan, Florence, and Siena. Southward, in the "boot" of Italy and in Sicily, there was similar economic recovery; along the western coast of Italy, Pisa and Genoa took the lead in driving the Moslem fleets out of the western Mediterranean and in taking over the trade of this area.

About the same time, economic revival was occurring in the north. It began in Flanders, whose strategic location made it comparable to Venice. Besides a fine location on the North Sea, into which so many of northern Europe's rivers emptied, Flanders also had a temperate and moist climate conducive to the production of superb woolen cloth that was vied for by all western Europe. Already in the tenth century, after the Vikings ceased their raids and turned their maritime talents to trade, we hear of Flanders as a center for northern trade. By the eleventh century it had become the economic hub of northern Europe, fulfilling the same role as Venice did for the south. Soon such economic recovery occurred in all areas well located for trade. Along the great rivers of Germany and France, on the routes of Champagne, and in southern England, the eleventh century was swept up in a remarkable revival that in the next two centuries was to transform the social, economic, and political structure of western Europe.

The most striking result of Europe's commercial rebirth was the great urban growth which peppered the countryside with towns, the first real towns to exist in western Europe since the fifth and sixth centuries. Along the coasts of the Mediterranean, the Atlantic, and the North Sea, wherever rivers flowed and joined, and at the inter- sections of overland routes, towns took form in the late tenth and eleventh centuries. Generally they developed at the site of an old Roman *civitas* or camp, or around a feudal castle or walled monas- tery. As spots familiar to the itinerant merchant who would peddle his wares and stop for the night, they began to attract a permanent settlement of merchants. At old Roman towns or camps such as Cologne, Mainz, Bordeaux, and York the merchants would first fill up the vacant areas within the masonry walls and then spread out- side the walls. At a castle such as the *château* of the counts of Flanders at Ghent, they would settle outside the castle walls. These settlements were called *faubourgs* (suburbs) because they were out- side the castle or *Burg.* The merchants would eventually throw a wall around their houses, and the process would be repeated as the town expanded. It should be understood, however, that the Roman *civitas,* the castle, or the monastery only lent their names, sites, and protec- tion to the new settlements which became the towns. In these new towns the merchant and the artisan lived by trade and industry and were entirely distinct from the feudal lord and functionaries of the castle, from the cleric of the cathedral, and from the peasant on the manors. These new towns resulted from the economic revival and the men who lived in them formed a new class — the bourgeois or middle class.

It is evident that the mercantile and industrial occupations of the new middle class set it apart from the feudal aristocracy and peas- antry; but it must also be understood that because of its profession the middle class acquired social, economic, legal, and political rights that established it as a privileged class, one that came to be known as the third estate. In order to succeed, the middle class had to have personal freedom and concessions that would release it from restric- tive economic and legal shackles. Although some lords and princes were reluctant to grant these privileges, most realized the economic benefits derived from thriving towns on their territories and willingly conceded liberties to the townsmen. Generally the first stage in this development was the donation of elementary bourgeois liberties consisting of social and economic privileges. It was thus that the bourgeois came to enjoy free status, that any man living for a year and a day in a town secured complete liberty and became emancipated from the peasantry with its servile status and services. A town was in reality an island of freedom in the midst of the unfree manorial countryside and became a great force for the emancipation of the medieval peasant. Another privilege was that of free tenure, which meant that a man paid but a nominal quitrent for his plot of land and house, could sell or lease his land, and could even dispose of it by will. All the bourgeois of a town also had the right of selling freely at the local market and were relieved of arbitrary and restrictive tolls and duties. Along with this right went another, freeing townsmen from payment to a feudal lord of an arbitrary tax known as the *taille*. Legal concessions were of prime importance because they helped to guarantee the privileged social and economic condition of the bourgeois. It was provided that no townsmen should be tried outside the town in a feudal or manorial court, because feudal and manorial law could not cope with the legal problems arising from trade and urban life. Each town had its own court which developed a special law merchant, practical and swift, that was tailored to the needs of the new middle class who composed the court and meted out justice.

Such were the elementary bourgeois liberties granted to most of the towns in the eleventh and twelfth centuries. They could be found in all the older and famous towns as well as in the hundreds of new towns (*villes neuves*) that were founded outright by lords during the eleventh, twelfth, and thirteenth centuries. Louis VI of France (1108–1137), for example, founded the town of Lorris and granted it a charter of elementary bourgeois liberties which became the model for scores of similar foundations. Freiburg-im-Breisgau, founded by the duke of Zähringen in 1120, became the model for new towns founded in southern Germany and Switzerland. Wherever one looks in western Europe the same process was occurring. With these privileges the new towns lured the peasants from the manor and accelerated the process of emancipation. By the thirteenth century an unfree peasantry had completely disappeared in the areas most advanced economically, such as Flanders and Normandy.

But towns with elementary bourgeois privileges did not enjoy self-government, that is, political rights. Such rights came only after the elementary privileges had been acquired and were by no means obtained by all the towns. Feudal princes were more reluctant to surrender political rights over the towns and had to be convinced that local urban self-government was not necessarily detrimental to their political interests. Rarely did a prince voluntarily offer political rights to a town, but some princes could be more easily persuaded than others. In general, townsmen who had enjoyed the elementary liberties would see the advantage of self-government and would negotiate with the prince. Experienced in business and legal matters and familiar with cooperation by virtue of their membership in the town guild, they were well qualified for both negotiation and self-government.

One cannot generalize too widely, but it may be said that the rulers of France, Flanders, and Normandy were reasonably enlightened and granted the right of self-government after peaceful negotiation. In Germany and particularly in Italy, where central government was weak or nonexistent, the towns obtained political power almost by default. In England the kings were reluctant to give their boroughs self-government, and not until the end of the twelfth century did London acquire the right. In parts of northeastern France where ecclesiastical princes ruled, many of the towns had to revolt to secure charters of self-government. In the late eleventh century we hear of bitter fighting between the townsmen of Cambrai and their bishop. It was common in most of the towns for the citizens to organize themselves into associations known as communes for securing political rights by negotiation or by force. For this reason towns with self-government came to be called communes whether or not they acquired this status by means of a commune. The twelfth century was the age of the commune. In the first half of the century the great Flemish towns of Ghent, Bruges, and Ypres became communes. In France there were the communes of Soissons, Laon, Beauvais, and numerous others. The German towns along the Rhine and Danube rivers achieved self-government, as did most of the towns in northern Italy.

When communal status was acquired it meant that princes and their representatives no longer concerned themselves with urban government. The citizens of a commune would designate an executive council — the town council or *échevinage* — which assumed the responsibility for governing the town. It dispensed justice, assessed and collected taxes, looked to the defense of the town, built and repaired buildings and streets, regulated local commerce and industry, and preserved law and order. Invariably it served as the representative of the town in dealings with the prince. Where there was strong central government the communes continued to respect the authority of the ruler, to pay him taxes, to obey his territorial laws, and to fight for him when necessary. This was the case in France and England. In Flanders the counts almost lost control over their powerful communes. In Germany and Italy the rulers did lose control. The great Italian communes and many of the German free cities became *de facto* independent states that declared war and concluded treaties. Political rights, however obtained, and the emergence of communes, however powerful they became, were essential developments in the political education of western Europe; they opened the way for later states to achieve constitutional government that restricted the power of the ruler by representative assemblies composed of the first, second, and third estates.

The number of towns granted social, economic, legal, and political privileges during the eleventh and twelfth centuries testifies to a large and important urban population such as Europe had not seen since the Roman Empire. Although not even the largest medieval town approached a modern city in size or complexity, when compared to the situation in early medieval Europe towns seemed large. By the end of the thirteenth century Venice may have had a population of 100,000, a figure approximated by other northern Italian communes. In Flanders a few of the towns came close to 50,000. Towns of this size, however, were rare; most were smaller. London had a population of only 25,000 in the thirteenth century. An average town had from 5,000 to 10,000 inhabitants.

What must be emphasized is that these towns were sustained by trade and industry rather than by agriculture. Each town had its market for local business. Towns strategically located, such as those of Champagne, became the centers of great fairs that served as international clearing houses for trade and finance. To these affairs came merchants from all over Europe and the Middle East to transact business on a wholesale level. Each town had a guild merchant that was an association for the regulation of trade and the negotiation of economic agreements with the ruler and with other towns. This organization took an active role in local politics, promoted social functions, and assisted in charitable causes. With the growth of industry, craft guilds split off from the guild merchant. To these belonged the artisan who gained economic solidarity and an organization for the regulation of the quality and price of the goods he fabricated. Towards the end of the thirteenth century the craft guilds were powerful enough to agitate for better working conditions and wages and for participation in town government. Such agitation brought the craft guilds into bitter conflict with the powerful merchants and led to the social and economic tension prevalent in most of the great towns during the fourteenth century. Both merchant and craft guilds had great civic pride and were responsible for lovely *hôtels de ville,* guild houses and halls, chapels and church windows, and the organization of communal schools.

As good currencies struck by great territorial princes became prominent in the late eleventh and twelfth centuries, the trade of Europe ceased to be local or even regional and expanded from the Atlantic to Kievan Russia, from the North Sea to North Africa, and from Europe to the Middle East. Northern Europe sent its raw materials and woolen cloth to the south in return for the fine fabricated goods of the Mediterranean basin. To facilitate this trade were new roads, canals, and improved ships with navigational aids and instruments. The expansion of business operations forced the merchant to devise new commercial and banking techniques. Various types of economic associations were formed to increase credit and capital as well as to acquire business skills. Specialization of economic activity became common. Some merchants dealt only with the production of woolen cloth, others marketed it, and others transported it. This specialization spread to all the important industries and trade. The man who both fabricated and marketed became increasingly rare. Some merchants, especially the Italian, excelled in banking. They began to loan money for interest, accepted deposits, and facilitated commercial operations by developing the bill of exchange and letter of credit. A successful merchant would often take his surplus funds and invest them in land and buildings which he would rent or resell at a profit. One can say without exaggeration that by the thirteenth century much of Europe's economy was capitalistically organized, that the motive and desire for profit were as strong as in the modern period. Medieval Europe had created towns inhabited by a privileged bourgeois class, occupied with commerce and industry, whose new mentality was to produce much of the thought and culture regarded as typical of our modern western civilization.

4. THE TRIUMPH OF THE CHURCH

As political anarchy and economic hibernation characterized most of the Early Middle Ages, stagnation typified the Christian church. The occasional bright spots, such as the spread of Benedictine monasticism, the pontificate of Pope Gregory the Great (590–604), the Christianization of western Europe, and the cultural achievements of the Anglo-Saxon monks, were not typical. The church could not escape the impact of the political and economic plunge of western Europe; it had also to suffer.

The decentralized political structure and localized economy of early medieval Europe undermined the unity so essential for the church and produced ecclesiastical fragmentation. Too often the popes at Rome lost effective communication with and control over the church and became the puppets of local Italian political factions. The church locally fell under the control of lords whose only interest was political and economic gain. They appropriated lands of the church and even appointed bishops and abbots, who had to become their vassals, hold church lands in fief, and render military and political service. As the church was feudalized during the eighth and ninth centuries, the bishops and abbots in turn became lords of other vassals. One has the impression that numerous bishops and abbots occupied themselves more with war and politics than with spiritual obligations. Meanwhile Benedictine monasticism lost its early ardor and fell away from the ideals of St. Benedict's Rule. Supported by plentiful lands and established in comfortable buildings, the monks ceased to be overly industrious or zealous in their devotion to Christian ideals. Everywhere the morals and discipline of the church suffered. That church offices were sold and bought, that the clergy commonly married and kept mistresses — such facts show that the interests of the clergy were other than unworldly. The majority of the clergy was abysmally ignorant; only a few could read and write Latin, and some did not even know enough to perform the divine services. In the early tenth century the future of the church was clearly uncertain; it wallowed in unfriendly seas, deprived of any effective guidance from the papacy.

How the church began the revival that was to lead to unparalleled triumphs in the twelfth and thirteenth centuries is not clear, but the change must have stemmed from the political and economic betterment of Europe. We know that it began in the tenth century with monastic reform and then spread throughout the entire church, enabling a strong line of popes to say truly that they were the recognized heads of the church universal. The Cluniac reform movement, begun at the new monastery of Cluny founded in Burgundy in 910 by the duke of Aquitaine, proclaimed and worked for many of the religious objectives that helped to save the church. It emphasized devotion to a simple and pure Christian faith, urged strict obedience to the Benedictine Rule, worked for clerical celibacy, called for an end to simony (the purchase of church offices), and denounced the feudalization of the church and secular control over the bishoprics and monasteries. Soon many of the great monasteries joined the so-called Congregation of Cluny, and the new zeal for reform began to have an effect upon the church. Benedictine monasticism regained vigor, and many of the monks it trained became bishops and abbots devoted to Cluniac principles. Even secular rulers were impressed by the Cluniac movement and lent their support to critical issues, one of which was the revitalization of the papacy. It was thus that Henry III, emperor of the Holy Roman Empire (1039–1056), became a convert to the Cluniac ideas, worked to remove simony from Germany and Italy, and installed a vigorous pope, Leo IX (1042–1054), whose pontificate marked the resumption by the papacy of spiritual leadership in Europe. Leo and his successors were devoted to the Cluniac ideals and promoted them systematically throughout Europe.

One result of this spiritual transformation, certainly unforeseen by the kings and princes who helped to make it possible, was the battle that ensued to defeudalize the church and to free its great officers, such as the bishops and abbots, from secular control. This struggle was begun in earnest by the great pope Gregory VII (1073–1085) who, even as archdeacon under Leo IX, had been responsible for a decree providing that popes should be freely elected by the cardinal clergy of Rome and not be designated by the Holy

Roman Emperor. This decree, if enforced, would have liberated the papacy from the control of the emperor and would have set a precedent for the free election of bishops and abbots by cathedral clergy and monks. Upon elevation to the papacy Gregory vigorously pursued this fight. In the early phases he was aided by the fact that the new emperor, Henry IV (1056–1106), was a young boy in no position to contest Gregory's claims or actions. When Henry had matured and established political mastery over Germany he challenged Gregory's claims, particularly those stating that lay rulers should not invest bishops with their spiritual offices but that this should be done by properly constituted ecclesiastical authority.

In 1075 Gregory prohibited lay investiture and thereby tossed the gauntlet to Henry, who realized that this act would deprive him of control over the German bishops who, since the time of Otto the Great, had helped the emperors govern their land. In early 1076 Henry angrily deposed Gregory, who then immediately excommunicated Henry and later, taking advantage of a baronial revolt, persuaded the barons to renounce their obedience to Henry unless he gained papal absolution. Temporarily at a disadvantage, Henry quickly sought out Gregory in northern Italy and made his humble submission at Canossa in early 1077. But this was merely a ruse to gain time; as soon as Henry had subdued the barons he marched against Gregory, who fled and died in exile at Salerno in 1085. The immediate victory was Henry's, but his dramatic submission at Canossa plus the momentum of the reform movement insured the ultimate triumph of Gregory's ideals. In the early twelfth century compromises were made in Germany and England in the matter of lay and spiritual investiture which guaranteed that bishops would not be invested with their offices by lay rulers.

Although no other struggle between spiritual and secular authority was as bitter as the investiture struggle, other issues continued to disrupt the harmony of western Christendom. When the broad lines of the investiture compromise were applied to individual cases, conflict inevitably arose. Princes feared that the church would grow too powerful in their realms and deprive them of traditional political authority. Differences arose over the proper jurisdiction of ecclesiastical and secular courts. The church in turn worried about the taxes levied upon its lands and goods by the princes. The disputes over these issues are celebrated. Thomas Becket, after becoming archbishop of Canterbury in 1162 with the support of Henry II, confounded his royal master, whom he had loyally served as chancellor, by refusing to cooperate with the royal attempt to limit the jurisdiction of church courts. The two fought in particular over Henry's attempt to have royal officers observe the trials of criminous clergy in church courts and punish those clergy found guilty. For eight years Becket and Henry fought, and then in 1170 Becket was murdered in Canterbury Cathedral by some of Henry's men. The death of Becket, immediately construed as martyrdom for a great cause, forced Henry to abandon his attempt to obtain greater control over church courts. This problem continued to plague the relations of church and state and was one of the points most bitterly contested at the end of the thirteenth century by Philip IV of France and Pope Boniface VIII. During the tug of war in the early thirteenth century between King John of England and Pope Innocent III, it was evident that John was not inclined to abandon what Henry IV had fought for in the eleventh century and that Innocent sincerely believed his plenitude of power entitled him to hegemony over the rulers of western Christendom.

While the church thus fought to free itself from secular entanglement, and while an energetic papacy not only assumed respected leadership over the church and its reform but also claimed the right to supreme leadership of western Christendom, there continued to be monastic reform that filled the ranks of the church with men devoted to the highest Christian ideals. When the Cluniac movement began to flag in the late eleventh century new monastic orders arose dedicated to emulating the life of Christ. In 1084 a group of men pledged to extreme asceticism and to a semi-anchorite way of life formed the Carthusian Order. Soon thereafter the clergy of the cathedrals began to embrace strict rules of Christian conduct resembling those of monasticism. In the twelfth century orders of canons were organized, of which the Praemonstratensian and Augustinian became the best known and had the largest number of chapters. Of all the orders founded in this period the most successful was the Cistercian. Taking root at Cîteaux in Burgundy in the late eleventh century, this order, with its call to the old Benedictine order and Cluniac congregation to return to St. Benedict's ideals, established numerous houses throughout western Europe. Typical of the men who joined the Cistercians was St. Bernard of Clairvaux (1090–

1153), who stimulated the foundation of monasteries, inspired able men to join the order, and took a leading role in the spiritual affairs of western Europe. From the Cistercians came some of the popes, bishops, and abbots responsible for the triumphs of the church in the twelfth and thirteenth centuries. In their search for peace and tranquility the Cistercians generally located their monasteries in the isolation of forests, moors, or marshlands and converted these areas into lands suitable for crops, cattle, and sheep — a work of prime importance in the vast land clearance that transformed the countryside in the twelfth and thirteenth centuries.

These monastic orders reflected an age dominated by feudalism and an agrarian economy. They sought to locate their monasteries in isolated spots, derived their living from the land, and recruited many of their members from feudal families. None of the orders except those of cathedral clergy were located in or concerned with the towns. The monk, it must be emphasized, was essentially a man desiring to escape from the entanglements of the world and hoping by his ascetic life to attain salvation. He was repelled by urban life and disinterested in the problems of others. By the thirteenth century, however, there was serious need for the church to consider its responsibility to the growing population of the towns. Neglected and left to their own resources, the townsmen in a search for spiritual consolation often embraced movements which, though dedicated to Christian ideals, deviated from Christian orthodoxy and taught heretical doctrines. In this category were the movements inspired by Peter Waldo in southern France and by Arnold of Brescia in Italy during the twelfth century. A heresy more grave was the Albigensian, which engulfed most of southern France by the early thirteenth century. Antagonistic to much of the doctrine and organization of the church, the Albigensians threatened Christian unity. The church could no longer remain aloof; it had to meet the threat of these heresies and accept the responsibilities created by the social and economic transformation of Europe in the twelfth and thirteenth centuries.

St. Dominic (1170–1221) and St. Francis of Assisi (1182–1226) confronted these spiritual problems in the early thirteenth century. Preaching during his early career among the Albigensians in Toulouse, Dominic became convinced that only men thoroughly trained in theology and preaching could successfully combat heresy. He therefore devoted himself to the task of winning back heretics and enlisted others by his example. By 1215 his enterprise was sanctioned by the pope and shortly thereafter given a rule for the guidance of those swelling the ranks of his intrepid followers. Thus began the Dominican Order or Friars Preachers, who concentrated on extirpating heresy and systematically trained themselves in theology and philosophy. From these friars came some of the greatest thinkers and scholars of the thirteenth century.

Another great order of friars, the Franciscans or Friars Minor, was meanwhile taking form under the inspiration of St. Francis, who rejected an early life spent amidst luxury but without purpose and came to believe that he must model his life after Christ's and devote his energies to helping his brothers. Clothed in rags and dependent upon Christian charity, Francis passed his life in helping the poor and sick of the towns and in preaching the message of Christ. Around this joyful and enthusiastic servant of Christ gathered a great band of followers who by word and deed showed the men of the towns the true significance of the Christian faith. Less interested in books and learning than the Dominicans, the Franciscans emphasized service to others and simple manual labor. In 1223 they received a rule that set forth their ideals and formalized their organization. Essentially a continuation of the successive reform movements that had characterized the church since the time of St. Benedict, the Franciscans and Dominicans were largely responsible for the success of the church in triumphing over heresy and in meeting the new challenges posed by the towns. Only when this stream of reform began to dry up and the church proved incapable of fulfilling the spiritual needs of medieval men did it fall into decline and suffer the setbacks of the fourteenth and fifteenth centuries.

There is no better commentary on the respected position that spiritual revival and reform gave to the church and papacy than the crusades. Cut off for centuries from the Holy Land under Moslem domination and lacking the political power, economic resources, or religious unity and zeal needed to advance into the eastern Mediterranean, western Europe endured this virtual truce until she had the strength to mount an offensive against the East, the first since Rome had conquered the eastern Mediterranean. In 1095, when Pope Urban II delivered a famous sermon at Clermont calling upon western Europe to unite and to drive the Seljuk Turks out of the

Holy Land, he symbolized a revived and strong Europe that could be led into battle by a respected papacy. Although the success of the military operations was due primarily to the military ability of the Norman leaders and the economic resources of the Italian ports, it was religious zeal that unified the crusading forces long enough to retake Jerusalem. Despite this spiritual zeal, dissension almost wrecked the venture. From contemporary accounts comes a story of political jealousy among the leaders, cynicism and skepticism among the Normans, and political and military naïveté among the clergy.

During the next century the church proclaimed more crusades, but never again was it able to unify and to lead. Increasingly, economic and political objectives triumphed over religious ideals, until by the Fourth Crusade (1201–1204) only economic and political interests were at stake. Whatever the motivations responsible for the movement of western Europe into the eastern Mediterranean during the twelfth and thirteenth centuries, the fact of prime importance is that Europe had the strength and was expanding. When weakened in the fourteenth century by political strife, by economic dislocation and social tension, and by deterioration of the church, Europe reverted to the defensive and retreated before the new forces from the East. Not until the fifteenth century was she again to expand and show the vitality that characterized her in the twelfth and thirteenth centuries.

5. THE MEDIEVAL CULTURAL ACHIEVEMENT

With the collapse of the great urban structure of the Roman Empire in the West, the social, economic, and intellectual under-pinnings vital to original thinking and creative art disintegrated. Even prior to the German occupation of the Roman Empire culture had badly decayed and was no longer creative. The few who could still read and write Latin compiled texts and compendia that merely condensed and preserved traditional learning. Artistic creation ceased as men forgot the advanced techniques of masonry, sculpture, and painting. Here and there appeared an exceptional mind like that of St. Augustine, but it was engulfed by the ignorance that seeped over western Europe, especially in the seventh century, when the Arab sweep around the Mediterranean cut off the West from normal contact with the East. The valiant efforts of Charlemagne to restore the essentials of learning were praiseworthy; they resulted in the education of some clergy who on becoming abbots and bishops cultivated learning at other places besides the imperial court at Aachen. The copying of important texts preserved some of the ancient learning. This cultural flurry rapidly lost momentum, however, and the later efforts of Alfred the Great and Otto the Great were not enough to create any sustained cultural activity. The late ninth and tenth centuries were culturally as barren as the centuries before Charlemagne. Then in the eleventh century, with the establishment of some political stability and the upturn in the economic and religious life of western Europe, one detects the return of concentrated intellectual endeavor that led to the glorious achievements of the twelfth and thirteenth centuries.

The intellectual revival of Europe in the eleventh century centered not around the rural monasteries but around the cathedral schools such as those at Reims, Chartres, Paris, and Laon, growing urban centers where the atmosphere was conducive to new ideas and the exchange of knowledge. At the cathedral school of Reims, for example, Gerbert (946–1003), later Pope Silvester II, made his reputation as the first great teacher in western Europe. Men eager for knowledge came to him and later went out to teach and to become the masters of schools throughout France and Germany. Gerbert tells us that he loved the Latin classics and taught his students to study the texts in the original so that they could understand true classical learning. Gerbert also became famous for his teaching of new mathematical and scientific knowledge which he had acquired during a brief sojourn in Arabic Spain. It was Gerbert who probably introduced the abacus into Europe and who enthralled his students with his lectures on astronomy. He even constructed visual aids such as an armillary sphere to illustrate the new principles he was introducing. At other cathedral schools there was similar activity. Liège became noted for mathematical study. Chartres concentrated on the *trivium* and under the famous master Fulbert became the center of literary study. At all the cathedral schools students were well grounded in Latin, so that they could study the extant classical works and writings of the church fathers and so that they could write in Latin. The few extant works of Aristotle on logic were restudied and related to the theology of the church, which since St. Augustine had been oriented toward Platonic philosophy.

These masters and students, however appreciative of classical literature and knowledge for their intrinsic beauty and value, desired also to use ancient learning to interpret better the truths of Christian revelation. Most of the teaching at these cathedral schools, therefore, concentrated upon funneling classical knowledge into the service of Christian theology. As Europe expanded and established contact with the Arabs she was introduced to much more of the culture of the ancient world. Latin translations were made from the Greek and Arabic, and scholars of western Europe had to labor even harder to assimilate Graeco-Roman-Arabic ideas and to make them substantiate Christian truth. This was particularly true of the major philosophical works of Aristotle, which became known in western Europe for the first time since the end of the Roman Empire in the West. Renowned masters such as Berengar of Tours, Roscellinus, Anselm of Bec, and William of Champeaux lectured on the significance of the new Aristotelianism and the traditional Augustinian-Platonic philosophy for Christian theology. The supporters of the traditional orthodox position came to be known as realists because they held that all knowledge is based on divine ideas implanted in the human reason by God, and that these ideas or universals are both in and apart from things (*res*). Those who denied the existence of universal ideas apart from things were generally influenced by Aristotle. Some who argued that universals are but names (*nomina*) were known as nominalists. This position, which actually denied the existence of the unity of the Divine Persons of the Father, Son, and Holy Ghost because they were considered as three Divine Persons, amounted to heresy and was strongly attacked by the orthodox theologians.

The most celebrated master of the early twelfth century was Peter Abelard (1079–1142) who, after studying with a number of well-known teachers, decided that he knew more than they (which he did) and began to lecture at Paris. Here his brilliant teaching attracted students from all over Europe, and he rode the crest of success. The proud master was soon humbled, however, when some of his ideas were branded heretical, and his turbulent love affair with Héloïse disbarred him from ecclesiastical preferment. The intellectual accomplishments of Abelard matched the drama of his life. Plunging into the dialectical battle between the realists and nominalists, he supported the latter but deviated somewhat, arguing that it is pointless to talk about universal ideas in terms of names or things because such ideas have meaning and should therefore be understood as concepts. Disturbed by the disagreement and confusion over fundamental questions of Christian faith and reason, Abelard wrote a great book known as *Sic et Non* ("Yes and No") that introduced the academic world to systematic theology. First he set forth all the propositions he could find from the authorities, and then he attempted to show which were closest to the truth. Where necessary he worked to remove contradictions in the authorities and to supply a satisfactory answer. Like his contemporaries, Abelard wished ultimately to reconcile all knowledge with Christian truth. It was Abelard who made Paris the intellectual center of western Europe. Due to his teaching the cathedral school there pulled ahead of the others, and from it arose the University of Paris in the late twelfth and thirteenth centuries.

The use of reason and the new Aristotelianism by Abelard and others to help explain Christian truth was not accepted without a struggle. The austere St. Bernard denounced the rationalistic study of Abelard and pleaded in his sermons for a return to simple faith in revealed truth. A similar position was taken by Hugh of St. Victor (1096–1141), who asserted that the nature of truth could never be explained by dialectical debate, that truth came only from divine revelation. Other scholars, such as John of Salisbury (1110–1180), decried the emphasis placed on "bloodless and barren" dialectic and appealed for more attention to the *trivium,* the study of literature and humanistic learning. But such criticism was not to prevail against the new intellectual currents of the twelfth century which developed into scholasticism, the dominant medieval system of thought and education.

At the new universities the masters preferred to write and to teach according to the methods of the new scholasticism. During the twelfth century, for example, Peter Lombard (1100?–1160) in his *Four Books of Sentences* collected opinions (*sententiae*) on controversial theological questions, reconciling divergent opinions when possible. About the same time Gratian did similar work with the canon law, collecting the numerous canons and explaining their principles as they applied to theological questions. Scholars meanwhile were studying Roman Law, rediscovered in the *Code* and *Digest.* Such intellectual labor increased as western Europe had to assimilate more and more classical and Arabic learning in the form of Latin translations of Greek and Arabic works on philosophy, mathematics, and science. All this new knowledge had to be worked into the pattern of Christian truth. To this end were organized all the courses of instruction at the French and Italian universities in the twelfth and thirteenth centuries. It was generally accepted that students should first study logic, mathematics, and general science as preparation for professional training in theology, law, and medicine. All students had to be adept in Latin, the language of scholars and academic learning, but it was regarded primarily as a tool, rarely as a subject to be studied for its rich literature. The faculties of universities like Bologna and Paris came to be organized around professional subjects, and thus developed the faculties of art, theology, law, and medicine.

Intellectual activity, which began to stir in the eleventh century and to know a veritable renaissance in the twelfth, reached maturity during the thirteenth century; it was then that medieval thought achieved some of its most remarkable triumphs. By this time Europe was in possession of most of the classical and Arabic knowledge it was to know until the Renaissance of the fourteenth and fifteenth centuries. The famous masters worked to assimilate all this new learning into vast encyclopedias of knowledge with the explication of Christian truth as their ultimate purpose. The Dominican Vincent of Beauvais wrote the enormous *Speculum Maius* ("The Greater Mirror") which with its three mirrors of nature, doctrine, and history attempted to embrace the whole range of man's knowledge. Another Dominican, the famous Albertus Magnus (1200?–1280), compiled a similar work with special attention to the implications of Aristotelian logic and science for Christian truth. The greatest *summa* (compendium of knowledge) was written by Thomas Aquinas (1226–1274), the brilliant Dominican master of the University of Paris. In a number of important works, but above all in his *Summa Theologica,* Thomas produced an intellectual tour de force which had as its purpose the presentation and reconciliation of the truths of reason and truths of revelation. The former, he argued, are most ably expounded by Aristotle, whereas the latter are of course derived from the precepts of the church. The two truths, he contended, must ultimately agree, and therefore his task was to make the truth of Aristotelian philosophy support and agree with the supreme truth of Christian revelation. Whether or not one agrees with the final conclusions, he must recognize this work as an intellectual achievement of the highest order, symbolizing the capabilities of the best minds in the thirteenth century.

While the masters of the universities were absorbed in scholastic learning, there developed outside the formal academic centers an amazingly rich culture. Composed during the eleventh and twelfth centuries was the beautiful Latin lyrical poetry known as Goliardic. This poetry served as a preparation for the vernacular writing, especially French, in which men came to compose the romance and the poetry of the *courtoisie* ("courtesy"). Along with Latin works on theology, law, philosophy, political theory, and medicine, histories began to appear that were more than annals or simple chronicles with but local perspective. If one accepts the fact that the histories composed in the twelfth and thirteenth centuries reflected a philosophy of history grounded in Christian teleology, then he can read these works with understanding and see that some represent historical writing of high quality. In the twelfth century Bishop Otto of Freising wrote a historical version of the eternal and terrestrial cities, just as St. Augustine had long before masterfully interpreted the two cities in theological terms. In the same century William of Tyre wrote what by rigid standards of objectivity and perspective was the best history of the First Crusade. In the thirteenth century the English monk Matthew Paris demonstrated a capacity to write both universal and English history with a remarkable catholic view. By the thirteenth century good works were also appearing in the vernacular. Villehardouin wrote a swiftly flowing account of the Fourth Crusade; Joinville, in the early fourteenth century, dictated his celebrated life of St. Louis; and Dante (1265–1321) wrote not only excellent Latin for a scholarly audience, but also beautiful Italian when composing his poetic masterpieces.

What attention was given to science in the universities was limited primarily to theory and to understanding the pertinent texts on science and mathematics that had come from the classical and Arabic worlds. What we would call engineering or technology was ignored. Robert Grosseteste, the thirteenth-century theologian, bishop, and scholar who tinkered with gadgets and experimented in science, was a man rare for the age. Roger Bacon (1214?–1294), however little he himself may have contributed to the knowledge of engineering and technology, rendered an inestimable service in popularizing what was known and in making a plea for the study of these fields in the university. Despite formal academic indifference to these important subjects, the period between 1000 and 1200 witnessed amazing progress. Although we have few written sources we can learn from a study of the great monuments what skills had been acquired. If one closely examines a Romanesque or Gothic cathedral or a tremendous stone castle, he realizes that there were not only men skilled in masonry, carpentry, sculpturing, and glassmaking, but also men with the mathematical and structural knowledge required to plan, draw, and execute buildings of exquisite beauty and amazing strength. From the few accounts of architecture that are extant as for example those of Abbot Suger of St. Denis, the monk Gervase of Canterbury, and the architect Villard de Honnecourt, we know that by the thirteenth century the Middle Ages had outpaced the mathematical and engineering knowledge of the Graeco-Roman world. However acquired, the knowledge of the engineers and architects was sound and expert enough to achieve not only the Gothic masterpieces of stone and glass, but also the more practical cloth hall, *hôtel de ville,* town wall, canal, lock, wharf, and the machines that lightened the burdens of medieval men. It is no exaggeration to say that the technological triumphs associated with our western civilization had their origin in the twelfth and thirteenth centuries.

The thirteenth century saw the spirit, knowledge, and talents of medieval men bloom and combine to produce a synthesis of rare achievement dedicated to the service of God and Christian truth. If one understands the architectural principles, the sculptured themes, and the stained-glass pictures of a cathedral such as Chartres or Amiens, he understands the High Middle Ages.

6. THE MEDIEVAL POLITICAL LEGACY

Had the tough feudal lords of the late tenth and eleventh centuries not succeeded in defending western Europe against attack from without and restoring the political stability essential for the normal occupations of society, there undoubtedly would not have been the dynamic economic recovery, the spiritual revitalization, and the cultural advance that unfolded in the three centuries after 1000. At the dawn of the High Middle Ages the rough and ready fighter was admirably suited to the needs of European society. When, however, he had achieved the first step in the political recovery of Europe, the need for men of military ability was replaced by one for men capable of erecting institutions that could sustain strong government. In areas where such rulers appeared, there emerged powerful states encompassing large tracts of land. The tenth-century empire of Otto the Great could have become a great political entity but was instead shattered by the futile imperial policy of Otto and his successors, by the investiture struggle, and by German particularism. Flanders never developed into a large state but became strong and stable, probably the most powerful state in northern Europe during the twelfth century. The rich kingdom of Sicily created by Roger I and Roger II (1101–1154) produced the stability that fertilized the brilliant culture of southern Italy and provided the principal bridge for the passage of Arabic culture into the West. The duchy of Normandy served as a springboard for the Norman conquest of England, which united two strong states and supplied the resources and administrative talent essential for the construction of the Angevin Empire under Henry II (1154–1189). Meanwhile the Capetian kings of the twelfth century secured firm control over the royal domain and began the steady expansion that was to create a great French state.

Along with military ability, the rulers of the new states had the political capacity to develop the administrative, judicial, and financial institutions needed to forge effective government. All of them exercised tremendous power in order to control their officers and unruly subjects. They revised feudal custom whenever it served their purposes and consistently disregarded the restrictions imposed by feudal law which did not recognize arbitrary power and held a lord responsible for the fulfillment of obligations to his vassals who, if necessary, could bring legal action against him or take up arms to obtain right. Despite justification for strong rulers in this early period, despotism would have resulted had they continued to flout the restrictions of feudal law.

When a prince met with success in military and political ventures his vassals and other subjects generally had to submit to his strong government. Henry II of England, despite a policy of increasing royal power, met little opposition because he was exceptionally successful in war and politics. This was true also with Philip Augustus (1180–1223) of France. Though less successful in war, St. Louis

(Louis IX, 1226–1270) had little trouble in strengthening the crown because he did so judiciously and equitably and was highly respected for his personal integrity and Christian virtue. More than any other king of western Christendom, he symbolized the ideal Christian ruler who obeyed God's law, respected feudal obligations, and concerned himself with the welfare of his subjects, but at the same time upheld the powers implicit in the royal prerogative. But most medieval kings, lacking the capacity of a Henry II or the virtue of a St. Louis, frequently met opposition from groups that feared or suffered from royal power. Feudal uprisings occurred when vassals felt that their lord had not fulfilled his obligations or had demanded exorbitant taxes and services. Towns protested or revolted when their liberties were impinged upon or when demands for money were too frequent. There was constant friction between rulers and the church over the authority each should have.

These conflicts, which disrupted the peace of western Europe, caused men to think and write about the just powers of the prince and his proper relations with subjects and church. The men concerned with political theory accepted without question the supremacy of God's law over royal authority. A king who flouted the law ceased to be a lawful ruler and became a tyrant deserving excommunication by the church and removal from office by his subjects. This was the position of all the political theorists who supported the papacy. John of Salisbury (1110–1180) went so far as to defend tyrannicide. Unlike most medieval political theorists, he argued that it was the duty of the subject to exterminate a ruler who could not be persuaded to obey God's law and respect the laws and customs of the realm.

So firmly was kingship entrenched in medieval Europe that its right to exist was seldom questioned. Thomas Aquinas, however, did write a treatise in which he examined the different forms of political authority and contended that kingship was the most just and effective form of government. He agreed with contemporary political theorists that when a king broke the laws of God and of his kingdom he could be removed by his subjects. The most realistic comments on the proper authority of the king came from the thirteenth-century English lawyer Henry de Bracton who wrote the first great treatise on the English common law. Taking for granted God's law, he concentrated upon the powers granted to the king by the laws and customs of the realm and upon the relations between king and subject. From Bracton, a judge close to the political and legal life of England in a time when political forces were regrouping and constructing a political solution that was to produce a limited monarchy by preserving and limiting royal power, one gains the clearest understanding of the medieval political ideas and practices that led to workable constitutional government.

Although many of the ideas developed by medieval political thinkers have become an accepted part of our western political tradition and have repeatedly inspired men in their struggle against despotic government, the medieval political precedents formed by attempts to restrict arbitrary authority and to work out practical political solutions which would protect the basic rights of the subject were of greater importance for the development of constitutional government. These attempts, which occurred throughout western Europe during the thirteenth and fourteenth centuries, appeared first and were most successful in England, the only state to emerge from the Middle Ages as a limited monarchy. In the fourteenth century, after a long struggle to restrict royal power, the English parliament became an institution able to control the king by withholding consent to taxes and political policies. It should be remembered, however, that Magna Carta, despite its feudal character and its concern primarily with the rights of the feudal aristocracy, was the first effective step taken to curb despotic government and to provide a realistic definition of the rights of king and subject. It declared that the king was under the law, that he could not arbitrarily levy taxes, that he must respect certain basic human rights, and that he could not punish or dispossess a man of his land or goods until after a lawful trial. To affirm that a man was entitled to trial in court rather than subject to arbitrary and extralegal action was to enunciate one of the most basic of legal principles in the western political tradition. This privilege and others in Magna Carta had to be defeudalized and extended to all royal subjects before one can truly say they constituted the fundamental legal and political liberties of English subjects; but as subsequent historical events translated these concepts into effective rights it was not forgotten that they were first proclaimed by Magna Carta, which symbolized the victory of the baronage over King John and despotic government in 1215.

To argue that in the long drama of western civilization the period between 1000 and 1300 was one of the most creative would be indefensible, but to claim it as one of the most decisive is justified. With the end of the Roman Empire in the West most of the institutions and human activities associated with a thriving culture withered or died. Between the fourth and eleventh centuries western Europe lay dormant. In this economically prostrate and politically disorganized age most men exhausted their energies in an effort to obtain sustenance and to preserve their lives; they had neither the resources nor the time for endeavors essential to political, social, economic, and cultural achievement. Even the new Christian church which had emerged from the fourth and fifth centuries as a dynamic religious movement and organization could not triumph over the alien forces and lost its momentum.

Happily this stagnation characteristic of the Early Middle Ages was arrested in the early eleventh century and was replaced on all fronts by a phenomenal recovery that made possible the achievements of the twelfth and thirteenth centuries. To label the accomplishments between 1000 and 1300 as typically medieval or as having developed exclusively in these three centuries would be historically inaccurate. One may, however, point to various contributions of the High Middle Ages that had an integral part in the molding of subsequent European history. Much of modern European political history with its national rivalries stems from this period. The traditional rivalry of France and England may be traced back to the eleventh century. The particularism that postponed the development of national states in Germany and Italy was firmly established in these lands by the thirteenth century. The governments of both England and France had begun to assume the forms that were to be retained for centuries. From the medieval town and the social and economic forces that it set in motion came such features of our modern civilization as the bourgeoisie, an emancipated peasantry, municipal self-government, free tenure of land, and many of the business, industrial, and banking practices regarded as typically capitalistic. Closely associated with this economic and social progress were the accomplishments in engineering and technology that facilitated transportation and permitted the construction of buildings, canals, docks, and other essential equipment. With scientific and engineering knowledge used to improve the material lot of mankind, applied science made its debut.

These centuries are even more significant for their cultural heritage. To the High Middle Ages must be ascribed the revival of the Latin language and the development of a rich vernacular literature noted for the romances, grand epic poems, and fine prose compositions that rank among the world's masterpieces. Who can deny the beauty of Romanesque and Gothic architecture, or of the sculptured art and stained glass that accompanied it? The revival of learning in the eleventh and twelfth centuries gave rise to the universities which became the centers of intellectual endeavor and the models for higher learning in the modern age. Scholasticism, the system of learning and education developed at the cathedral schools and universities, cannot be dismissed as futile quibbling over minute theological questions but must be praised for its solid academic accomplishments. From it came our faculties of arts, theology, law, and medicine. As far as it went, the knowledge of these subjects is still valid. Few are the scholars today who do not envy the medieval scholar's mastery of Latin grammar and composition. Much of our logic is still that of Peter Abelard and his generation. The theology of Peter Lombard and Thomas Aquinas is the official theology of the Catholic church, which attained the peak of its power in the twelfth and thirteenth centuries. Whoever studies law today, be it canon, common, or the systems derived from the Roman law, soon becomes aware that the typical method of deduction from authoritative legal precepts is derived from medieval scholasticism. The mathematical and scientific knowledge of medieval schoolmen, though considered elementary by our standards, was equal to that of the Greeks and Romans and prepared the way for the splendid mathematical and scientific achievements of the seventeenth and eighteenth centuries.

For neither the Early nor the Late Middle Ages does the record list achievements like those that unfolded between 1000 and 1300. What made the High Middle Ages even more remarkable and unique was the capacity and flair of the men of that age for the development of practical political ideas and workable forms of government that provided not only strong orderly states, but also effective control over despotic power. From long familiarity with feudal institutions, medieval men understood that obligations between ruler and subject could and should be reciprocal, that the basic individual rights of the subject were best preserved when the ruler was kept under the law and forced to fulfill his just responsibilities to the governed. If the ruler was, as Bracton insisted he should be, "under God and under the law, because the law makes the king," then he would rule so justly that his subjects would have the liberty and motivation for creative and productive lives. If only for the creation of this political environment, so vital for individual liberty and creativity, the High Middle Ages deserve to be regarded as one of the decisive periods of our western civilization. Without this sympathetic political atmosphere the great accomplishments that the western world was to witness would have been impossible.

1

Medieval Europe About the Year 1000

UNTIL some fifty years ago books dealing with the Middle Ages stated that around the year 1000 men were convinced that the world was coming to an end and that the Day of Last Judgment was imminent. Apparently this belief stemmed from the famous passage in the Apocalypse of St. John predicting the end of the world 1,000 years after Christ's death, and from the extraordinary number of physical and human catastrophes then befalling Europe. When the year 1000 passed, however, and the world did not end, men took heart, worked industriously, and planned for the future. This renewed vigor and activity was supposedly responsible for the great economic, political, religious, and cultural revival that began in the eleventh century and flourished in the twelfth and thirteenth centuries. Although historians now discredit this explanation and advance more reliable, sophisticated reasons for the upturn in the fortunes of eleventh-century Europe, they accept the account of the terrors and catastrophes of the year 1000 by the eleventh-century Burgundian monk Ralph Glaber as evidence of the miserable state of western Europe prior to the remarkable improvement in its life during the eleventh century.

Ralph Glaber, Historiarum Libri Quinque ("The Five Books of His Histories")

WARNED by the prophecy of Holy Writ, we see clearer than daylight that in process if the Last Days, as love waxed cold and iniquity abounded among mankind, perilous times were at hand for men's souls. For by many assertions of the ancient fathers we are warned that, as covetousness stalks abroad, the religious Rules or

From G. G. Coulton, LIFE IN THE MIDDLE AGES, 2nd ed. (Cambridge, 1930), I, 1–7. Reprinted by permission of the Cambridge University Press.

Orders of the past have caught decay and corruption from that which should have raised them to growth and progress. . . . From this [covetousness] also proceed the constant tumult of quarrels at law, and frequent scandals arise, and the even tenour of the different Orders is rent by their transgressions. Thus also it cometh to pass that, while irreligiousness stalks abroad among the clergy, froward and incontinent appetites grow among the people, until lies and deceit and fraud and manslaughters, creeping abroad among them, draw almost all to perdition! And, since the mist of utter blindness hath darkened the eye of the Catholic Faith (that is, the prelates of the Church), therefore their flocks, ignorant of the way to salvation, fall into the ruin of their own perdition. . . . For whensoever religion hath failed among the pontiffs, and strictness of the Rule hath decayed among the abbots, and therewith the vigour of monastic discipline hath grown cold, and by their example the rest of the people are become prevaricators of God's commandments, what then can we think but that the whole human race, root and branch, is sliding willingly down again into the gulf of primaeval chaos? . . . And because, in fulfilment (as we see) of the Apostle's prophecy,[1] love waxeth cold and iniquity aboundeth among men that are lovers of their own selves, therefore these things aforesaid befel more frequently than usual in all parts of the world about the thousandth year after the birth of our Lord and Saviour.

For, in the seventh year before that date, Mount Vesuvius (which is also called Vulcan's Caldron) gaped far more often than his wont and belched forth a multitude of vast stones mingled with sulphurous flames which fell even to a distance of three miles around; and thus by the stench of his breath he began to make all the surrounding province uninhabitable. . . . It befel meanwhile that almost all the cities of Italy and Gaul were ravaged by flames of fire, and that the greater part even of the city of Rome was devoured by a conflagration. During which fire, the flames caught the beams of St Peter's church, beginning to creep under the bronze tiles and lick the carpenters' work. When this became known to the whole multitude that stood by, then, finding no possible device for averting this disaster, they turned with one accord and, crying with a terrible voice, hastened to the Confession[2] even of the Chief of the Apostles, crying upon him with curses that, if he watched not over his own, nor showed himself a very present defender of his church, many throughout the world would fall away from their profession of faith. Whereupon the devouring flames straightway left those beams of pine and died away. . . . At this same time a horrible plague raged among men, namely a hidden fire which, upon whatsoever limb it fastened, consumed it and severed it from the body.[3] Many were consumed even in the space of a single night by these devouring flames. . . . Moreover, about the same time, a most mighty famine raged for five years throughout the Roman world, so that no region could be heard of which was not hungerstricken for lack of bread, and many of the people were starved to death. In those days also, in many regions, the horrible famine compelled men to make their food not only of unclean beasts and creeping things, but even of men's, women's, and children's flesh, without regard even of kindred; for so fierce waxed this hunger that grown-up sons devoured their mothers, and mothers, forgetting their maternal love, ate their babes. [The chronicler then goes on to speak of two heresies which arose in France and Italy, of the piety of King Robert of France, etc., etc.]

So on the threshold of the aforesaid thousandth year, some two or three years after it, it befel almost throughout the world, but especially in Italy and Gaul, that the fabrics of churches were rebuilt, although many of these were still seemly and needed no such care; but every nation of Christendom rivalled with the other, which should worship in the seemliest buildings. So it was as though the very world had shaken herself and cast off her old age, and were clothing herself everywhere in a white garment of churches. Then indeed the faithful rebuilt and bettered almost all the cathedral churches, and other monasteries dedicated to divers saints, and smaller parish churches. . . . When therefore, as we have said, the whole world had been clad in new church buildings, then in the days following — that is, in the eighth year following the aforesaid thousandth after the Incarnation of our Saviour — the relics of very many saints, which had long lain hid, were revealed by divers proofs and testimonies; for these, as if to decorate this revival, revealed themselves by God's will to the eyes of the faithful, to whose minds also they brought much consolation. This revelation is known to have begun first in the city of Sens in Gaul, at the church of the blessed Stephen, ruled in those days by the archbishop Leoteric, who there discovered certain marvellous relics of ancient holy things; for, among very many other things which lay hidden, he is said to have found a part of Moses' rod, at the report whereof all the faithful flocked together not only from the provinces of Gaul but even from well-nigh all Italy and from countries beyond the sea; and at the same time not a few sick folk returned thence whole and sound, by the intervention of the saints. But, as most frequently befalleth, from that source whence profit springeth to men, there they are wont to rush to their ruin by the vicious impulse of covetousness; for the aforesaid city having, as we have related, waxed most wealthy by reason of the people who resorted thither through the grace of piety, its inhabitants conceived an excessive insolence in return for so great benefits. . . . At that time, moreover, that is in the ninth year after the aforesaid thousandth anniversary, the church at Jerusalem which contained the sepulchre of our Lord and Saviour was utterly overthrown at the command of the prince of Babylon.[4] . . . After that it had been overthrown, as we have said, then within a brief space it became fully evident that this great iniquity had been done by the wickedness of the Jews. When therefore this was spread abroad through the whole world, it was decreed by the common consent of Christian folk that all Jews should be utterly driven forth from their lands or cities. Thus they were held up to universal hatred and driven forth from the cities; some were slain with the sword or cut off by manifold kinds of death, and some even slew themselves in divers fashions; so that, after this well-deserved vengeance had been wreaked, scarce any were found in the Roman world. Then also the bishops published decrees forbidding all Christians to associate themselves with Jews in any matter whatsoever; and ordaining that, whosoever would be converted to baptismal grace and utterly eschew the customs or manners of the Jews, he alone should be received. Which indeed was done by very many of them for love of this present life, and impelled rather by fear of death than by the joys of the life everlasting; for all such of them as simulated this conversion returned impudently within a brief while to their former way of life. . . .

After the manifold signs and prodigies which came to pass in the world, some earlier and some later, about the thousandth year from our Lord's birth, it is certain that there were many careful and sagacious men who foretold other prodigies as great when the thousandth year from His Passion should draw nigh. [Glaber here goes on to relate the rival claims of the Greek Church, the growth of heresy in Italy, the success of false miracles wrought by evil spirits, and another three years of famine and cannibalism; after which a series of church councils were held for peace and reform.] Then were innumerable sick folk healed in those conclaves of Holy men; and, lest men should think lightly of mere bursten skin or rent flesh in the straightening of arms and legs, much blood flowed forth also when the crooked limbs were restored; which gave faith to the rest who might have doubted. At this all were inflamed with such ardour that through the hands of their bishops they raised the pastoral staff to heaven, while themselves with outspread palms and with one voice cried to God: Peace, peace, peace! that this might be a sign of perpetual covenant for that which they had promised between themselves and God; on condition that, after the lapse of five years, the same covenant should marvellously be repeated by all men in the world in confirmation of that peace. That same year, moreover, so great was the plenty and abundance of corn and wine and other fruits of the earth, that men dared not hope to have so much during all the five years next to come; for no human food was aught accounted of save flesh or choice victuals, and this year was like unto the great Jubilee of ancient Mosaic times. Next year again, and again in the third and fourth years, the fruits were no less abundant. But, alas for shame! the human race, forgetful of God's lovingkindness and prone from its very beginning to evil, like the dog returning to his own vomit again or the sow that was washed to her wallowing in the mire, made the covenant of their own promise of none effect in many ways; and, as it is written, they waxed fat, and grew thick, and kicked. For even the princes of both orders, spiritual and secular, turned to covetousness and began to sin in theft and greed as grievously as before, or even worse. Then those of middle rank and the poorer people, following the example of the greater, declined into horrible crime. For who ere now had heard of such incests, adulteries, and illicit alliances between close kindred, such mockery of concubines and such emulation of evil men? Moreover, to fill up the measure of so great wickedness, since there were few or none among the people to correct the rest, and to rebuke such crimes, therefore the prophecy was fulfilled which saith, "And it shall be as with the people, so with the priest"; seeing especially that all the rulers in those days, both secular and spiritual, were mere boys. For in those days, through the sins of the people, that saying of Solomon's was fulfilled: "Woe to thee, O land, when thy king is a child." For even the universal Pope of Rome himself, the nephew of the two popes Benedict and John who had preceded him, was a boy scarce ten years old, whose money and treasures had procured his election by the Romans; by whom in process of time he was dishonourably treated and oftentimes cast forth, so that he had no power. Moreover, as we have already said, the rest of the prelates in those days owed their promotion rather to their gold and silver than to their merit. Alas for shame! It is of such that the Scripture saith — nay, rather God's own mouth — "They have been princes, and I knew not." At this same time so innumerable a multitude began to flock from all parts of the world to the sepulchre of our Saviour at Jerusalem, as no man could before have expected; for the lower orders of people led the way, after whom came those of middle rank, and then all the greatest kings and counts and bishops; lastly (a thing which had never come to pass before), many noble ladies and poorer women journeyed thither. For many purposed and desired to die before they should see their homes again. . . . Moreover, some of those who were then most concerned in these matters, being consulted by many concerning the signification of this concourse to Jerusalem, greater than the past age had ever heard of, answered with some caution that it portended no other than the advent of that reprobate Antichrist, whose coming at the end of this world is prophesied in Holy Scripture.

NOTES

1. *The Revelation of St. John the Divine,* xx. 1–15.
2. The part of the church choir in which the celebrant makes his confession before saying Mass.
3. A disease known in the Middle Ages as St. Anthony's fire.
4. A local Moslem ruler.

2

The Quest for Peace in a Feudal State

ESSENTIAL for the spectacular economic and cultural revival of Europe in the eleventh and twelfth centuries was political stability. Where this condition was established there soon followed the revival of commerce, the growth of towns, the rise of a middle class, and an awakening in art, literature, and thought. Political stability first came in such powerful feudal states as Flanders, Normandy, Capetian France, and Norman England, but even under strong princes the struggle against disorder was won only after desperate fighting and pertinacious devotion to weeding out the forces of chaos and particularism. Fortunately there has survived a contemporary account of such struggle in early twelfth-century Flanders. An eyewitness to much that he describes, the notary Galbert of Bruges vividly tells how the Flemish count Charles the Good (1119–1127) was murdered because of his efforts towards peace and how, in the civil war that followed, such thriving Flemish towns as Bruges, Ghent, and St. Omer secured political concessions from the contenders for the countship. The selection from Galbert's account also illustrates the roughness of feudal life, the importance of the feudal contract, the typical trial by combat, and the operation of the inquest system. One may discern throughout the growth of political strength and consciousness in the middle-class inhabitants of the towns.

Galbert of Bruges, De Multro, Traditione et Occisione Gloriosi Karoli Comitis Flandriarum ("The Murder of Charles the Good, Count of Flanders")

1] *Charles becomes count of Flanders in 1119; his concern for peace and justice, 1119–24*

CHARLES, son of Canute, king of Denmark, and born of a mother who was descended from the blood of the counts of the land of Flanders, because of this relationship grew up from boyhood to manly strength of body and mind in our fatherland. After he was armed with the honors of knighthood he fought with distinction against his enemies and gained a fine reputation and glory for his name among the rulers of the earth. Our barons had for many years shown a preference for him as prince if by chance such a possibility should occur. Therefore when Count Baldwin, that extraordinarily brave youth, was dying, he, together with the barons, handed the realm over to his cousin Charles and commended it to him under oath. The pious count, acting with the prudence of his predecessor, now took such measures to strengthen the peace, to reaffirm the laws and rights of the realm, that little by little public order was restored in all parts, and by the fourth year of his reign, thanks to his efforts, everything was flourishing, everything was happy and joyful in the security of peace and justice. When he saw that such a great boon of peace made everyone happy, he gave orders that throughout the limits of the realm all who frequented markets or dwelt in towns should live together in quiet and security without resort to arms; otherwise they would be punished by the very arms they bore. To enforce this, bows and arrows and subsequently all arms were laid aside not only in those places already protected by the count's peace but in other places as well.

Thanks to this boon of peace, men governed themselves in accord-

From J. B. Ross, THE MURDER OF CHARLES THE GOOD COUNT OF FLANDERS BY GALBERT OF BRUGES (New York, 1960), pp. 81–84, 118–119, 201–207, 212–213, 258–259, 278–280. Reprinted by permission of the Columbia University Press.

ance with laws and justice, devising by skill and study every kind of argument for use in the courts, so that when anyone was attacked he could defend himself by the strength and eloquence of <u>rhetoric</u>, or when he was attacking, he might ensnare his enemy, who would be deceived by the wealth of his oratory. Rhetoric was now used both by the educated and by those who were naturally talented, for there were many illiterate people, endowed by nature herself with the gift of eloquence and rational methods of inference and argument, whom those who were trained and skilled in the rhetorical art were not able to resist or refute. But, on the other hand, because these by their deceits brought action in the courts against the faithful and the lambs of God, who were less wary, God, who sees all from on high, did not fail to chastise the deceivers so that He might reach by scourges those whom He had endowed with the gift of eloquence for their salvation because they had used this gift for their own perdition.

15] *The murder of Count Charles, Tuesday, March 2, 1127*

In the year one thousand one hundred and twenty-seven, on the sixth day before the Nones of March, on the second day, that is, after the beginning of the same month, when two days of the second week of Lent had elapsed, and the fourth day was subsequently to dawn, on the fifth Concurrent, and the sixth Epact, about dawn, the count at Bruges was kneeling in prayer[1] in order to hear the early Mass in the church of Saint Donatian, the former archbishop of Rheims. Following his pious custom he was giving out alms to the poor, with his eyes fixed on reading the psalms, and his right hand outstretched to bestow alms; for his chaplain who attended to this duty had placed near the count many pennies which he was distributing to the poor while in the position of prayer.

The office of the first hour was completed and also the response of the third hour,[2] when "Our Father" is said, and when the count, according to custom, was praying, reading aloud obligingly; then at last, after so many plans and oaths and pacts among themselves, those wretched traitors, already murderers at heart, slew the count, who was struck down with swords and run through <u>again and again</u>, while he was praying devoutly and giving alms, humbly kneeling before the Divine Majesty. And so God gave the palm of the martyrs to the count, the course of whose good life was washed clean in the rivulets of his blood and brought to an end in good works. In the final moment of life and at the onset of death, he had most nobly lifted his countenance and his royal hands to heaven, as well as he could amid so many blows and thrusts of the swordsmen; and so he surrendered his spirit to the Lord of all and offered himself as a morning sacrifice to God. But the bloody body of such a great man and prince lay there alone, without the veneration of his people and the due reverence of his servants. Whosoever has heard the circumstances of his death has mourned in tears his pitiable death and has commended to God such a great and lamented prince, brought to an end by the fate of the martyrs.

55] *The count grants charters to the chapter of Saint Donatian and the citizens of Bruges and Aardenburg, April 5 and 6, 1127*

On April 5, Tuesday, "Aqua sapientiae,"[3] at twilight, the king[4] with the newly elected Count William, marquis of Flanders, came into our town at Bruges. The canons of Saint Donatian had come forth to meet them, bearing relics of the saints, and welcoming the king and new count joyfully in a solemn procession worthy of a king.

On April 6, Wednesday, the king and count assembled with their knights and ours, with the citizens and many Flemings in the usual field where reliquaries and relics of the saints had been collected. And when silence had been called for, the charter of liberty of the church and of the privileges of Saint Donatian was read aloud before all, in the presence of the king and count, in order that neither the king in his person, nor the count, should ever arrogantly violate what had been written down in the pages of the privileges and sanctioned by the Roman Catholic pontiffs, and what had never been impaired by any of the Catholic kings and counts; he should rather honor what had been sanctioned by the prerogative of his royal dignity and confirm it by the authority of his office. The brothers of the same church asserted that they had the liberty of electing the provost canonically and without simony by grant of the lord pope, as was affirmed in the text of his privilege. After the provost had been elected canonically and without simony, the king, if he was present, by virtue of his own authority, should confirm the provost in the office and dignity of the prelacy, and install him in the seat of the prelacy; but if the king should not be present, the count, exercising by delegation the latter's authority, should perform the investiture of the canonically elected provost and install him personally in his place according to the custom of his predecessors, the Catholic princes.

There was also read the little charter of agreement reached between the count and our citizens about the remission of the toll and the ground rent on their houses. As the price of their election and acceptance of the person of the new count, they were to receive from the count this liberty, that neither they nor their successors in our place should pay toll or rent henceforth to the count or his successors. And having been granted this liberty in perpetuity, as it was written in the charter of agreement, they should receive confirmation of this same liberty by an oath which they demanded of both king and count, to the effect that neither king nor count, either in person or through their agents, would any longer disturb our citizens, or their successors in our place, about paying the toll and rent but would respect inviolably the privileges of the canons as well as the remission of tolls and rent, honestly and fairly, without reservation. Binding themselves to accept this condition, the king and count took an oath on the relics of the saints in the hearing of the clergy and the people. Subsequently the citizens swore fidelity to the count, according to custom, and did homage and pledged loyalty to him, as they had done formerly to his predecessors, the lawful princes and lords of the land. In order to make our citizens well disposed towards himself, the count granted to them in addition the right freely to correct their customary laws from day to day and to change them for the better as circumstances of time and place demanded.

Finally when everything had been confirmed by the oath of the swearers, the king and the count returned to their quarters where there was produced in the hearing of all the following letter from the leading men of Aardenburg[5] who had taken part in the siege.

"We, who have also shared in the siege, will proceed on our part to elect the newly chosen count of Flanders, but on this condition, that you will condemn and completely free us and the inhabitants of our vicinity from expeditions about which we have not been consulted, and do away with the evil exactions of the barons and the new tolls which were levied recently and contrary to the customary law of the land on the crafty advice of Lambert of Aardenburg; and also on condition that our farmers secure the liberty of going out and pasturing their flocks on the land which is called 'Mor' without the evil payment levied by Lambert. Moreover, concerning the very burdensome payment on the houses in Aardenburg, we want to propose to the king and count that each of those pennies which sons, on the death of their fathers, formerly redeemed for sixteen pennies by reason of the location of the houses, should henceforth be redeemed by only twelve pennies. We have also enacted a law for ourselves, that if an expedition on the count's part is announced to us, anyone who does not have a legitimate excuse, shall pay to the count twenty shillings. Concerning all these things, we beg your approval, lord king, and concession and confirmation from the new count, so that he may confirm by oath all those things that we have written down in this charter and that have been announced in the hearing of all. And we warn and beseech the person and authority both of king and count never again to permit the provost Bertulf and his brothers, Wulfric Cnop, the castellan Hacket, Robert the Young, Lambert of Aardenburg together with their sons, Borsiard and the other traitors,[6] to become owners of property in the county of Flanders."

And when the charter had been read through in the sight of all, the new count took an oath to confirm it and to grant honestly and fairly and without reservation everything they had demanded from him. And then throughout all the rest of the day those who had formerly been enfeoffed by the most pious Count Charles did homage to the count, receiving now in the same way their fiefs and offices and whatever they had held before rightfully and lawfully.

56] *The new count receives homages, April 7–10, 1127*

On April 7, Thursday, homages to the count were again performed; they were carried out in this order in expression of faith and loyalty. First they did homage in this way. The count asked each one if he wished to become wholly his man, and the latter replied, "I so wish," and with his hands clasped and enclosed by those of the count, they were bound together by a kiss. Secondly, he who had done homage pledged his faith to the count's spokesman in these words: "I promise on my faith that I will henceforth be faithful to Count William and that I will maintain my homage toward him completely against everyone, in good faith and without guile." And in the third place he swore an oath to this effect on the relics of the saints. Then the count, with a wand which he held in his hand, gave investiture to all those who by this compact had promised loyalty and done homage and likewise had taken an oath.

On the same day, Eustace of Steenvoorde, seized earlier by the citizens in Saint Omer and later thrown into the conflagration of the house where he had fled, was burned to ashes; being marked with the stigma of the treachery, he deserved to suffer such a death. On the same day in Bruges the count gave Baldwin of Aalst four hundred pounds minus twenty because by his strength and counsel he had done more for him in the county than anyone save the king.

On April 8, Friday, homages were done to the count in the same way.

58] *Guy of Steenvoorde is defeated in single combat and hanged, April 11, 1127*

At the same time, Guy,[7] a famous and strong knight, who had been one of the chief counselors of the counts of Flanders, had conspired in the very same treachery because he had married the niece of the provost, that is, Isaac's sister. For this reason Herman the Iron, a strong knight, immediately after the murder of Count Charles, had, in the presence of that false count of Ypres, challenged Guy to single combat because he had vilely betrayed his lord. But Guy asserted that he was ready at any time to defend himself against the charge of treason. And the day was set for their conflict, the same on which the provost had borne the torments of his death.[8] As soon as the provost was dead, everyone present went out to the manor where the combat between Herman the Iron and Guy had been called and where both sides fought bitterly. Guy had unhorsed his adversary and kept him down with his lance just as he liked whenever Herman tried to get up. Then his adversary, coming closer, disemboweled Guy's horse, running him through with his sword. Guy, having slipped from his horse, rushed at his adversary with his sword drawn. Now there was a continuous and bitter struggle, with alternating thrusts of swords, until both, exhausted by the weight and burden of arms, threw away their shields and hastened to gain victory in the fight by resorting to wrestling. Herman the Iron fell prostrate on the ground, and Guy was lying on top of him smashing the knight's face and eyes with his iron gauntlets. But Herman, prostrate, little by little regained his strength from the coolness of the earth, as we read of Antaeus,[9] and by cleverly lying quiet made Guy believe he was certain of victory. Meanwhile, gently moving his hand down to the lower edge of the cuirass where Guy was not protected, Herman seized him by the testicles, and summoning all his strength for the brief space of one moment he hurled Guy from him; by this tearing motion all the lower parts of the body were broken so that Guy, now prostrate, gave up, crying out that he was conquered and dying.

Then the count, wishing above all to look after his own reputation in this fight, ordered Guy to be hanged next to the dead provost on the same gallows so that just as they had been equals in treachery so they should die as equals in torment. After this they placed the bodies of both men on the wheel of a cart, fastened to a high tree, and exposed them to the gaze of all the passers-by; bending their arms around each other's necks as if in a mutual embrace, they made those dead men look as if they were plotting and conspiring for the death of their lord, the most glorious and pious Count Charles, even after they had been dead for three days.

So it was related by a squire who came to us and in the presence of the king told us of their fate; he had been present on that day and had seen the provost and Guy hanged at Ypres. Those who were besieged in the tower were at once informed by shouting how their lord the provost had been captured and put to death and told that nothing now remained to them except to surrender to the king to be dealt with according to their evil deeds. Then sorrow and anxiety, lamentations and sighs, prevailed among those wretches, now deprived of all hope of life; fear and desperation assailed them more effectively than the barons of the siege.

87] *The count orders a sworn inquest, September 16, 1127*

On September 16, Friday, on the eve of Saint Lambert, the count ordered the best and most faithful men from among the citizens of Bruges and from all the vicinities around us and also the castellan, Gervaise, to swear that they would declare by true assertion, for the honor of the land, the names of those

who had killed Count Charles and

who had slain those who were killed along with the count and

who had seized as booty the property of the count and of those killed with him, and of his vassals and members of his household and

who had lent aid to those traitors after the death of the lord of the whole fatherland and

who had stood by those most impious men before or after the siege and

who had led out those traitors and their accomplices, without the permission of the barons who were besieging the castle and the very same men inside, and as reward had secretly received from them money and treasure belonging to Count Charles and

who had afterwards given them refuge and lent them aid

— all of whom the king and count with the common consent of the barons of the land had condemned and proscribed. Then after taking the oath they assembled in the count's house and they accused one hundred and twenty-five among us and thirty-seven at Aardenburg together with Lambert,[10] whom they had marked with the stigma of treachery.

102] *The barons and burghers elect Thierry as count at Bruges, March 30, 1128*

On March 30, Friday, the people of Bruges were expecting the return of Daniel and Ivan who earlier had gone out of the town secretly with their vassals. For they had agreed upon this day with our citizens as the time when they would do homage and pledge loyalty to Thierry of Alsace, and also the people of Ghent and of Bruges and those who had sworn with them. Now this day was Friday in this bissextile year whereas it was Wednesday before Easter in the previous year.[11] On the same day, at evening,

Ivan and Daniel returned to us in Bruges, and with them came Hugh of Saint Pol. And it was reported that the captive William of Ypres had been given his liberty by Count William the Norman. Immediately after eating, the barons and the people came together at the exit of the town, at the Sands, and there they all elected Thierry of Alsace as count of all Flanders,[12] and Ivan and Daniel did homage to him in the presence of everyone. And the law was laid down for all who had been proscribed on account of the betrayal of Count Charles, that they might return to the court of this new count, and, if they dared, offer satisfaction according to the judgment of the barons and feudatories of the land, that is, anyone who was a knight and had belonged to the count's court; anyone else who was accused could purge himself according to the judgment of the magistrates of the land. In addition the count granted to his barons and to the people of the land, the right to amend all the laws and judgments and customs and usages of the inhabitants of the land in matters concerning the common welfare and the honor of the land.

And it should be noted that on the very same day, in the year before, the barons of the siege had returned from Arras, the ones who had gone out from us to elect the count of the land according to the counsel and order of King Louis — Ivan of Aalst and his brother Baldwin, Walter of Vladslo, and other peers of the land. Coming back to us in happy spirits, they had announced to us that they, together with the king of France, had elected the young William of Normandy freely and lawfully as count and lord of our whole land. And it should be noted that while Count William was sitting with his barons in a certain gallery at Ypres, considering what he should do against the newly elected Thierry, count only of the people of Ghent and Bruges and their confederates, the gallery fell to the ground and also all those sitting in it, so that one of them almost died of suffocation in the crash.

103] *Thierry is acknowledged as count at Bruges, March 31 and April 1, 1128*

On March 31, Saturday, the clergy and people returned to the Sands, and the count took an oath on the shrine of Saint Donatian, as we have said above, and Ivan and Daniel were named as pledges between the count and the clergy and people, to make sure the count would fulfill everything he had sworn and not consciously violate anything. Then the men of Ghent swore fealty to the count and then the men of Bruges, and they performed homages. On the same day Lambert of Aardenburg came to Bruges in order to clear himself of the charge of treachery.

NOTES

1. Reckoning of time in the Middle Ages was extremely complicated, but Galbert is, in effect, saying that Count Charles was praying at the church of St. Donatian on March 2, 1127.

2. The canonical hours or offices of Prime and Tierce.

3. The beginning of the Introit of the Mass for the day.

4. King Louis VI (1108–1137) of France.

5. A small port to the northeast of Bruges.

6. The party of conspirators responsible for the murder of Count Charles.

7. Guy of Steenvoorde.

8. A reference to Bertulf, provost of St. Donatian and leader of the conspiracy.

9. A mythical Libyan giant and invincible wrestler who regained his strength by touching the earth, his mother.

10. The brother of Bertulf.

11. This means that March 30 fell on Friday in 1128 but on Wednesday in 1127. The year 1128 was a leap year.

12. Thierry of Alsace was ultimately the successful victor in the contest for the countship.

3

An Early Medieval Merchant

A PERPLEXING problem for historians is to explain satisfactorily the origin of the medieval merchants from whom developed the middle class of the new towns. There is little contemporary evidence on the social background of the early merchants or their methods of making money. Of the few records extant perhaps the best is that of St. Godric of Finchale, who was born of peasant parents in Lincolnshire at the end of the eleventh century. Parting from the traditional agrarian life of his father, Godric wandered from job to job, finally becoming a peddler. By careful management of his slim resources he soon acquired enough money to join other merchants in the selling of wares at markets and fairs. Eventually a group of merchants, including Godric, pooled their resources in order to buy cargo for ships plying the English coast and sailing to Scotland, Denmark, and Flanders. Godric prospered, became rich, finally retired, gave his goods to the poor, and ended his life as a hermit. Here is a fine picture of a man shrewd, intelligent, and with a sense for business, who was eager for profit and labored to acquire capital. Godric was typical of thousands of merchants who brought about the economic revival of the eleventh and twelfth centuries, who possessed the capitalistic spirit which some historians argue did not develop until the sixteenth century.

Reginald of Durham, Libellus de Vita et Miraculis S. Godrici, Heremitae de Finchale ("The Book on the Life and Miracles of St. Godric, Hermit of Finchale")

THIS holy man's[1] father was named Ailward, and his mother Edwenna; both of slender rank and wealth, but abundant in righteousness and virtue. They were born in Norfolk, and had

From G. G. Coulton, SOCIAL LIFE IN BRITAIN FROM THE CONQUEST TO THE REFORMATION (Cambridge, 1918), pp. 415–420. Reprinted by permission of the Cambridge University Press.

long lived in the township called Walpole. . . . When the boy had passed his childish years quietly at home; then, as he began to grow to manhood, he began to follow more prudent ways of life, and to learn carefully and persistently the teachings of worldly forethought. Wherefore he chose not to follow the life of a husbandman, but rather to study, learn and exercise the rudiments of more subtle conceptions. For this reason, aspiring to the merchant's trade, he began to follow the chapman's[2] way of life, first learning how to gain in small bargains and things of insignificant price; and thence, while yet a youth, his mind advanced little by little to buy and sell and gain from things of greater expense. For, in his beginnings, he was wont to wander with small wares around the villages and farmsteads of his own neighbourhood; but, in process of time, he gradually associated himself by compact with city merchants. Hence, within a brief space of time, the youth who had trudged for many weary hours from village to village, from farm to farm, did so profit by his increase of age and wisdom as to travel with associates of his own age through towns and boroughs, fortresses and cities, to fairs and to all the various booths of the market-place, in pursuit of his public chaffer. He went along the high-way, neither puffed up by the good testimony of his conscience nor downcast in the nobler part of his soul by the reproach of poverty. . . .

Seeing that he then dwelt by the sea-shore, he went down one day to the strand to seek for some means of livelihood. . . . The place is called Wellstream, hard by the town of Spalding; there, when the tide was out, the country-folk were wont to scour and explore the stretches of sand, discovering and converting to their own use whatever wreckage or drift the sea might have brought to shore; for hence they sometimes get wealth, since they are free to seize there upon whatsoever goods or commodities they may find by the shore. The saint, then, inspired by such hopes, roamed one day over these stretches of foreshore; and, finding nothing at first, he followed on and on to a distance of three miles, where he found three porpoises lying high and dry, either cast upon the sands by the waves or left there by the ebb-tide. Two were still alive and struggling: the third, in the midst, was dead or dying. Moved with pity, he left the living untouched, cut a portion from the dead fish, and began carrying this away upon his back.[3] But the tide soon began to flow; and

Godric, halting under his burden, was overtaken by the waves; first they wet his feet, then his legs; then his upper body was compassed about by the deep; at length the waters went even over his head; yet Godric, strong in faith, bare his burden onwards even under the waves, until, by God's help, he struggled out upon the very shore from which he had gone forth. Then, bringing the fish to his parents, he told them the whole tale, and exhorted them to declare the glory of God.

Yet in all things he walked with simplicity; and, in so far as he yet knew how, it was ever his pleasure to follow in the footsteps of the truth. For, having learned the Lord's Prayer and the Creed from his very cradle, he oftentimes turned them over in his mind, even as he went alone on his longer journeys; and, in so far as the truth was revealed to his mind, he clung thereunto most devoutly in all his thoughts concerning God. At first, he lived as a chapman for four years in Lincolnshire, going on foot and carrying the smallest wares; then he travelled abroad, first to St. Andrews in Scotland and then for the first time to Rome. On his return, having formed a familiar friendship with certain other young men who were eager for merchandise, he began to launch upon bolder courses, and to coast frequently by sea to the foreign lands that lay around him. Thus, sailing often to and fro between Scotland and Britain, he traded in many divers wares and, amid these occupations, learned much worldly wisdom. . . . He fell into many perils of the sea, yet by God's mercy he was never wrecked; for He who had upheld St. Peter as he walked upon the waves, by that same strong right arm kept this His chosen vessel from all misfortune amid these perils. Thus, having learned by frequent experience his wretchedness amid such dangers, he began to worship certain of the Saints with more ardent zeal, venerating and calling upon their shrines, and giving himself up by wholehearted service to those holy names. In such invocations his prayers were oftentimes answered by prompt consolation; some of which prayers he learned from his fellows with whom he shared these frequent perils; others he collected from faithful hearsay; others again from the custom of the place, for he saw and visited such holy places with frequent assiduity. Thus aspiring ever higher and higher, and yearning upward with his whole heart, at length his great labours and cares bore much fruit of worldly gain. For he laboured not only as a merchant but also as a shipman . . . to Denmark and Flanders and Scotland; in all which lands he found certain rare, and therefore more precious, wares, which he carried to other parts wherein he knew them to be least familiar, and coveted by the inhabitants beyond the price of gold itself; wherefore he exchanged these wares for others coveted by men of other lands; and thus he chaffered most freely and assiduously. Hence he made great profit in all his bargains, and gathered much wealth in the sweat of his brow; for he sold dear in one place the wares which he had bought elsewhere at a small price.

Then he purchased the half of a merchant-ship with certain of his partners in the trade; and again by his prudence he bought the fourth part of another ship. At length, by his skill in navigation, wherein he excelled all his fellows, he earned promotion to the post of steersman. . . .

For he was vigorous and strenuous in mind, whole of limb and strong in body. He was of middle stature, broad-shouldered and deep-chested, with a long face, grey eyes most clear and piercing, bushy brows, a broad forehead, long and open nostrils, a nose of comely curve, and a pointed chin. His beard was thick, and longer than the ordinary, his mouth well-shaped, with lips of moderate thickness; in youth his hair was black, in age as white as snow; his neck was short and thick, knotted with veins and sinews; his legs were somewhat slender, his instep high, his knees hardened and horny with frequent kneeling; his whole skin rough beyond the ordinary, until all this roughness was softened by old age. . . . In labour he was strenuous, assiduous above all men; and, when by chance his bodily strength proved insufficient, he compassed his ends with great ease by the skill which his daily labours had given, and by a prudence born of long experience. . . . He knew, from the aspect of sea and stars, how to foretell fair or foul weather. In his various voyages he visited many saints' shrines, to whose protection he was wont most devoutly to commend himself; more especially the church of St. Andrew in Scotland, where he most frequently made and paid his vows. On the way thither, he often-times touched at the island of Lindisfarne, wherein St. Cuthbert had been bishop, and at the isle of Farne, where that Saint had lived as an anchoret,[4] and where St. Godric (as he himself would tell afterwards) would meditate on the Saint's life with abundant tears. Thence he began to yearn for solitude, and to hold his merchandise in less esteem than heretofore....

And now he had lived sixteen years as a merchant, and began to think of spending on charity, to God's honour and service, the goods which he had so laboriously acquired. He therefore took the cross as a pilgrim to Jerusalem, and, having visited the Holy Sepulchre, came back to England by way of St. James [of Compostella]. Not long afterwards he became steward to a certain rich man of his own country, with the care of his whole house and household. But certain of the younger household were men of iniquity, who stole their neighbours' cattle and thus held luxurious feasts, whereat Godric, in his ignorance, was sometimes present. Afterwards, discovering the truth, he rebuked and admonished them to cease; but they made no account of his warnings; wherefore he concealed not their iniquity, but disclosed it to the lord of the household, who, however, slighted his advice. Wherefore he begged to be dismissed and went on a pilgrimage, first to St. Gilles and thence to Rome the abode of the Apostles, that thus he might knowingly pay the penalty for those misdeeds wherein he had ignorantly partaken. I have often seen him, even in his old age, weeping for this unknowing transgression....

On his return from Rome, he abode awhile in his father's house; until, inflamed again with holy zeal, he purposed to revisit the abode of the Apostles and made his desire known unto his parents. Not only did they approve his purpose, but his mother besought his leave to bear him company on this pilgrimage; which he gladly granted, and willingly paid her every filial service that was her due. They came therefore to London; and they had scarcely departed from thence when his mother took off her shoes, going thus barefooted to Rome and back to London. Godric, humbly serving his parent, was wont to bear her on his shoulders....

Godric, when he had restored his mother safe to his father's arms, abode but a brief while at home; for he was now already firmly purposed to give himself entirely to God's service. Wherefore, that he might follow Christ the more freely, he sold all his possessions and distributed them among the poor. Then, telling his parents of this purpose and receiving their blessing, he went forth to no certain abode, but whithersoever the Lord should deign to lead him; for above all things he coveted the life of a hermit.

NOTES

1. The holy man is St. Godric.
2. A peddler.
3. A porpoise was valuable for its fat.
4. A hermit.

4

Liberties and Privileges in a Medieval Town

ONE of the most significant results of the medieval urban revival was the acquisition of liberties and privileges by inhabitants of towns during the eleventh and twelfth centuries. Most towns gradually came to enjoy rights which set them apart from the unfree seignorial countryside and bestowed upon their inhabitants a status superior to that of the peasant. The merchants and artisans of the towns developed into a distinct class that came to be known as the middle class or bourgeoisie. In almost all towns this new middle class possessed elementary social, legal, and economic liberties that released it from the seignorial obligations of the peasant, gave it freedom of movement, enabled it to possess property, to buy and sell goods, to practice a profession, and to be tried under a new merchant law, which accorded swift and practical justice. Men with such rights were liberated from the peasantry, were relieved of the servile obligations which had enchained the great majority of men for centuries. Thus began a movement that emancipated most of western Europe's population by the end of the Middle Ages. Some of the towns that received the elementary bourgeois liberties were founded outright by feudal princes. Such a town was Lorris, near Orléans, in the French royal domain. It was founded by Louis VI some time between 1108 and 1137. The following charter granted by Louis VI to Lorris illustrates the typical social, economic, and legal privileges men enjoyed when they came to reside in such a new town.

Carta Franchesie Lorriaci ("Charter of the Liberties of Lorris")

Louis etc. Be it known to all now and hereafter that:

1] Whoever shall have a house in the parish of Lorris should pay for his house and for each arpent [one and one-half acres] of land that he shall have in this parish 6d. only as a quitrent; and each arpent that he shall acquire he should hold for the same quitrent that he pays for his house.

2] None of the men of the parish of Lorris should render toll or any duty for his food; neither should he render grain taxes from his yearly income which he will have from his labor or from the labor of any of his animals; nor should he render wine dues for his wine which he will have from his vineyards.

3] None of them should go on a military expedition or on riding service unless he can return the same day to his home if he should wish to do so.

4] None of them should render tolls up to Étampes, or up to Orléans, or up to Milly which is in the district of the Gâtinais, or up to Melun.

5] Whoever shall have his own property in the parish of Lorris should lose none of it on account of any misdeed unless he shall have committed a misdeed against us or any of our household.

6] No one coming to or returning from the fairs or markets of Lorris should be seized or disturbed unless he shall have committed a misdeed that same day.

And no one on the day of the market or fair of Lorris should seize bail given as security unless that bail shall have been given on a market or fair day.

7] A forfeiture of 60s. should be reduced to 5s., and a forfeiture of 5s. should be reduced to 12d.; and in cases of justice the fee of the prévôt should be 4d.

8] None of the men of Lorris should go out of Lorris to obtain justice from the lord king.

9] No one, either ourselves or anyone else, should impose upon

From Maurice Prou, LES COUTUMES DE LORRIS ET LEUR PROPAGATION AUX XIIᵉ ET XIIIᵉ SIÈCLES (Paris, 1884), pp. 445–457. Translation by Bryce Lyon.

the men of Lorris a tallage,[1] or an arbitrary tax, or any pecuniary exaction.

10] No one of Lorris should sell wine with public notice except the king, who should sell his own wine in his cellar.

11] At Lorris, moreover, we will have credit in food for fifteen full days for our work and that of the queen.

And if anyone will have security of the lord king or another, he will not hold it more than eight days unless he so desires.

12] And if anyone will have quarreled with another without violating the peace of the castle or the *bourg*,[2] and will have reached an agreement without bringing a complaint before the prévôt,[3] no fine should be due on this account to us or to our prévôt; and if a complaint will have been made, they should be permitted to come to an agreement when they shall have paid the fine; and if one will have made a complaint against the other, and neither will have paid a fine to the other, nothing should be owed by these men to us or to our prévôt.

13] If anyone shall have made an oath to another, the latter should be permitted to remit it.

14] If men of Lorris will have rashly given pledges for a duel and will have come to an agreement with the consent of the prévôt before hostages are handed over, each should pay 2*s*. 6*d*.; and if hostages will have been given, each should pay 7*s*. 6*d*.

And if a duel will have been fought by authorized men, the hostages of the defeated man should pay 112*s*.

15] None of the men of Lorris should perform corvée[4] to us unless to convey our wine once a year to Orléans; nor should any do this except those who will have horses and carts, and they will be given notice and will not receive payment for their expenses from us. Also, the villeins should bring wood for our kitchen.

16] No one of Lorris should be held captive if he is able to give bail for coming to justice.

17] Anyone of Lorris may sell his possessions if he so desires and after selling them, if he wishes to leave the town, may do so freely and unmolested unless he will have committed a misdeed in the town.

18] Whoever will have remained in the parish of Lorris for a year and a day with no claim following him and without having been denied the right to remain by us or by our prévôt, may thereafter remain free and undisturbed.

19] No one will plead against another unless for the sake of receiving and prosecuting his rights.

20] When the men of Lorris will go to Orléans with merchandise, they should pay upon departure from the town 1d. for their cart when they do not go for the fair. And when they will go in March for the fair, they should pay for their cart 4d. when leaving Orléans and 2d. when entering.

21] At marriages in Lorris, by custom, the town crier will receive no fee, nor will the watchman.

22] No one of the parish of Lorris who cultivates the land with a plow should render at harvest time more than one *mine* [78 liters] of rye to all the serjeants of Lorris.

23] If any knight or serjeant will have found horses or other animals of the men of Lorris in our woods, he should not lead them away except to the prévôt of Lorris.

And if any animal of the parish of Lorris, put to flight by bulls or driven by flies, will have entered our forest or enclosures, he whose animal it is and who is able to swear that it had entered in spite of the keeper ought to pay no fine on this account to the prévôt. And if any animal will have entered with the knowledge of the keeper, the owner will pay for that animal 12d.; and if there will have been more, he should pay a like amount for each.

24] For use of the ovens of Lorris there will be, by custom, no fees.

25] At Lorris there will be, by custom, no watch.

26] Anyone of Lorris, if he will have taken his salt or wine to Orléans, will pay only 1d. for his cart.

27] None of the men of Lorris should pay fines to the prévôt of Étampes, or to the prévôt of Pithiviers, or in all of the Gâtinais.

28] None of them will pay tolls at Ferrières, or at Château-Landon, or at Puiseaux, or at Nibelle.

29] The men of Lorris may take dead wood out of the forest for their use.

30] Whoever will have bought or sold anything at the market of Lorris and, through forgetfulness, will not have paid his toll, should pay it eight days afterwards without any penalty if he is able to swear that he had not withheld it knowingly.

31] None of the men of Lorris, having a house, or a vineyard, or a meadow, or a field, or any building in the domain of Saint Benedict, shall be under the jurisdiction of the abbot of Saint Benedict or of his serjeant unless he owes something for his rent in kind or for his quitrent; and then he will not go out of Lorris for the sake of obtaining justice.

32] If any of the men of Lorris will have been accused by another and the accuser is not upheld by a witness, the accused shall clear himself against the charge of his accuser by his oath alone.

33] No one, moreover, from the same parish will pay a duty for whatever he will have sold or bought within the precincts of Lorris for his own use or for whatever he will have bought on Wednesday at the market.

34] Moreover, these customs, just as they have been conceded to the men of Lorris, likewise are common to the men who live at Courpalais, at Mairie-Chanteloup, and in the *bailliage*[5] of Hapardière.

35] In a like manner we have ordained that, whenever the prévôt will be replaced in the town, one after the other should swear that he will firmly preserve these customs; and new serjeants should do likewise when they are instituted.

So that this may be firmly established etc. Given at Orléans in the year of our Lord 1155.

NOTES

1. An infamous tax levied by feudal lords on peasants.
2. Inhabited area around the castle.
3. Local officer of the king.
4. Labor service.
5. Administrative district.

5

The Winning of a Commune

DURING the eleventh and twelfth centuries it was normal for the bourgeois of any important town to acquire elementary social, economic, and legal privileges. This development always preceded another, that of self-government — the final stage of urban government — which generally involved the right to have a town council of magistrates who replaced the officials of the feudal prince and assumed the responsibility of governing the town. Although many towns never acquired political power, most important ones did. In some areas, such as Flanders and the French royal domain, rulers were sympathetic to urban self-government and it was achieved by peaceful negotiation. But in other parts of Europe, for example in northern Italy and in northeastern France, townsmen often had to organize themselves into an association known as a commune and fight for this right. During the late eleventh and early twelfth centuries numerous French towns in Picardy and adjacent areas revolted against ecclesiastical and secular lords and became communes. Among them were Cambrai, St. Quentin, Beauvais, and Noyon. We have, however, the most information on how the town of Laon became a commune in 1115. The abbot Guibert of Nogent-sous-Coucy vividly described the violent struggle between the townsmen of Laon and the bishop. Although Guibert feared the "pestilential communes" and gives a biased account, it is the account of one personally involved in the struggle.

Guibert of Nogent, De Vita Sua ("His Life")

CHAPTER VII] Now after some time when he[1] had set out for England to extract money from the English king, whom he had served, and who had formerly been his friend, the Archdeacons Walter and Guy, with the nobles of the city, devised the following plan: Of old time such ill-fate had settled upon that city that

From C. C. Swinton Bland, THE AUTOBIOGRAPHY OF GUIBERT ABBOT OF NOGENT-SOUS-COUCY (London, 1925), pp. 152–166, 173–180. Reprinted by permission of Routledge and Kegan Paul Ltd.

neither God nor any lord was feared therein, but according to each man's power and lust the state was involved in rapine and murder. For to begin with the source of the plague, whenever it happened that the king came there, he who ought to have exacted respect for himself with royal severity, was himself first shamefully fined on his own property. When his horses were led to the water morning or evening, his grooms were beaten and the horses carried off. It was known that the very clergy were held in such contempt, that neither their persons nor their goods were spared, as it is written, "Like as the people, so the priest." But what shall I say about the baser people? No one of the countrymen came into the city, no one except under the safest conduct approached it, who was not thrown into prison and held to ransom, or was not, as opportunity served, drawn without cause into a lawsuit.

As an example let me adduce one practice, which occurring amongst barbarians or Scythians, men having no code of laws, would be regarded as most inquitous. When on the Saturday the country populace from different parts came there to buy and sell, the town-folk carried round as for sale, beans, barley or any kind of corn in cup and platter or other kind of measure in the marketplace, and when they had offered them for sale to the countrymen seeking such things, the latter having settled the price promised to buy. "Follow me," said the seller, "to my house that you may there see the rest of the corn which I am selling you, and when you have seen it, may take it away." He followed, but when he came to the bin, the honest seller, having raised and held up the lid, would say, "Bend your head and shoulders over the bin, that you may see that the bulk does not differ from the sample which I shewed you in the market-place." And when the buyer getting up on the pediment of the bin leaned his belly over it, the worthy seller standing behind lifted up his feet and pushed the unwary man into the bin, and having put the lid down on him as he fell, kept him in safe prison until he ransomed himself. Such and like things were done in the city. No one was safe going out at night. There remained for him nothing but plunder, capture or murder.

The clergy with the archdeacons considering this, and the nobles catching at pretexts for exacting money from the people, offered them through agents the choice of making composition by paying a sum to cover them. Now Commune is a new and a bad name of an arrangement for all the poorest classes to pay their usual due of servitude to their lords once only in the year, and to make good any breach of the laws they have committed by the payment fixed by law, and to be entirely free from all other exactions usually imposed on serfs. The people seizing on this opportunity for freeing themselves gathered huge sums of money to fill the gaping mouths of so many greedy men. And they, pleased with the shower poured upon them, took oaths binding themselves in the matter.

A pledge of mutual aid had been thus exchanged by the clergy and nobles with the people, when the Bishop returned with much wealth from England and being moved to anger against those responsible for this innovation, for a long time kept away from the city. But a quarrel full of honour and glory began between him and Walter, the archdeacon, his accomplice. The Archdeacon made very unbecoming remarks about his Bishop on the subject of the death of Gerard. Whether the Bishop had any talk on the matter with others I know not, but this I do know, that he complained to me about him saying, "Lord Abbot, if it should so happen that Walter should start any charges against me at any council, would you take it without offence? Is it not he, who at the time when you left your fellow-monks and went to Ely, openly flattered you, but secretly raised dissensions against you, publicly taking your side, but privately stirring me up against you?" With such speeches did he try to win me to oppose that dangerous man, conscious of the weight of his charges, fearful and suspicious of universal condemnation.

Saying therefore that he was moved with relentless wrath against those who had taken that oath and the principals in the transaction, in the end his loud-sounding words were suddenly quieted by the offer of a great heap of silver and gold. Therefore he swore that he would maintain the rights of the Commune according to the terms duly drawn up at Noyon and Saint-Quentin. The King too was induced by a bribe from the people to confirm the same by oath. O my God, who could say how many disputes arose when the gifts of the people were accepted, how many after oath had been sworn to reverse what they had agreed to, whilst they sought to bring back the serfs who had been freed from the oppression of their yoke, to their former state. At least there was implacable hate by the Bishop and nobles against the citizens, and whereas he has not the power to crush the freedom of the French, after the fashion of Normandy and England, the pastor is weak and forgetful of his sacred calling through his insatiable greed. Whenever one of the people entered a court of law, where he was dependent not on the justice of God, but on his ability to please his judges, if I may say so, he was drained of his substance to the last penny.

Hence because the taking of gifts is wont to be attended by the subversion of all justice, the coiners of the currency, knowing that if they did wrong in their office, they could save themselves by money bribes, corrupted the coinage with so much base metal that through this very many were reduced to poverty. For as they made coins of the cheapest bronze, which in a moment by certain dishonest arts they made brighter than silver, (shame on them!) fond men were deceived, and giving up their goods of great or little value, got in exchange nothing but dross. And the patient suffering of this by the Lord Bishop was well rewarded, and thus not only within the province of Laon but in all directions the ruin of many was hastened. And when he was deservedly powerless to uphold the value of his own currency wickedly debased by himself, he instituted pence of Amiens, also most debased, to be current in the city for some time; but when he could by no means keep that up, he struck an impression of his own time, on which he had stamped a pastoral staff to represent himself. This was received with such laughter and scorn, that it had less value than the debased coinage.

Meantime since, on the issue of each of these new coins, proclamation was made that no one should criticise the wretched impression, there ensued frequent occasion for accusing the people of speaking evil of the Bishop's ordinances, and hence exaction of all sorts of heavy fines could be carried out. Moreover a certain monk of the very worst reputation in every respect, named Theodorus of Thorn, of which place he was a native, brought very large quantities of silver from Flanders. Bringing all this down to the false standard of the Laon mint, he scattered it all over the surrounding province. By appealing to the greed of the rich with his hateful presents and bringing in lies, perjury and want, he robbed his country of truth, justice and wealth. No act of an enemy, no plunderings, no burnings have hurt the province more ever since the Roman walls contained the ancient mint of the city.

But since "Impiety long hidden does violence at times to the show of honour artfully drawn over it, and things evident cannot be concealed; as bright light pierces through glass, so does it through the countenance," that which he did to Gerard hiding his hand in it, he did to another Gerard some time afterwards and gave manifest proof of his cruelty. It was an older Gerard, perhaps a foreman over the countrymen who belonged to him; and because he was more attached to Thomas, reputed son of Enguerrand, of whom we have spoken before, the most wicked man we have known in this generation, the Bishop regarded him as a general enemy. Seizing him therefore and thrusting him into prison in the palace, he had his eyes put out at night by the hands of his negro servant.[2] By this deed he brought open shame upon himself and the old story of what he had done to the first Gerard, was renewed, both clergy and people being aware that the canon of Toledo, if I am not mistaken, forbade the infliction of death or the passing of a sentence of death or mutilation by bishops, priests and clergy and the very rumour of such acts raised the anger of the King. Perhaps too, it reached the ears of the Apostolic See; at least I know the Pope suspended him from his office, and I believe, for no other reason. But to make matters worse, during his suspension he dedicated a church. Therefore he goes to Rome and by persuasive words the Pope's anger is assuaged, and he is sent back to us with his authority restored. And so, God seeing that pastors and flock were by act and will partners in wickedness, could no longer restrain his judgment and at last permitted the malice that had been conceived to break out into open rage, which in its headlong mad career was through the vengeance of God shattered by a dreadful fall.

Having therefore summoned the nobles and certain of the clergy on the last day of Lent in the holy days of the Passion of our Lord, he determined to urge the annulment of the Commune, to which he had sworn, and had by bribes induced the King to swear, and the day before the Passover, that is to say, on the day of the Lord's Supper, he summoned the King to this pious duty and instructed the King and all his people to break their oaths, in which snare he had first placed his own neck, on the day, that is, on which his predecessor, Ascelin, had betrayed his King as aforesaid. For on that day, when he should have performed that most glorious of all a prelate's duties, the consecration of the oil and the absolution of the people from their sins, he was not even seen to enter the church. He was intriguing with the King's courtiers for the annulment of the Commune and for the restoration by the King of the laws of the city to their former state. But the citizens fearing their overthrow, promised four hundred (perhaps more) pounds to the King and his courtiers. In reply the Bishop begged the nobles to go with him to interview the King. They promised on their part seven hundred pounds, and King Louis,[3] son of Philip, of conspicuous person and a mighty warrior, hating sloth in business, of dauntless courage in adversity, and in other respects a good man, in this was not very just that he gave ear and attention too much to worthless persons debased by greed. And this redounded to his own great loss and blame and the ruin of many, which it is certain took place here and elsewhere.

The King's craving for money being turned therefore, as I said, to feed upon the larger promise, through his consent the oaths of the Bishop and the nobles became void without any regard for honour or the sacred season. That night because of the outbreak of disorder caused by his most unjust blow, although the King had a lodging elsewhere, he was afraid to sleep outside the Bishop's palace. Very early in the morning the King departed and the Bishop assured the nobles they need have no fear about the agreement to pay so much money, knowing that he himself would pay whatever they had promised. "And," said he, "if I do not perform my promise, hand me over to the king's prison for ransom."

The compact of the Commune being broken, such rage, such amazement seized the citizens that all the officials abandoned their duties and the stalls of the craftsmen and cobblers were closed and nothing was exposed for sale by the innkeepers and hucksters, who expected to have nothing left when the lords began plundering. For at once the property of all was calculated by the Bishop and nobles, and whatever any man was known to have given to arrange the Commune, so much was demanded of him to procure its annulment. These events took place on the day of the Passover, which is called the preparation, and on the holy Sabbath when their minds were being prepared to receive the body and blood of the Lord, they were made ready for murders only here, for perjury there. Why say more? All the efforts of the prelate and the nobles in these days were reserved for fleecing their inferiors. But those inferiors were no longer moved by mere anger, but goaded into a murderous lust for the death of the Bishop and his accomplices and bound themselves by oath to effect their purpose. Now they say that four hundred took the oath. Such a mob could not be secret and when it came to the ears of Anselm towards evening of the holy Sabbath, he sent word to the Bishop, as he was retiring to rest, not to go out to the early morning service, knowing that if he did he must certainly be killed. But he, infatuated with excessive pride said, "Fie, surely I shall not perish at the hands of such." Yet notwithstanding his scornful words, he did not dare to rise for matins or to enter the church. The next day, as he followed the clergy in procession, he ordered his household people and all the soldiers coming behind him to carry short swords under their garments. In this procession, when a little disorder, as is likely in a crowd, began to arise, one of the citizens coming out of the crypt and thinking the time had come for the murder, to which they were sworn, began to cry out in a loud voice as a signal, "Commune, Commune!" over and over again. And because it was a feast day, this was easily stopped, yet it brought suspicion on the other party. And so, when the service of the mass was over, the Bishop summoned a great number of countrymen from the episcopal manors and manned the towers of the church and gave orders that his palace should be guarded, although he was almost as much hated by them, as they knew that the piles of money, which he had promised the King, must be drained from their own purses.

Now on the second day after Easter it is the custom for the clergy to assemble at St. Vincent's. Since therefore the conspirators had been anticipated the day before, they had decided to act on this day, and would have done so, if they had seen that all the nobles were with the Bishop. For they had found one of the nobles in the suburb, a harmless man, who had recently married a young cousin of mine, a woman of modest character. But they were unwilling to attack him fearing to put others on their guard. Having therefore reached the third day of Easter and feeling more secure the Bishop allows those men to depart, whom he had put in the towers and palace to protect him. On the fourth day I went to him, because I had been plundered of my supply of corn and of some legs of pork, called bacon, through his disorders. When interviewed by me and requested to relieve the city of these great disturbances, he replied, "What do ye think they can do by their riots? If John, my moor, were to take by the nose the most powerful man amongst them, he would not dare so much as to grunt. For just now I have compelled them to renounce what they call their Commune for so long as I live." I spoke, and then seeing the man overcome with pride, I refrained from saying more. Yet before I left the city, by reason of his instability we quarrelled with mutual recriminations. But although he was warned by many of the imminent peril, he took no notice of any one.

CHAPTER VIII] The next day, that is, the fifth in Easter week, after midday, as he was engaged in business with Archdeacon Walter about the getting of money, behold there arose a disorderly noise throughout the city, men shouting "Commune!" and again through the middle of the chapel of the Blessed Mary through that door by which the murderers of Gerard had come and gone, there citizens now entered the Bishop's court with swords, battle-axes, bows and hatchets, and carrying clubs and spears, a very great company. As soon as this sudden attack was discovered, the nobles rallied from all sides to the Bishop, having sworn to give him aid against such an onset, if it should occur. In this rally Guinimon, the châtelain, an aged nobleman of handsome presence and guiltless character, armed only with shield and spear, ran out through the church and as he entered the Bishop's hall, was the first to fall, struck on the back of the head with a battle-axe by a certain Rainbert, who was his fellow-citizen. Immediately afterwards Regnier, of whom I spoke before as married to my cousin, hurrying to enter the palace, was struck from behind with a spear when trying to enter by mounting on the pulpitum[4] of the Bishop's chapel, and there falling headlong was at once consumed by the fire of the palace from his waist downwards. Ado, the Vidame, quarrelsome, but brave, separated from the rest and able to do little by himself among so many, as he was striving to reach the Bishop's palace, encountered the full force of the attack, but with spear and sword made such a stand that in a moment he struck down two of those who came on.

Then mounting the dining-table in the hall, wounded now in the knees and other parts of the body and at last only supporting himself on his knees, whilst striking at his assailants all round him, he kept them off for a long time, until, becoming exhausted, he was struck through the body with a lance and after a little was reduced to ashes by the fire in that house.

Next the outrageous mob attacking the Bishop and howling before the walls of his palace, he with some who were succouring him fought them off by hurling of stones and shooting of arrows. For he now, as at all times, shewed great spirit as a fighter; but because he had wrongly and in vain taken up another sword, by the sword he perished. Therefore being unable to stand against the reckless assaults of the people, he put on the clothes of one of his servants and flying to the vaults of the church hid himself in a cask, shut up in which with the head fastened on by a faithful follower he thought himself safely hidden. And as they ran hither and thither demanding where, not the Bishop, but the hangdog, was, they seized one of his pages, but through his faithfulness could not get what they wanted. Laying hands on another, they learn from the traitor's nod where to look for him. Entering the vaults, therefore, and searching everywhere, at last they found him in the following manner.

There was a pestilent fellow, a bondman of the church of the Blessed Vincent, but for a long time an official and overseer of Enguerrand of Coucy, who being set over the collection of tolls paid for crossing the bridge called Soord, sometimes watched until there were only a few travellers passing, and having robbed them of all their property, in order that they might make no complaint against him, threw them into the river with a weight round their necks. How often he had done this, God only knows. The number of the thefts and robberies being more than any one could count, the unchecked wickedness of his heart, and one as might say, was displayed also in the truculence of his looks. This man having incurred the displeasure of Enguerrand, went over wholly to the party of the Commune in Laon. He who had spared neither monk nor clerk nor stranger, in fact no sex, was last of all to be the slayer of a bishop. He the leader and instigator of this attack searched most diligently for the Bishop, whom he hated more bitterly than the rest.

And so, as they sought for him in every vessel, this fellow halted in front of that cask, where the man was hiding, and having broken in the head, asked again and again who was there. And he, hardly able to move his frozen lips under his blows, said "A prisoner." Now the Bishop was wont in mockery to call him Isengrin, I suppose, because of his wolfish look, for so some people call wolves. The wretch, therefore, says to the Bishop, "Is this my Lord Isengrin stored away?" Renulf[5] therefore, sinner though he was, yet the Lord's anointed, was dragged forth from the cask by the hair, beaten with many blows and brought out into the open air in the narrow lane of the clergy's cloister before the house of the chaplain Godfrey. And as he piteously implored them, ready to take oath that he would henceforth cease to be their Bishop, that he would give them unlimited riches, that he would leave the country, and as they with hardened hearts jeered at him, one named Bernard and surnamed de Brueys, lifting his battle-axe brutally dashed out the brains of that sacred, though sinner's, head, and he slipping between the hands of those who held him, was dead before he reached the ground stricken by another thwart blow under the eye-sockets and across the middle of the nose. There brought to his end, his legs were cut off and many another wound inflicted. But Thibaut seeing the ring on the finger of the erstwhile prelate and not being able to draw it off, cut off the dead man's finger and took it. And so stripped to his skin he was thrown into a corner in front of his chaplain's house. My God, who shall recount the mocking words that were thrown at him by passers-by, as he lay there, and with what clods and stones and dirt his corpse was covered? But before I go on to other matters, I must say that a certain act did much to bring about his end. Two days, I think, before his death there was a meeting of the chief of his clergy, because he had recently told the King when staying in the city, that the clergy were not to be considered, because they were almost all of them born king's serfs. When confronted with his words, he denied them, speaking after this manner, "May the Holy Communion, which I have just received at that altar" — stretching out his right hand towards it — "turn to my ruin, and I call down the sword of the Holy Spirit on my soul, if I spoke such words to the King about you." When they heard this, some were utterly confounded and swore (by the Sacrament) that they heard him out of his own mouth tell the King that. Manifestly the instability of his character and his false tongue brought on him his ruin.

CHAPTER IX] Meantime one part of the raging mob made their way to the house of Raoul, who was the Bishop's serving-man and had been one of the friends of Gerard of Crecy, a man of small stature but heroic spirit. He in breastplate and helmet and light harness resolved to resist, but seeing the numbers too great and fearing to be thrown into the fire, cast away his arms and exposed himself unprotected to their mercy with his arms stretched out in the shape of a cross. They with no thought of God cruelly butchered him, as he lay prostrate. He himself before the murder of Gerard in the church saw the following vision: He thought he was in the church of the Blessed Mary and that there assembled men of wicked disposition, who began to play foreign games and to exhibit to some who sat round, strange sights. Whilst that went on, other men from the house of Guy, the Treasurer, came forth bearing cups, in which was contained a drink of such foul odour that it was intolerable for those who smelled it, and this was carried along the rows of spectators. The meaning of this is clearer than daylight. What a horrible and hateful sport of demons leapt forth there, what monstrous stench of wickedness everywhere poured out of that same house, is now manifest. For the maddened populace first threw brands into that house from which the fire leapt into the church and lastly seized the Bishop's palace.

CHAPTER XI] Now when the wicked citizens had duly weighed the enormity of the crime done by them, they were consumed with dread, fearing greatly the King's judgment, and hence when they ought to have sought a cure for their hurt, they only added wound to wound. For they decided to call in Thomas, the son of de Coucy, who had the castle of Marne, to defend them against the King's attack. He, it appears, attained power to ruin hosts of people by preying from early youth on the poor, and pilgrims to Jerusalem. So unheard-of in our times was his cruelty, that men considered cruel seem more merciful in killing cattle than he in murdering men. For he did not merely kill them outright with the sword and for definite offenses, as is usual, but by butchery after horrible tortures. For when he was compelling prisoners to ransom themselves, he hung them up by their testicles, sometimes with his own hands, and these often breaking away through the weight of the body, there followed at once the breaking out of their vital parts. Others were suspended by their thumbs or even their private parts and were weighted with a stone placed on their shoulders, and he himself walking below them, when he failed to extort what he could not get by other means, beat them madly with cudgels until they promised what satisfied him, or perished under punishment.

No one can tell how many expired in his dungeons and chains by starvation, disease and torture. But it is certain that two years before, when he had gone to the mountains of Soissons to give aid against some countrymen, three of these hid themselves in a cave and coming to the entrance into the cave with his lance he drove his weapon into the mouth of one of them with so hard a thrust, that the iron of the lance breaking through the entrails passed out by the anus. Why go on with instances that have no end? The two left in it both perished by his hand. Again, one of his prisoners being wounded could not march. He asked the man why he did not go faster. He replied that he could not. "Stop," said he, "I will make you hurry and be sorry for it." Leaping down from his horse, he cut off both his feet, and of that the man died. Of what use is it to recount these horrors, when later there will be like occasion for mentioning them? I will return to my matter.

This man long gave shelter to the murderers of Gerard, whilst under excommunication, and long encouraged them, cherishing none but the worst criminals, and to him is applicable rather than to Catiline the saying of Sallust, "Out of mere delight was he evil and cruel." To set the crown upon their wrong doing, they turned to him with a request that he would come and protect them against the King, and when at last he did so, they admitted him into the city. After hearing their petition, he consulted his friends what he should do, and was unanimously advised by them that his strength was not sufficient to hold the city against the King, counsel which he dared not make known for some time to the madmen whilst in their city. Therefore, he told them to come out into the open country where he would reveal to them his intentions. When they had gone about two miles outside, he told them this: "Since this city is the capital of the realm, it cannot be held against the King by me. But if ye fear the royal troops, follow me into my land and take me for your patron and friend." At those words they were exceedingly dismayed. Maddened therefore, with fear because of what they had done and thinking the King was threatening their lives, a countless host of the people fled with him. Teudegold too, the slayer of the bishop, who, sword in hand, had searched the ceilings, the vaults and the claustral recesses of the church of the Blessed Vincent to find fugitives to kill, who displaying the episcopal ring on his finger proved his right to be their head, he, with his accomplices did not dare to return to the city and followed Thomas almost in destitution. Moreover, Thomas had set free William, son of Hadwin, and other persons in the city. But rumour with the speed of Pegasus flying abroad, roused the men of the neighbouring country as well as those of the towns with the tale that the city was emptied of inhabitants. Then all the villagers rush upon the deserted city and see the houses full of property and with no one to defend them. Even wealthy people disguised themselves in mean dress, for they were afraid to draw the eyes of the nobles upon themselves.

At that time the unlawful and incestuous wife of Enguerrand under guise of continence covering her contempt for Enguerrand because of his age and bulk, yet could not live without enjoyment of lovers. Enamoured therefore, of a handsome youth and kept from all converse with him by Enguerrand, she suddenly became so mad with lust for the man that having summoned him to her side, she gave her little daughter to him in marriage to cover their wicked intrigue and made him the defender of her land against Thomas, for whom his so-called father cherished an implacable hatred and whom she wished to disinherit. He being at Coucy and threatening Thomas with enmity by every means in his power, but having insufficient resources to venture upon a difficult task, was befriended by fortune in the following manner:

Now Enguerrand and Guy, as he was called, learning that Thomas had left the city followed by the people, went to Laon and found the houses filled with an abundance of everything, but without inhabitants. Such plenty was there that if it had been carefully guarded by the rulers to save it from waste by hangers-on and thieves, all attempts to drive out that young man would have been in vain, and he would have felt no want for the rest of his life. Who should say, or saying would be believed, what money, what clothing, what provisions of all kinds were found there? For when the crowds of rustics and those in the outskirts, moreover, the people of Montaign and Pierrepoint and La Fere too came there before those of Coucy, wonderful to say, what did the first comers find, what did they carry off, when our people arriving later boasted that they had found everything in order and almost untouched! But what consideration or self-restraint could there be amongst brutes and fools? The wine and corn they happened to find having no value and because there were no means on the spot of carrying them off, were wantonly and shockingly wasted. Then the proceeds of their plundering began to give rise to quarrels and any booty passed out of the hands of the weaker into the possession of the stronger. Two, if they met a third, were certain to plunder him. So wretched was the state of the city. Those who had fled from it, had pillaged and burnt the houses of the clergy and nobles, whom they hated; but now the nobles remaining there lost all their property and furnishings down to the bars and bolts.

Not a single monk then could enter the city in safety or go out of it without being deprived of his horse or stripped of the clothes on his body. Guilty and innocent alike had collected at St. Vincent's with a great quantity of goods. What swords, Lord God, were drawn over monks willing to surrender their lives as well as their property! There, William, the son of Hadwin, forgetting the deliverance granted him by God, allowed a countryman of his, to whom he had just promised security for life and limb and had drawn him into his power through trust in his promises, to be taken and condemned by the servants of the nobles, Guinimar and Regnier, who had been slain. For being fastened by his feet to the tail of a horse by the son of that castellan, his brains were quickly dashed out and he was then placed on the gallows. Now he was called Robert and surnamed Manducans and was a rich and upright man. But the steward of the Vidame mentioned above and called, I believe, Everard, who slew his master on the very day he had eaten with him, the servant his master, was exalted to great heights of arrogance. Others too were done to death in similar ways. It is an impossible task to ravel out all that happened anywhere in the punishment inflicted on monks and secular. But it should be known that on the day after the slaughter, that is, on the sixth day, Thomas came into the city and left on the Sabbath, and on Sunday, God quickly sent punishment on them for their great crime.

These events took place in the year 1115 of the Incarnation of our Lord, on the sixth day of Easter and the 30th of April. Assuredly that Bishop was of unbounded levity, so that whatever foolish and worldly thought he conceived, his tongue very readily gave him absolution. Certainly I saw that cousin whom I have mentioned, conducting herself when recently married with the greatest possible modesty; but he in my hearing called her a coarse hoyden, because she absented herself from the talk and sight of strangers, and was far from forcing herself on his notice like other women. Certainly too, I had written a book on the Crusade to Jerusalem, which, he desiring to see it, was sent to him, but he was much displeased with it, because he saw it was dedicated in the introduction to my Lord, the Bishop Lisiard of Soissons. After that he would deign to read no more, whereas he had valued my other works more than I deserved. And although he was so successful in gathering wealth, he quickly squandered the whole of it on useless causes. But those evils came to early fruition in his times.

It should be known that evil flourished not in him alone, but resulted from the great wickedness of others too, in fact of the whole population. For in the whole of France there nowhere occurred such crimes as amongst the people of Laon. A very little time before these things happened, a certain priest whilst sitting in his own house near the fire, was struck from behind and killed by a servant with whom he had been too familiar. Taking up the body he hid it in a more secret chamber, locking it up. And when after some days, because of the disappearance of his master, people asked the servant where he had gone, he lied to them, saying the man had gone on business somewhere. And when, by reason of the unusual stench, the body could no longer be kept in the house, having collected his master's property and laid the body face downwards on the ashes of the house fire and thrown down the shelf hanging above, which they call the drying-shelf, that it might be thought its fall had crushed him, he then fled away with the goods.

The Deans also just before the first of the month used to transact the business of the priests in their districts. And when a certain Burgundian priest, very talkative and ready, had accused the priest next to him of some trifling matter, the Dean fined him for the offence only sixpence. He, being more than a little annoyed at the fine, when the Burgundian returned home at night, the priest who had lost the money, lay in wait for him. And he, climbing the steps to his house with a lantern, was struck on the head by the other from behind and died of the blow, intestate.

Another also a priest at Essey, catching a priest celebrating mass before the altar, ordered his attendant to shoot him down with an arrow. Although he did not die of the wound, yet the author and cause of it was not guiltless of a crime of murder and a sacrilege unheard of among Christians. Other such acts are related, done at the same time and in the same parts.

There appeared also visions foreshowing the calamities I have described. A man thought he saw a moon-shaped ball fall over Laon, which meant that a sudden rebellion would arise in the city. Some one of our monks also saw before the knees of the crucifix in the chapel of the Blessed Mary three great bars in order placed opposite. Moreover, the place where Gerard perished, seemed to be covered with blood. The crucifix signified someone high up in the church, who was truly opposed by three bars, his poor entry on office, his sin against Gerard and, lastly, against the people, being the offences that brought about his end. That place in which Gerard had perished was covered with blood in that the wickedness done was wiped out by no punishment. Besides there were heard, I have learnt from the monks of St. Vincent, certain noises, it was supposed of malignant spirits, and there was the appearance of flames in the air at night in the city. There was born also some days before a boy who was double down to the buttocks, having that is, two heads and right down to the loins two bodies, each with its own arms: being double, therefore, above, it was single below. After it was baptized, it lived three days. In short, many portents were seen to occur, about which there was no doubt that they foreboded the great disaster which ensued.

NOTES

1. The new bishop of Laon.

2. Undoubtedly this negro servant was secured from Africa and was a victim of the slave trade carried on by Moslem merchants.

3. King Louis VI (1108–1137).

4. The *pulpitum* was a screen and loft separating the choir from the nave.

5. The bishop's name.

6

The Opulence of Constantinople

THE dramatic economic recovery of western Europe between 1000 and 1200 brought vast change. A phenomenal growth in population led men into land hitherto uncultivated and into the towns, which became centers of local and international trade. Some towns became noted for the products of their industries, others became banking centers. Everywhere new financial techniques, more efficient business organization, expanded transportation facilities, and renewed contact with the non-European world brought material prosperity and a better standard of living. An important by-product of this economic advance was, of course, a greater awareness of the non-European world and a realization of how far Europe had to progress before it could equal the material and cultural civilization of the Byzantine and Arab worlds. When the forces of the Fourth Crusade (1201–1204) were diverted from the Holy Land and ended by capturing Constantinople, the capital of the Byzantine Empire, thousands of ordinary Europeans were introduced for the first time to the amazing riches and artistic treasures of this famous queen of the Mediterranean. No account of the taking of Constantinople better describes western amazement at eastern wealth and artistic achievement than that of Robert of Clari, a knight from northern France who participated in the Fourth Crusade and was one of the first to enter Constantinople. In his account, note how the magnificence of Byzantine civilization is regarded by one steeped in the feudal mentality of western Europe.

Robert of Clari, La conquête de Constantinople ("The Conquest of Constantinople")

AFTERWARDS[1] it was ordered that all the wealth of the spoils should be brought to a certain church in the city. The wealth was brought there, and they took ten knights, high men, of the

From E. H. McNeal, THE CONQUEST OF CONSTANTINOPLE TRANSLATED FROM THE OLD FRENCH OF ROBERT OF CLARI (New York, 1936), pp. 101–112. Reprinted by permission of the Columbia University Press.

pilgrims and ten of the Venetians who were thought to be honorable, and they set them to guard this wealth. So the wealth was brought there. And it was so rich, and there were so many rich vessels of gold and silver and cloth of gold and so many rich jewels, that it was a fair marvel, the great wealth that was brought there. Not since the world was made, was there ever seen or won so great a treasure or so noble or so rich, not in the time of Alexander nor in the time of Charlemagne nor before nor after. Nor do I think, myself, that in the forty richest cities of the world there had been so much wealth as was found in Constantinople. For the Greeks say that two thirds of the wealth of this world is in Constantinople and the other third scattered throughout the world. And the very ones who were to guard the wealth took gold ornaments and whatever else they wanted and robbed the treasure. And each one of the rich men took gold ornaments or cloth of silk and gold or anything else he wanted and carried it off. So in this way they began to rob the treasure, so that nothing was shared with the common people of the host or the poor knights or the sergeants who had helped to win the treasure, save the plain silver, like the silver pitchers which the ladies of the city used to carry to the baths. And the other wealth that remained to be divided was concealed in such evil ways as I have told you. But in any event the Venetians had their half, and the precious stones and the great treasure that remained to be divided went such evil ways as I shall tell you later.

When the city was captured and the pilgrims were quartered, as I have told you, and the palaces were taken over, then they found in the palaces riches more than a great deal. And the palace of Boukoleon[2] was very rich and was made in such a way as I shall tell you. Within this palace, which was held by the marquis, there were fully five hundred halls, all connected with one another and all made with gold mosaic. And in it there were fully thirty chapels, great and small, and there was one of them which was called the Holy Chapel,[3] which was so rich and noble that there was not a hinge nor a band nor any other part such as is usually made of iron that was not all of silver, and there was no column that was not of jasper or porphyry or some other rich precious stone. And the pavement of this chapel was of a white marble so smooth and clear that it seemed to be of crystal, and this chapel was so rich and so noble that no one could ever tell you its great beauty and nobility. Within this chapel were found many rich relics. One found there two pieces of the True Cross as large as the leg of a man and as long as half a *toise,* and one found there also the iron of the lance with which Our Lord had His side pierced and two of the nails which were driven through His hands and feet, and one found there in a crystal phial quite a little of His blood, and one found there the tunic which He wore and which was taken from Him when they led Him to the Mount of Calvary, and one found there the blessed crown with which He was crowned, which was made of reeds with thorns as sharp as the points of daggers. And one found there a part of the robe of Our Lady and the head of my lord St. John the Baptist and so many other rich relics that I could not recount them to you or tell you all the truth.

Now there was still another relic in this chapel which we had forgotten to tell you about. For there were two rich vessels of gold hanging in the midst of the chapel by two heavy silver chains. In one of these vessels there was a tile and in the other a cloth. And we shall tell you where these relics came from. There was once a holy man in Constantinople. It happened that this holy man was covering the house of a widow with tile for the love of God. And as he was covering it, Our Lord appeared to him and said to him (now this good man had a cloth wrapped about him): "Give me that cloth," said Our Lord. And the good man gave it to Him, and Our Lord enveloped His face with it so that His features were imprinted on it. And then He handed it back to him, and He told him to carry it with him and touch the sick with it, and whoever had faith in it would be healed of his sickness. And the good man took it and carried it away; but before he carried it away, after God had given him back his cloth, the good man took it and hid it under a tile until vespers. At vespers, when he went away, he took the cloth, and as he lifted up the tile, he saw the image imprinted on the tile just as it was on the cloth, and he carried the tile and the cloth away, and afterwards he cured many sick with them. And these relics were hanging in the midst of the chapel, as I have told you. Now there was in this chapel still another relic, for there was an image of St. Demetrius which was painted on a panel. This image gave off so much oil that it could not be removed as fast as it flowed from the picture. [And there was another palace in the city, called the palace of Blachernae.] And there were fully twenty chapels there and at least two hundred chambers, or three hundred, all connected with one another and all made of gold mosaic. And this palace was so rich and so noble that no one could describe it to you or recount its great nobility and richness. In this palace of Blachernae there was found a very great treasure, for one found there the rich crowns which had belonged to former emperors and the rich ornaments of gold and the rich cloth of silk and gold and the rich imperial robes and the rich precious stones and so many other riches that no one could number the great treasure of gold and silver that was found in the palaces and in many other places in the city.

Then the pilgrims regarded the great size of the city, and the palaces and fine abbeys and churches and the great wonders which were in the city, and they marveled at it greatly. And they marveled greatly at the church of Saint Sophia and at the riches which were in it.

Now I will tell you about the church of Saint Sophia,[4] how it was made. Saint Sophia in Greek means Sainte Trinité ["Holy Trinity"] in French [sic]. The church of Saint Sophia was entirely round, and within the church were domes, round all about, which were borne by great and very rich columns, and there was no column which was not of jasper or porphyry or some other precious stone, nor was there one of these columns that did not work cures. There was one that cured sickness of the reins when it was rubbed against, and another that cured sickness of the side, and others that cured other ills. And there was no door in this church and no hinges or bands or other parts such as are usually made of iron that were not all of silver. The master altar of the church was so rich that it was beyond price, for the table of the altar was made of gold and precious stones broken up and crushed all together, which a rich emperor had had made. This table was fully fourteen feet long. Around the altar were columns of silver supporting a canopy over the altar which was made just like a church spire, and it was all of solid silver and was so rich that no one could tell the money it was worth. The place where they read the gospel was so fair and noble that we could not describe to you how it was made. Then down through the church there hung fully a hundred chandeliers, and there was not one that did not hang by a great silver chain as thick as a man's arm. And there were in each chandelier full five and twenty lamps or more. And there was not a chandelier that was not worth at least two hundred marks of silver. On the ring of the great door of the church, which was all of silver, there hung a tube, of what material no one knew; it was the size of a pipe such as shepherds play on. This tube had such virtue as I shall tell you. When an infirm man who had some sickness in his body like the bloat, so that he was bloated in his belly, put it in his mouth, however little he put it in, when this tube took hold it sucked out all the sickness and it made the poison run out of his mouth and it held him so fast that it made his eyes roll and turn in his head, and he could not get away until the tube had sucked all of the sickness out of him. And the sicker a man was the longer it held him, and if a man who was not sick put it in his mouth, it would not hold him at all, much or little.

Then in front of this church of Saint Sophia there was a great column which was fully three times the reach of a man's arms in thickness and was fully fifty *toises* in height. It was made of marble and of copper over the marble and was bound about with strong bands of iron. And on top of this column there lay a flat slab of stone which was fully fifteen feet in length and as much in width. On this stone there was an emperor made of copper on a great copper horse, and he was holding out his hand toward heathendom, and there were letters written on the statue which said that he swore that the Saracens should never have truce from him. And in the other hand he held a golden globe with a cross on it. The Greeks said that this was Heraclius the emperor.[5] And on the croup of the horse and on the head and round about there were fully ten nests of herons, who nested there every year.

Then elsewhere in the city there was another church which was called the church of the Seven Apostles. And it was said to be even richer and nobler than the church of Saint Sophia. There was so much richness and nobility there that no one could recount to you the richness and nobility of this church. And there lay in this church the bodies of seven apostles. There was also the marble column to which Our Lord was bound, before He was put on the cross. And it was said that Constantine the emperor lay there and Helena [Constantine's mother], and many other emperors.

Now there was elsewhere in the city a gate which was called the Golden Mantle. On this gate there was a golden globe which was made by such enchantment that the Greeks said as long as it was there no thunderbolt would fall in the city. On this globe there was an image cast of copper, with a golden mantle clasped about it, which it held out on its arm, and it had letters written on it which said: "Anyone," said the image, "who lives in Constantinople a year can have a golden mantle just as I have."

Elsewhere in the city there is another gate which is called the Golden Gate. On this gate there were two elephants made of copper which were so large that it was a fair marvel. This gate was never opened except when an emperor was returning from battle after conquering territory. And when an emperor returned from battle after conquering territory, then the clergy of the city would come out in procession to meet him, and the gate would be opened, and they would bring out a chariot of gold, which was made like a cart with four wheels, such as we call a *curre*. Now in the middle of this chariot there was a high seat and on the seat there was a throne and around the throne there were four columns which bore a canopy to shade the throne, which seemed as if it were all of gold. Then the emperor, wearing his crown, would take his seat on the throne, and he would enter through this gate and be borne in this chariot, with great joy and rejoicing, to his palace.

Now in another part of the city there was another marvel. There was an open place near the palace of Boukoleon which was called the Games of the Emperor.[6] This place was a good bowshot and a half long and nearly a bowshot wide. Around this place there were fully thirty rows of seats or forty, on which the Greeks used to mount to watch the games, and above these rows there was a loge, very dainty and very noble, where the emperor and the empress sat when the games were held, and the other high men and ladies. And if there were two sides playing at the same time, the emperor and the empress would wager with each other that one side would play better than the other, and so would all the others who watched the games. Along this open place there was a wall which was a good fifteen feet high and ten feet wide. Upon this wall there were figures of men and women, and of horses and oxen and camels and bears and lions and many other kinds of animals, all made of copper, and all so well made and formed so naturally that there is no master workman in heathendom or in Christendom so skillful as to be able to make figures as good as these. And formerly they used to play by enchantment, but they do not play any longer. And the French looked at the Games of the Emperor in wonder when they saw it.

Now there was elsewhere in the city another marvel. There were two statues made of copper in the form of women, well and naturally made, and more beautiful than a good deal. And neither of them was less than a good twenty feet in height. One of these figures held its hand out toward the West, and it had letters written on it which said: "From the West will come those who will capture Constantinople," and the other figure held its hand out toward a vile place and said: "Here," said the figure, "here is where they will throw them." These two figures were sitting in front of the Change, which used to be very rich there, for the rich money changers used to be there with great heaps of besants and of precious stones in front of them, before the city was taken, but there were not so many of them afterwards.

There was elsewhere in the city still another great marvel. There were two columns, each of them at least three times the reach of a man's arms in thickness and at least fifty *toises* in height. And hermits used to live on the tops of these columns in little shelters that were there, and there were doors in the columns by which one could ascend. On the outside of these columns there were pictured and written by prophecy all the events and all the conquests which have happened in Constantinople or which were going to happen. But no one could understand the event until it had happened, and when it had happened the people would go there and ponder over it, and then for the first time they would see and understand the event. And even this conquest of the French was written and pictured there and the ships in which they made the assault when the city was taken, and the Greeks were not able to understand it before it had happened, but when it had happened they went to look at these columns and ponder over it, and they found that the letters which were written on the pictured ships said that a people, short haired and with iron swords, would come from the West to conquer Constantinople. All these marvels which I have recounted to you here and still a great many more than we could recount, the French found in Constantinople after they had captured it, nor do I think, for my part, that any man on earth could number all the abbeys of the city, so many there were, both of monks and of nuns, aside from the other churches outside of the city. And it was reckoned that there were in the city a good thirty thousand priests, both monks and others. Now about the rest of the Greeks, high and low, rich and poor, about the size of the city, about the palaces and the other marvels that are there, we shall leave off telling you. For no man on earth, however long he might have lived in the city, could number them or recount them to you. And if anyone should recount to you the hundredth part of the richness and the beauty and the nobility that was found in the abbeys and in the churches and in the palaces and in the city, it would seem like a lie and you would not believe it.

NOTES

1. After the crusaders had taken Constantinople in April 1204.

2. This was the Great Palace located between the Hippodrome and the sea walls of Constantinople.

3. The famous church of the Blessed Virgin of the Pharos (lighthouse).

4. The celebrated church constructed by the emperor Justinian.

5. Actually this was an equestrian statue of the emperor Justinian.

6. The Hippodrome.

7

The Conflict Between Spiritual and Secular Authority

THE revival of western Europe in the eleventh century was characterized not only by economic growth and political stability but also by the reform of the church, the invigoration of spiritual life and the rise of the papacy to real leadership of western Christendom. The awakening of the church, which for over two centuries had been relatively decadent and under the control of secular rulers, was not accomplished without a struggle. Such powerful rulers as the emperors of the Holy Roman Empire, who had been partially responsible for the reform of the church and for the selection of abler popes, would not admit that their imperial authority was inferior to that of the papacy, that they should no longer appoint bishops and abbots and invest them with their spiritual offices, or that they should not exploit some of the church's landed wealth. From the second half of the eleventh century into the fourteenth a bitter struggle, known as the investiture controversy, was fought between secular princes and the papacy over these issues. The records that follow give the arguments advanced by both parties as well as some of the dramatic episodes of the conflict. In order of their appearance these records tell of the papal decree in 1059 providing for the election of the pope by the cardinal clergy, the opinions expressed on papal authority by Pope Gregory VII in 1075, the renunciation of obedience to Gregory VII by the emperor Henry IV in 1076, the deposition of Henry IV by Gregory VII in 1076, the submission of Henry IV to Gregory VII at Canossa in 1077, Gregory VII's eloquent exposition of papal power in a letter of 1081, the murder in 1170 of Thomas Becket, archbishop of Canterbury and enemy of Henry II of England, the statement of papal supremacy in a letter of Innocent III in 1214, and finally the bull UNAM SANCTAM (1302) of Boniface VIII, wherein the pope interpreted his authority especially as it related to Philip IV of France.

A Pope Nicholas II, Decree on Papal Elections (1059)

WE (Pope Nicholas II) decree and establish   3] that, on the death of the pontiff of this Roman universal church, the cardinal bishops shall first confer with most diligent consideration and then shall summon the cardinal clergy[1] to join them; and afterwards the rest of the clergy and people shall give their assent to the new election.   4] That, lest the disease of venality creep in by any means, godly men shall take the chief part in the election of the pontiff, and the others shall follow their lead. This method of election is regular and in accordance with the rules and decrees of the Fathers . . . especially with the words of St. Leo;[2] "No argument," he says, "will permit them to be considered bishops who have not been elected by the clergy, nor demanded by the people, nor consecrated by the bishops of the province with the approval of the metropolitan." But since the Apostolic See is raised above all churches in the world and therefore can have no metropolitan over it, the cardinal bishops without doubt perform the function of a metropolitan, when they raise the elected pontiff to the apostolic eminence.   5] They shall elect someone from out of this [Roman] church, if a suitable candidate be found; if not, he shall be chosen from another church. 6] Saving the honour and reverence due to our beloved son Henry,[3] who at present is acknowledged King and, it is hoped, will be Emperor, by God's grace; as we have granted to him and to such of his successors as obtain this right in person from the apostolic see. 7] But, if the perversity of evil and wicked men shall make it impossible to hold a pure, fair and free election in the city, the cardinal bishops with the godly clergy and catholic laymen, even though they be few, shall have the right and power to elect the pontiff of the Apostolic See in any place which they shall consider most convenient.   8] After an election has been clearly made, if the fierceness of war or the malignant endeavours of any man shall prevent him who is elected from being enthroned on the apostolic chair according to custom, the elected shall nevertheless have author-

From Henry Bettenson, DOCUMENTS OF THE CHRISTIAN CHURCH (London, 1950), pp. 140–141. Reprinted by permission of the Oxford University Press.

ity as Pope to rule the holy Roman church and to dispose of its resources, as we know that blessed Gregory did before his consecration. . . .

B Dictatus Papae (*"Dictates of the Pope,"* 1075)

THAT the Roman church was founded by God alone,

That the Roman pontiff alone can with right be called universal.

That he alone can depose or reinstate bishops.

That, in a council, his legate, even if a lower grade, is above all bishops, and can pass sentence of deposition against them.

That the pope may depose the absent.

That, among other things, we ought not to remain in the same house with those excommunicated by him.

That for him alone is it lawful, according to the needs of the time, to make new laws, to assemble together new congregations, to make an abbey of a canonry; and, on the other hand, to divide a rich bishopric and unite the poor ones.

That he alone may use the imperial insignia.

That of the pope alone all princes shall kiss the feet.

That his name alone shall be spoken in the churches.

That this is the only name in the world.

That it may be permitted to him to depose emperors.

That he may be permitted to transfer bishops if need be.

That he has power to ordain a clerk of any church he may wish.

That he who is ordained by him may *preside* over another church, but may not hold a subordinate position; and that such a one may not receive a higher grade from any bishop.

That no synod shall be called a general one without his order.

That no chapter and no book shall be considered canonical without his authority.

From E. F. Henderson, SELECT HISTORICAL DOCUMENTS OF THE MIDDLE AGES (London, 1896), pp. 366–367.

That a sentence passed by him may be retracted by no one; and that he himself, alone of all, may retract it.

That he himself may be judged by no one.

That no one shall dare to condemn one who appeals to the apostolic chair.

That to the latter should be referred the more important cases of every church.

That the Roman church has never erred; nor will it err to all eternity, the Scripture bearing witness.

That the Roman pontiff, if he have been canonically ordained, is undoubtedly made a saint by the merits of St. Peter; St. Ennodius, bishop of Pavia, bearing witness, and many holy fathers agreeing with him. As is contained in the decrees of St. Symmachus the pope.

That, by his command and consent, it may be lawful for subordinates to bring accusations.

That he may depose and reinstate bishops without assembling a synod.

That he who is not at peace with the Roman church shall not be considered catholic.

That he may absolve subjects from their fealty to wicked men.

C Letter of the Synod of Worms to Gregory VII (January 1076)

SIEGFRIED, Archbishop of Mainz, Udo of Trier, William of Utrecht, Hermann of Metz, Henry of Liége, Ricbert of Verden, Bibo of Toul, Hozemann of Speyer, Burckhard of Halberstadt, Werner of Strassburg, Burchard of Basel, Otto of Constance, Adalbero of Wurzburg, Rodbert of Bamberg, Otto of Regensburg, Ellinard of Freising, Udalric of Eichstadt, Frederick of Munster, Eilbert of Minden, Hezil of Hildesheim, Benno of Osnabrück, Eppo of Naumburg, Imadus of Paderborn, Tiedo of Brandenburg, Burchard of Lausanne, Bruno of Verona — to brother Hildebrand.

From Henry Bettenson, DOCUMENTS OF THE CHRISTIAN CHURCH (London, 1950), pp. 141–144. Reprinted by permission of the Oxford University Press.

Although, when thou didst first seize the control of the church, it was clear to us how unlawful and wicked a thing thou hadst presumed to do contrary to right and justice with thy well-known arrogance; nevertheless we thought fit to draw a veil of indulgent silence over the evil beginnings of thine inauguration, hoping that these iniquitous preliminaries would be emended and cancelled by the integrity and diligence of the rest of thy reign. But now, as the lamentable condition of the whole church sadly proclaims, thou art consistently and pertinaciously faithful to thine evil beginnings, in the increasing iniquity of thine actions and decrees. . . . The flame of discord, which thou didst arouse with baneful factions in the Roman church, thou hast spread with senseless fury throughout all the churches of Italy, Germany, Gaul and Spain. For to the utmost of thy power thou hast deprived the bishops of all the power, known to have been divinely given to them by the grace of the Holy Spirit, Who operates above all in ordinations. Thou hast given all oversight over ecclesiastical matters to the passions of the mob. None is now acknowledged a bishop or a priest, unless by unworthy subservience he has obtained his office from thy magnificence. Thou hast thrown into wretched confusion all the vigour of the apostolic institution and that perfect mutuality of the members of Christ, which the teacher of the gentiles so often commends and inculcates. Thus, because of thine ambitious decrees — with tears it must be said — the name of Christ has all but perished. Who is not astounded by thine unworthy conduct in arrogating to thyself a new and unlawful power in order to destroy the due rights of the whole brotherhood? For thou dost assert that, if the mere rumour of a sin committed by a member of our flocks reaches thee, none of us has henceforth any power to bind or loose him, but thou only or he whom thou shalt specially delegate for the purpose. Who, that is learned in the sacred scriptures, does not see that this decree exceeds all madness? Wherefore . . . we have decided, by common consent, to make known to thee that on which we have hitherto kept silence, namely why thou canst not now, nor ever couldst preside over the apostolic see. Thou didst bind thyself with a corporal oath in the time of Emperor Henry[1] of blessed memory that never in the Emperor's lifetime, nor in that of his son, our present reigning and glorious King, wouldst thou thyself accept the papacy, or, as far as in thee lay, wouldst thou suffer another to accept it, without the consent and approval of the father, while he was alive, or of the son while he lived. And there are to-day many bishops who witnessed that oath; who saw it with their eyes and heard it with their ears. Remember too how, when ambition to be pope moved several of the cardinals, to remove all rivalry on that occasion, thou didst bind thyself with an oath, on condition that they did the same, never to hold the papacy. See how faithfully thou hast kept these oaths!

Further, when a synod was held in the time of Pope Nicholas, whereat 125 bishops assisted, it was established and decreed under pain of anathema that none should ever be made Pope except by the election of the cardinals,[2] the approbation of the people and the consent and authorization of the king. And of that decision and decree thou thyself wast the author, sponsor and signatory.

Also thou hast, as it were, filled the whole church with the stench of a grave scandal by living more intimately than is necessary with a woman not of thy kin. This is a matter of propriety rather than of morality; and yet this general complaint is everywhere made, that at the apostolic see all judgments and all decrees are the work of woman, and that the whole church is governed by this new senate of woman. . . .

Wherefore henceforth we renounce, now and for the future, all obedience unto thee — which indeed we never promised to thee. And since, as thou didst publicly proclaim, none of us has been to thee a bishop, so thou henceforth wilt be Pope to none of us.

D Deposition of Henry IV by Gregory VII (February 1076)

BLESSED Peter, chief of the apostles, incline thine holy ears to us, I pray, and hear me, thy servant, whom from infancy thou hast nourished and till this day hast delivered from the hand of the wicked, who have hated and do hate me for my faithfulness to thee. . . . Especially to me, as thy representative, has been committed, and

From Henry Bettenson, DOCUMENTS OF THE CHRISTIAN CHURCH (London, 1950), pp. 144–145. Reprinted by permission of the Oxford University Press.

to me by thy grace has been given by God the power of binding and loosing in heaven and on earth. Relying, then, on this belief, for the honour and defence of thy church and in the name of God Almighty, the Father, the Son and the Holy Ghost, through thy power and authority, I withdraw the government of the whole kingdom of the Germans and of Italy from Henry the King, son of Henry the Emperor. For he has risen up against thy Church with unheard of arrogance. And I absolve all Christians from the bond of the oath which they have made to him or shall make. And I forbid anyone to serve him as king. For it is right that he who attempts to diminish the honour of thy church, shall himself lose the honour which he seems to have. And since he has scorned to show Christian obedience, and has not returned to the Lord whom he has deserted — holding intercourse with the excommunicate; committing many iniquities; despising my warnings, which, as thou art my witness, I have sent to him for his salvation, separating himself from thy church and trying to divide it — on thy behalf I bind him with the bond of anathema. Trusting in thee I thus bind him that the peoples may know and acknowledge that thou art Peter and that on thy rock the Son of the living God has built his church and that the gates of hell shall not prevail against it.

E Gregory VII, Letter to the German Princes Describing the Submission of Henry IV at Canossa (1077), Registrum ("Register"), Book IV

WHEREAS, for love of justice you have made common cause with us and taken the same risks in the warfare of Christian service, we have taken special care to send you this accurate account of the king's penitential humiliation, his absolution and the course of the whole affair from his entrance into Italy to the present time.

From Ephraim Emerton, THE CORRESPONDENCE OF POPE GREGORY VII. SELECTED LETTERS FROM THE REGISTRUM (New York, 1932), pp. 111–112. Reprinted by permission of the Columbia University Press.

According to the arrangement made with the legates sent to us by you we came to Lombardy about twenty days before the date at which some of your leaders were to meet us at the pass and waited for their arrival to enable us to cross over into that region. But when the time had elapsed and we were told that on account of the troublous times — as indeed we well believe — no escort could be sent to us, having no other way of coming to you we were in no little anxiety as to what was our best course to take.

Meanwhile we received certain information that the king was on the way to us. Before he entered Italy he sent us word that he would make satisfaction to God and St. Peter and offered to amend his way of life and to continue obedient to us, provided only that he should obtain from us absolution and the apostolic blessing. For a long time we delayed our reply and held long consultations, reproaching him bitterly through messengers back and forth for his outrageous conduct, until finally, of his own accord and without any show of hostility or defiance, he came with a few followers to the fortress of Canossa where we were staying. There, on three successive days, standing before the castle gate, laying aside all royal insignia, bare-footed and in coarse attire, he ceased not with many tears to beseech the apostolic help and comfort until all who were present or who had heard the story were so moved by pity and compassion that they pleaded his cause with prayers and tears. All marveled at our un-wonted severity, and some even cried out that we were showing, not the seriousness of apostolic authority, but rather the cruelty of a savage tyrant.

At last, overcome by his persistent show of penitence and the urgency of all present, we released him from the bonds of anathema and received him into the grace of Holy Mother Church, accepting from him the guarantees described below,[1] confirmed by the signa-tures of the abbot of Cluny, of our daughters, the Countess Matilda and the Countess Adelaide, and other princes, bishops and laymen who seemed to be of service to us.

And now that these matters have been arranged, we desire to come over into your country at the first opportunity, that with God's help we may more fully establish all matters pertaining to the peace of the Church and the good order of the land. For we wish you clearly to understand that, as you may see in the written guarantees, the whole negotiation is held in suspense, so that our coming and your unanimous consent are in the highest degree necessary. Strive, therefore, all of you, as you love justice, to hold in good faith the obligations into which you have entered. Remember that we have not bound ourselves to the king in any way except by frank statement — as our custom is — that he may expect our aid for his safety and his honor, whether through justice or through mercy, and without peril to his soul or to our own.

F Gregory VII, Letter to Bishop Hermann of Metz (1081)

BISHOP Gregory, servant of the servants of God, to his beloved brother in Christ, Hermann bishop of Metz, greeting and apostolic benediction. It is doubtless owing to a dispensation of God that, as we learn, thou art ready to endure trials and dangers in defence of the truth. For such is His ineffable grace and wonderful mercy that He never allows His chosen ones completely to go astray — never permits them utterly to fall or to be cast down. For, after they have been afflicted by a period of persecution — a useful term of probation as it were, — He makes them, even if they have been for a time fainthearted, stronger than before. Since, moreover, manly courage impels one strong man to act more bravely than another and to press forward more boldly — even as among cowards fear induces one to flee more disgracefully than another, — we wish, beloved, with the voice of exhortation, to impress this upon thee: thou shouldst the more delight to stand in the army of the Christian faith among the first, the more thou art convinced that the conquerors are the most worthy and the nearest to God. Thy request, indeed, to be aided, as it were, by our writings and fortified against the madness of those who babble forth with impious tongue that the authority of the holy and apostolic see had no authority to excommunicate Henry — a man who despises the Christian law; a destroyer of the churches and of the empire; a patron and companion of heretics — or to absolve any

From Henry Bettenson, DOCUMENTS OF THE CHRISTIAN CHURCH (London, 1950), pp. 145–153. Reprinted by permission of the Oxford University Press.

one from the oath of fealty to him, seems to us to be hardly necessary when so many and such absolutely decisive warrants are to be found in the pages of Holy Scripture. Nor do we believe, indeed, that those who (heaping up for themselves damnation) impudently detract from the truth and contradict it have added these assertions to the audacity of their defence so much from ignorance as from a certain madness.

For, to cite a few passages from among many, who does not know the words of our Lord and Saviour Jesus Christ who says in the gospel: "Thou art Peter and upon this rock will I build my church, and the gates of hell shall not prevail against it; and I will give unto thee the keys of the kingdom of Heaven; and whatsoever thou shalt bind upon earth shall be bound also in Heaven, and whatsoever thou shalt loose upon earth shall be loosed also in Heaven"? [Matthew xvi. 18, 19.] Are kings excepted here? Or are they not included among the sheep which the Son of God committed to St. Peter? Who, I ask, in view of this universal concession of the power of binding and loosing, can think that he is withdrawn from the authority of St. Peter, unless, perhaps, that unhappy man who is unwilling to bear the yoke of the Lord and subjects himself to the burden of the devil, refusing to be among the number of Christ's sheep? It will help him little to his wretched liberty that he shake from his proud neck the divinely granted power of Peter. For the more any one, through pride, refuses to bear it, the more heavily shall it press upon him unto damnation at the judgement.

The holy fathers, as well in general councils as in their writings and doings, have called the Holy Roman Church the universal mother, accepting and serving with great veneration this institution founded by the divine will, this pledge of a dispensation to the church, this privilege entrusted in the beginning and confirmed to St. Peter the chief of the apostles. And even as they accepted its statements in confirmation of their faith and of the doctrines of holy religion, so also they received its judgements — consenting in this, and agreeing as it were with one spirit and one voice: that all greater matters and exceptional cases, and judgements over all churches, ought to be referred to it as to a mother and a head; that from it there was no appeal; that no one should or could retract or reverse its decisions. . . .

Shall not an authority founded by laymen — even by those

who do not know God, — be subject to that authority which the providence of God Almighty has for His own honour established and in his mercy given to the world? For His Son, even as He is undoubtingly believed to be God and man, so is He considered the highest priest, the head of all priests, sitting on the right hand of the Father and always interceding for us. Yet He despised a secular kingdom, which makes the sons of this world swell with pride, and came of His own will to the priesthood of the cross. Who does not know that kings and leaders are sprung from men who were ignorant of God, who by pride, robbery, perfidy, murders — in a word, by almost every crime at the prompting of the devil, who is the prince of this world — have striven with blind cupidity and intolerable presumption to dominate over their equals, that is, over mankind? To whom, indeed, can we better compare them, when they seek to make the priests of God bend to their feet, than to him who is head over all the sons of pride[1] and who, tempting the Highest Pontiff Himself, the Head of priests, the Son of the Most High, and promising to Him all the kingdoms of the world, said: "All these I will give unto Thee if Thou wilt fall down and worship me"? who can doubt but that the priests of Christ are to be considered the fathers and masters of kings and princes and of all the faithful? Is it not clearly pitiful madness for a son to attempt to subject to himself his father, a pupil his master; and for one to bring into his power and bind with iniquitous bonds him by whom he believes that he himself can be bound and loosed not only on earth but also in Heaven? This the emperor Constantine the Great, lord of all the kings and princes of nearly the whole world, plainly understood — as the blessed Gregory reminds us in a letter to the emperor Maurice, when, sitting last after all the bishops in the holy council of Nicaea, he presumed to give no sentence of judgement over them, but addressed them as gods and decreed that they should not be subject to his judgement but that he should be dependent upon their will. . . .

Many pontiffs have excommunicated kings or emperors. For, if particular examples of such princes is needed, the blessed pope Innocent excommunicated the emperor Arcadius for consenting that St. John Chrysostom should be expelled from his see. Likewise another Roman pontiff, Zacchary, deposed a king of the Franks, not so much for his iniquities as because he was not fitted to exercise so great power. And in his stead he set up Pepin, father of the emperor

Charles the Great, in his place — releasing all the Franks from the oath of fealty which they had sworn him. As, indeed, the holy church frequently does by its authority when it absolves servitors from the fetters of an oath sworn to such bishops as, by apostolic sentence, are deposed from their pontifical rank. And the blessed Ambrose — who, although a saint, was still not bishop over the whole church — excommunicated and excluded from the church the emperor Theodosius the Great for a fault[2] which, by other priests, was not regarded as very grave. He shows, too, in his writings that gold does not so much excel lead in value as the priestly dignity transcends the royal power; speaking thus towards the beginning of his pastoral letter: "The honour and sublimity of bishops, brethren, is beyond all comparison. If one should compare them to resplendent kings and diademed princes it would be far less worthy than if one compared the base metal lead to gleaming gold. For, indeed, one can see how the necks of kings and princes are bowed before the knees of priests; and how, having kissed their right hands, they believe themselves strengthened by their prayers." And a little later: "Ye should know, brethren, that we have mentioned all this to show that nothing can be found in this world more lofty than priests or more sublime than bishops."

Furthermore every Christian king, when he comes to die, seeks as a pitiful suppliant the aid of a priest, that he may escape hell's prison, may pass from the darkness into the light, and at the judgement of God may appear absolved from the bondage of his sins. Who, in his last hour (what layman, not to speak of priests), has ever implored the aid of an earthly king for the salvation of his soul? And what king or emperor is able, by reason of the office he holds, to rescue a Christian from the power of the devil through holy baptism, to number him among the sons of God, and to fortify him with the divine unction? Who of them can by his own words make the body and blood of our Lord, — the greatest act in the Christian religion? Or who of them possesses the power of binding and loosing in heaven and on earth? From all of these considerations it is clear how greatly the priestly office excels in power.

Who of them can ordain a single clerk in the holy Church, much less depose him for any fault? For in the orders of the Church a greater power is needed to depose than to ordain. Bishops may ordain other bishops, but can by no means depose them without the authority of the apostolic see. Who, therefore, of even moderate understanding, can hesitate to give priests the precedence over kings? Then, if kings are to be judged by priests for their sins, by whom can they be judged with better right than by the Roman pontiff?

In short, any good Christians may far more properly be considered kings than may bad princes. For the former, seeking the glory of God, strictly govern themselves, whereas the latter, seeking the things which are their own and not the things of God, are enemies to themselves and tyrannical oppressors of others. Faithful Christians are the body of the true king, Christ; evil rulers, that of the devil. The former rule themselves in the hope that they will eternally reign with the Supreme Emperor, but the sway of the latter ends in their destruction and eternal damnation with the prince of darkness, who is king over all the sons of pride.

It is certainly not strange that wicked bishops are of one mind with a bad king, whom they love and fear for the honours which they have wrongfully obtained from him. Such men simoniacally ordain whom they please and sell God even for a paltry sum. As even the elect are indissolubly united with their Head, so also the wicked are inescapably leagued with him who is the head of evil, their chief purpose being to resist the good. But surely we ought not so much to denounce them as to mourn for them with tears and lamentations, beseeching God Almighty to snatch them from the snares of Satan in which they are held captive, and after their peril to bring them at last to a knowledge of the truth.

We refer to those kings and emperors who, too much puffed up by worldly glory, rule not for God but for themselves. Now, since it belongs to our office to admonish and encourage every one according to the rank or dignity which he enjoys, we endeavour, by God's grace, to arm emperors and kings and other princes with the weapon of humility, that they may be able to allay the waves of the sea[3] and the floods of pride. For we know that earthly glory and the cares of this world usually tempt men to pride, especially those in authority. So that they neglect humility and seek their own glory, desiring to lord it over their brethren. Therefore it is of especial advantage for emperors and kings, when their minds tend to be puffed up and to delight in their own glory, to discover a way of humbling themselves, and to realize that what causes their complacency is the thing which should be feared above all else. Let them, therefore, diligently consider how perilous and how much to be feared is the royal or imperial dignity. For very few are saved of those who enjoy it; and those who, through the mercy of God, do come to salvation are not so glorified in the Holy Church by the judgement of the Holy Spirit as are many poor people. For, from the beginning of the world until our own times, in the whole of authentic history we do not find seven emperors or kings whose lives were as distinguished for religion and so adorned by miracles of power as those of an innumerable multitude who despised the world — although we believe many of them to have found mercy in the presence of God Almighty. For what emperor or king was ever so distinguished by miracles as were St. Martin, St. Antony and St. Benedict — not to mention the apostles and martyrs? And what emperor or king raised the dead, cleansed lepers, or healed the blind? See how the Holy Church praises and venerates the Emperor Constantine of blessed memory, Theodosius and Honorius,[4] Charles and Louis[5] as lovers of justice, promoters of the Christian religion, defenders of the churches: it does not, however, declare them to have been resplendent with such glorious miracles. Moreover, to how many kings or emperors has the holy church ordered chapels or altars to be dedicated, or masses to be celebrated in their honour? Let kings and other princes fear lest the more they rejoice at being placed over other men in this life, the more they will be subjected to eternal fires. For of them it is written: "The powerful shall powerfully suffer torments."[6] And they are about to render account to God for as many men as they have had subjects under their dominion. But if it be no little task for any private religious man to guard his own soul: how much labour will there be for those who are rulers over many thousands of souls? Moreover, if the judgement of the Holy Church severely punishes a sinner for the slaying of one man, what will become of those who, for the sake of worldly glory, hand over many thousands to death? And such persons, although after having slain many they often say with their lips "I have sinned," nevertheless rejoice in their hearts at the extension of their (so-called) fame. They do not regret what they have done. Nor are they grieved at having sent their brethren down to Tartarus. As long as they do not repent with their whole heart, nor agree to give up what they have acquired or kept through bloodshed, their repentance remains without the true fruit of penitence before God.

Therefore they should greatly fear and often call to mind what we have said above, that out of the innumerable host of kings in all

countries from the beginning of the world, very few are found to
have been holy; whereas in one single see — the Roman — of the
successive bishops from the time of blessed Peter the Apostle, nearly
one hundred are counted amongst the most holy. And why is this,
unless because kings and princes, enticed by vain glory, prefer, as has
been said, their own things to things spiritual, whereas the bishops
of the Church, despising vain glory, prefer God's will to earthly
things? The former are quick to punish offences against themselves,
but lightly tolerate those who sin against God. The latter readily pardon those who sin against themselves, but do not readily forgive
offenders against God. The former, too bent on earthly achievements,
think little of spiritual ones; the latter, earnestly meditating on
heavenly things, despise the things of earth. . . .

Therefore let those whom Holy Church, of its own will and after
proper counsel, not for transitory glory but for the salvation of many,
calls to have rule or dominion, humbly obey. And let them always
beware in that point as to which St. Gregory in that same pastoral
book[7] bears witness: "Indeed, when a man disdains to be like to
men, he is made like to an apostate angel. Thus Saul, after having
possessed the merit of humility, came to be swollen with pride when
at the summit of power. Through humility, indeed, he was advanced; through pride, rejected — God being witness who said:
'When thou wast small in thine own eyes, did I not make thee head
over the tribes of Israel?' "[8] And a little further on: "Moreover,
strange to say, when he was small in his own eyes he was great in the
eyes of God; but when he seemed great in his own eyes he was small in
the eyes of God." Let them also carefully retain what God says in the
gospel: "I seek not my own glory"; and, "He who will be the first
among you shall be the servant of all." Let them always prefer the
honour of God to their own; let them cherish and guard justice by
observing the rights of every man; let them not walk in the counsel
of the ungodly but, with an assenting heart, always consort with
good men. Let them not seek to subject to themselves or to subjugate
the Holy Church as a handmaid; but above all let them strive, by
recognizing the teachers and fathers, to render due honour to the
eyes of the Church — the priests of God. For if we are ordered to
honour our fathers and mothers after the flesh — how much more
our spiritual ones! And if he who has cursed his father or mother
after the flesh is to be punished with death — what does he merit

who curses his spiritual father or mother? Let them not, led astray by worldly love, strive to place one of their own sons over the flock for which Christ poured forth His blood, if they can find some one who is better and more useful than he: lest, loving their son more than God, they inflict the greatest damage on the Holy Church. For he who neglects to provide to the best of his ability for such a want — and, one might say, necessity — of Holy Mother Church is openly convicted of not loving God and his neighbour as a Christian should.

For if this virtue, love, has been neglected, no matter what good any one does he shall be without any fruit of salvation. And so by humbly doing these things, and by observing the love of God and of their neighbour as they ought, they may hope for the mercy of Him who said: "Learn of Me, for I am meek and lowly of heart." If they have humbly imitated Him they shall pass from this servile and transitory kingdom to a true kingdom of liberty and eternity.

G The Murder of Thomas Becket, Archbishop of Canterbury (29 December 1170)

so then the aforesaid men,[1] no knights forsooth but miserable wretches, as soon as they landed, summoned the king's officials, whom the archbishop had already excommunicated, and by falsely proclaiming that they were acting with the king's approval and in his name, they got together a band of knights and their followers. For they were easily persuaded to this crime by the knights' statement that they had come to settle the affair by order of the king. They then collected in a body, ready for any impious deed, and on the fifth day after the Nativity of Christ,[2] that is, on the morrow of the Feast of the Holy Innocents, they gathered together against the innocent. The hour of dinner being over, the saint had already withdrawn with

From Edward Grim, VITA SANCTI THOMAE ("The Life of Saint Thomas"), in D. C. Douglas and G. W. Greenaway, ENGLISH HISTORICAL DOCUMENTS, 1042–1189 (New York, 1953), pp. 761–768. Reprinted by permission of the Oxford University Press.

some of his household into an inner chamber to transact some business, leaving the crowd awaiting his return in the hall without. The four knights with one attendant forced their way in. They were received with respect as servants of the king and well known to the archbishop's household; and those who had waited on the archbishop, being now themselves at dinner, invited them to share their table. They scorned the offer, thirsting rather for blood than for food. By their order the archbishop was informed that four men had arrived who wished to speak with him on behalf of the king. On his giving consent, they were permitted to enter. For a long time they sat in silence and neither saluted the archbishop nor spoke to him. Nor did the man of wise counsel salute them immediately they came in, in order that, according to the Scriptures, "By thy words shalt thou be justified," he might discover their intentions from their questions. After a while, however, he turned to them and, carefully scanning the face of each, he greeted them in a friendly manner; but the unhappy wretches, who had made a pact with death, straightway answered his greeting with curses and ironically prayed that God might help him. At these words of bitterness and malice the man of God flushed deeply, for he now realized that they had come to work him injury. Whereupon fitz Urse, who seemed to be their leader and more prepared for the crime than the others, breathing fury, broke out in these words: "We have somewhat to say to thee by the king's command; say if thou wilt that we tell it here before all." But the archbishop knew what they were about to say and answered, "These things should not be spoken in private or in the chamber, but in public." Now these wretches so burned for the slaughter of the archbishop that if the door-keeper had not called back the clerks — for the archbishop had ordered them all to withdraw — they would have killed him with the shaft of his cross which stood by, as they afterwards confessed. When those who had gone out returned, he, who had before reviled the archbishop, again addressed him saying, "When the king made peace with you and all disputes were settled, he sent you back to your own see, as you requested; but you, in contrary fashion, adding insult to injury, have broken the peace, and in your pride have wrought evil in yourself against your lord. For those, by whose ministry the king's son was crowned and invested with the honours of sovereignty, you with obstinate pride have condemned with sentence of suspension. You have also bound with the chain of anathema those servants of the king by whose counsel and prudence the business of the kingdom is transacted. From this it is manifest that you would take away the crown from the king's son if you had the power. But now the plots and schemes you have hatched in order to carry out your designs against your lord the king are known to all men. Say therefore whether you are prepared to come into the king's presence and make answer to these charges." The archbishop replied, "Never was it my wish, as God is my witness, to take away the crown from my lord the king's son or to diminish his power; rather would I wish him three crowns and help him to obtain the greatest realms of the earth, so it be with right and equity. But it is unjust that my lord the king should be offended because my people accompany me through the towns and cities and come out to meet me, when for seven years now they have been deprived through my exile of the consolation of my presence. Even now I am ready to satisfy my lord wherever he pleases, if in anything I have done amiss; but he has forbidden me with threats to enter any of his cities and towns or even villages. Moreover, it was not by me, but by the lord pope that the prelates were suspended from office." "It was through you," said the infuriated knights, "that they were suspended; do you absolve them?" "I do not deny," he answered, "that it was done through me, but it is beyond my power and utterly incompatible with my dignity to absolve those whom the lord pope has bound. Let them go to him, on whom redounds the injury and contempt they have shown towards me and their mother, the Church of Christ at Canterbury."

"Well then," said these butchers, "this is the king's command, that you depart with all your men from the kingdom and the lands which own his dominion; for from this day forth there can be no peace betwixt him and you or any of yours, for you have broken the peace." To this the archbishop answered, "Cease your threats and still your brawling. I put my trust in the King of Heaven who for his own suffered on the Cross; for from this day forth no one shall see the sea between me and my church. I have not come back to flee again; here shall he who wants me find me. It is not fitting for the king to issue such commands; sufficient are the insults received by me and mine from the king's servants, without further threats." "Such were the king's commands," they replied, "and we will make them good, for whereas you ought to have shown respect to the king's majesty and submitted your vengeance to his judgment, you have followed the impulse of your passion and basely thrust out from the Church his ministers and servants." At these words Christ's champion, rising in fervour of spirit against his accusers, exclaimed, "Whoever shall presume to violate the decrees of the holy Roman see or the laws of Christ's Church, and shall refuse to come of his own accord and make satisfaction, whosoever he be, I will not spare him, nor will I delay to inflict ecclesiastical censures upon the delinquent."

Confounded by these words, the knights sprang to their feet, for they could no longer bear the firmness of his answers. Coming close up to him they said, "We declare to you that you have spoken in peril of your head." "Are you then come to slay me?" said he. "I have committed my cause to the great Judge of all mankind; wherefore I am not moved by threats, nor are your swords more ready to strike than is my soul for martyrdom. Go, seek him who would fly from you; me you will find foot to foot in the battle of the Lord." As they retired amidst tumult and insults, he who was fitly surnamed "the bear"[3] brutishly cried out, "In the king's name we command you, both clerks and monks, to seize and hold that man, lest he escape by flight ere the king take full justice on his body." As they departed with these words, the man of God followed them to the door and cried out after them, "Here, here will you find me"; putting his hand on his neck, as though marking beforehand the place where they were to strike.

The archbishop then returned to the place where he had before been seated, consoled his clerks and exhorted them not to fear; and, so it seemed to us who were present, he sat there waiting as unperturbed, although his death alone was sought, as if they had come to invite him to a wedding. Ere long back came the murderers in full armour, with swords, axes and hatchets, and other implements suitable for the crime on which their minds were set. Finding the doors barred and unopened at their knocking, they turned aside by a private path through an orchard till they came to a wooden partition, which they cut and hacked and finally broke down. Terrified by the noise and uproar, almost all the clerks and the servants were scattered hither and thither like sheep before wolves. Those who remained cried out to the archbishop to flee to the church; but he, mindful of his former promise that he would not through fear of death flee from those who kill the body, rejected flight. For in such case it were not meet to flee from city to city, but rather to set an example to those subject to him, so that every one of them should choose to die by the sword rather than see the divine law set at naught and the sacred canons subverted. Moreover, he who had long since yearned for martyrdom, now saw that the occasion to embrace it had seemingly arrived, and dreaded lest it should be deferred or even altogether lost, if he took refuge in the church. But the monks still pressed him, saying that it was not becoming for him to absent himself from vespers, which were at that very moment being said in the church. He lingered for a while motionless in that less sacred spot,[4] deliberately awaiting that happy hour of consummation which he had craved with many sighs and sought with such devotion; for he feared lest, as has been said, reverence for the sanctity of the sacred building might deter even the impious from their purpose and cheat him of his heart's desire. For, being confident that after martyrdom he would pass from this vale of misery, he is reported to have said in the hearing of many after his return from exile, "You have here a martyr, Alphege, beloved of God and a true saint; the divine compassion will provide you with yet another; he will not tarry." O pure and trustful was the conscience of that good shepherd, who in defending the cause of his flock would not delay the hour of his own death, when it was in his power to do so, nor shun the executioner, that the fury of the wolves, satiated with the blood of the shepherd, might spare the sheep. But when he would not be persuaded by argument or entreaties to take refuge in the church, the monks seized hold of him in spite of his resistance, and pulled, dragged and pushed him; without heeding his opposition and his clamour to let him go, they brought him as far as the church. But the door, which led to the monks' cloister, had been carefully barred several days before, and as the murderers were already pressing on their heels, all hope of escape seemed removed. But one of them, running forward, seized hold of the bolt, and to the great surprise of them all, drew it out with as much ease as if it had been merely glued to the door.

After the monks had retreated within the precincts of the church, the four knights came following hard on their heels with rapid strides. They were accompanied by a certain subdeacon called Hugh, armed with malice like their own, appropriately named Mauclerc,[5] being one who showed no reverence either to God or his saints, as he proved by his subsequent action. As soon as the archbishop entered the monastic buildings, the monks ceased the vespers, which they had already begun to offer to God, and ran to meet him, glorifying God for that they saw their father alive and unharmed, when they had heard he was dead. They also hastened to ward off the foe from the slaughter of their shepherd by fastening the bolts of the folding doors giving access to the church. But Christ's doughty champion turned to them and ordered the doors to be thrown open, saying, "It is not meet to make a fortress of the house of prayer, the Church of Christ, which, even if it be not closed, affords sufficient protection to its children; by suffering rather than by fighting shall we triumph over the enemy; for we are come to suffer, not to resist." Straightway these sacrilegious men, with drawn swords, entered the house of peace and reconciliation, causing no little horror to those present by the mere sight of them and the clash of their armour. All the onlookers were in tumult and consternation, for by this time those who had been singing vespers had rushed up to the scene of death.

In a spirit of mad fury the knights called out, "Where is Thomas Becket, traitor to the king and the realm?" When he returned no answer, they cried out the more loudly and insistently, "Where is the archbishop?" At this quite undaunted, as it is written, "The righteous shall be bold as a lion and without fear," he descended from the steps, whither he had been dragged by the monks through their fear of the knights, and in a perfectly clear voice answered, "Lo! here am I, no traitor to the king, but a priest. What do you seek from me?" And whereas he had already told them that he had no fear of them, he now added, "Behold, I am ready to suffer in His Name who redeemed me by His Blood. Far be it from me to flee from your swords, or to depart from righteousness." Having thus said, he turned aside to the right, under a pillar, having on one side the altar of the blessed Mother of God, Mary ever-Virgin, on the other, that of the holy confessor, Benedict, by whose example and prayers, having crucified the world and its lusts, he endured whatsoever the murderers did to him with such constancy of soul, as if he were no longer in the flesh. The murderers pursued him. "Absolve," they cried, "and restore to communion those whom you have excommunicated, and the functions of their office to the others who have been suspended." He answered, "There has been no satisfaction made, and I will not absolve them." "Then you shall die this instant," they cried, "and receive your desert." "I, too," said he, "am ready to

die for my Lord, that in my blood the Church may obtain peace
and liberty; but in the name of Almighty God I forbid you to harm
any of my men, whether clerk or lay." Thus did the noble martyr
provide piously for his followers, and prudently for himself, in that
no one standing near should be hurt nor the innocent oppressed, lest
any serious mishap befalling any that stood by him should dim the
lustre of his glory as his soul sped up to Christ. Most fitting was it
that the soldier-martyr should follow in the footsteps of his Captain
and Saviour, who, when the wicked sought to take him, said, "If ye
seek me, let these go their way."[6]

Then they made a rush at him and laid sacrilegious hands upon
him, pulling and dragging him roughly and violently, endeavouring
to get him outside the walls of the church and there slay him, or
bind him and carry him off prisoner, as they afterwards confessed
was their intention. But as he could not easily be moved from the
pillar, one of them seized hold of him and clung to him more
closely. The archbishop shook him off vigorously, calling him a pan-
dar and saying, "Touch me not, Reginald; you owe me fealty and
obedience; you are acting like a madman, you and your accomplices."
All aflame with a terrible fury at this rebuff, the knight brandished
his sword against that consecrated head. "Neither faith," he cried,
"nor obedience do I owe you against my fealty to my lord the king."
Then the unconquered martyr understood that the hour was approaching that should release him from the miseries of this mortal
life, and that the crown of immortality prepared for him and
promised by the Lord was already nigh at hand. Whereupon, inclining his head as one in prayer and joining his hands together and
uplifting them, he commended his cause and that of the Church to
God and St. Mary and the blessed martyr, St. Denys. Scarce had he
uttered the words than the wicked knight, fearing lest he should be
rescued by the people and escape alive, leapt suddenly upon him and
wounded the sacrificial lamb of God in the head, cutting off the
top of the crown which the unction of the sacred chrism had dedicated to God, and by the same stroke he almost cut off the arm of
him who tells the story.[7] For he, when all the others, both monks
and clerks had fled, steadfastly stood by the saintly archbishop and
held his arms around him, till the one he opposed to the blow was
almost severed. Behold the simplicity of the dove, the wisdom of the
serpent in this martyr who presented his body to the strikers that

he might preserve his head, that is to say, his soul and the Church, unharmed, nor would he take any forethought or employ any stratagem against those who slay the body whereby he might escape. O worthy shepherd, who gave himself so boldly to the wolves, in order that his flock might not be torn to pieces! Because he had cast away the world, the world in seeking to crush him unconsciously exalted him.

Next he received a second blow on the head, but still he stood firm and immovable. At the third blow he fell on his knees and elbows, offering himself a living sacrifice and saying in a low voice, "For the Name of Jesus and the protection of the Church I am ready to embrace death." But the third knight[8] inflicted a terrible wound as he lay prostrate. By this stroke the sword was dashed against the pavement and the crown of his head, which was large, was separated from the head in such a way that the blood white with the brain and the brain no less red from the blood, dyed the floor of the cathedral with the white of the lily and the red of the rose, the colours of the Virgin and Mother and of the life and death of the martyr and confessor. The fourth knight[9] warded off any who sought to intervene, so that the others might with greater freedom and licence perpetrate the crime. But the fifth — no knight he, but that same clerk who had entered with the knights[10] — that a fifth blow[11] might not be wanting to the martyr who in other things had imitated Christ, placed his foot on the neck of the holy priest and precious martyr and, horrible to relate, scattered the brains and blood about the pavement, crying out to the others, "Let us away, knights; this fellow will rise no more."

In all his sufferings the illustrious martyr displayed an incredible steadfastness. Neither with hand nor robe, as is the manner of human frailty, did he oppose the fatal stroke. Nor when smitten did he utter a single word, neither cry nor groan, nor any sound indicative of pain. But he held motionless the head which he had bent to meet the uplifted sword until, bespattered with blood and brains, as though in an attitude of prayer, his body lay prone on the pavement, while his soul rested in Abraham's bosom.

H The Submission of King John of England to Pope Innocent III (1214)

Innocent, bishop, servant of the servants of God, to his well-beloved son in Christ, John illustrious king of the English, and to his legitimate free-born heirs for ever.

THE King of kings and Lord of lords, Jesus Christ, a priest for ever after the order of Melchisedech,[1] has so established in the Church His kingdom and His priesthood that the one is a kingdom of priests and the other a royal priesthood, as is testified by Moses in the Law and by Peter in his Epistle;[2] and over all He has set one whom He has appointed as His Vicar on earth, so that, as every knee is bowed to Jesus, of things in heaven, and things in earth, and things under the earth, so all men should obey His Vicar and strive that there may be one fold and one shepherd. All secular kings for the sake of God so venerate this Vicar, that unless they seek to serve him devotedly they doubt if they are reigning properly. To this, dearly beloved son, you have paid wise attention; and by the merciful inspiration of Him in whose hand are the hearts of kings which He turns whithersoever He wills, you have decided to submit in a temporal sense yourself and your kingdom to him to whom you knew them to be spiritually subject, so that kingdom and priesthood, like body and soul, for the great good and profit of each, might be united in the single person of Christ's Vicar. He has deigned to work this wonder, who being alpha and omega has caused the end to fulfill the beginning and the beginning to anticipate the end, so that those provinces which from of old have had the Holy Roman Church as their proper teacher in spiritual matters should now in temporal things also have her as their peculiar sovereign. You, whom God has chosen as a suitable minister to effect this, by a devout and spontaneous act of will and on the general advice of your barons have offered and yielded, in the form

LETTER OF POPE INNOCENT III TO KING JOHN OF ENGLAND from REGISTRUM ("Register"), in C. R. Cheney and W. H. Semple, SELECTED LETTERS OF POPE INNOCENT III CONCERNING ENGLAND (1198–1216) (Edinburgh, 1953), pp. 177–183. Reprinted by permission of Thomas Nelson and Sons Ltd.

of an annual payment of a thousand marks, yourself and your kingdoms of England and Ireland, with all their rights and appurtenances, to God and to SS Peter and Paul His apostles and to the Holy
Roman Church and to us and our successors, to be our right and our
property — as is stated in your official letter attested by a golden seal,
the literal tenor of which is as follows:

"John, by the grace of God king of England, lord of Ireland,
duke of Normandy and Aquitaine, count of Anjou, to all the faithful
of Christ who may see this charter, greeting in the Lord.

"By this charter attested by our golden seal we wish it to be known
to you all that, having in many things offended God and Holy
Church our mother and being therefore in the utmost need of
divine mercy and possessing nothing but ourselves and our kingdoms that we can worthily offer as due amends to God and the
Church, we desire to humble ourselves for the sake of Him who for
us humbled Himself even unto death; and inspired by the grace
of the Holy Spirit — not induced by force nor compelled by fear,
but of our own good and spontaneous will and on the general
advice of our barons — we offer and freely yield to God, and to
SS Peter and Paul His apostles, and to the Holy Roman Church
our mother, and to our lord Pope Innocent III and his catholic
successors, the whole kingdom of England and the whole kingdom
of Ireland with all their rights and appurtenances for the remission
of our sins and the sins of our whole family, both the living and
the dead. And now, receiving back these kingdoms from God and
the Roman Church and holding them as feudatory vassal, in the
presence of our venerable father, lord Nicholas, bishop of Tusculum,
legate of the Apostolic See, and of Pandulf, subdeacon and member
of household to our lord the Pope, we have pledged and sworn our
fealty henceforth to our lord aforesaid, Pope Innocent, and to his
catholic successors, and to the Roman Church, in the terms herein-
under stated; and we have publicly paid liege homage for the said
kingdoms to God, and to the Holy Apostles Peter and Paul, and
to the Roman Church, and to our lord aforesaid, Pope Innocent
III, at the hands of the said legate who accepts our homage in
place and instead of our said lord, the Pope; and we bind in
perpetuity our successors and legitimate heirs that without question
they must similarly render fealty and acknowledge homage to the
Supreme Pontiff holding office at the time and to the Roman

Church. As a token of this our perpetual offering and concession we will and decree that out of the proper and special revenues of our said kingdoms, in lieu of all service and payment which we should render for them, the Roman Church is to receive annually, without prejudice to the payment of Peter's pence,[3] one thousand marks sterling — five hundred at the feast of St. Michael and five hundred at Easter — that is, seven hundred for the kingdom of England and three hundred for the kingdom of Ireland, subject to the maintenance for us and our heirs of our jurisdiction, privileges, and regalities. Desiring all these terms, exactly as stated, to be forever ratified and valid, we bind ourselves and our successors not to contravene them; and if we or any of our successors shall presume to contravene them, then, no matter who he be, unless on due warning he come to his senses, let him lose the title to the kingdom, and let this document of our offer and concession remain ever valid.

"I, John, by grace of God king of England and lord of Ireland, will from this hour henceforward be faithful to God and Saint Peter and the Roman Church and my lord Pope Innocent III and his catholic successors. I will not take part in deed, word, agreement, or plan whereby they should lose life or limb or be treacherously taken prisoners; any injury to them, if aware of it, I will prevent and will check if I can; and otherwise, I will notify them as soon as possible, or inform a person whom I can trust without fail to tell them; any counsel they have entrusted to me either personally or by envoys or by letter I will keep secret, nor will I wittingly divulge it to anyone to their disadvantage. I will help in maintaining and defending, to the utmost of my power, against all men, the patrimony of Saint Peter, and particularly the kingdom of England and the kingdom of Ireland. So help me God and the Holy Gospels of God whereon I swear.

"To prevent any questioning of these terms at any time in the future, and for the greater surety of our offer and concession, we have caused this charter to be made and to be sealed with our golden seal; and as tribute for this the first year we pay a thousand marks sterling to the Roman Church by the hand of the said legate.

"Witnessed by his lordship Stephen archbishop of Canterbury, and by their lordships William bishop of London, Peter bishop of Winchester, Eustace bishop of Ely, and Hugh bishop of Lincoln, and by our Chancellor, Walter de Gray, our brother William earl of Salisbury, Ranulf earl of Chester, William Marshal earl of Pembroke, William earl of Ferrers, Saer earl of Winchester, Robert de Ros, William Briwerre, Peter FitzHerbert, Matthew FitzHerbert, and Brian de Lisle our steward.

"By the hand of Master Richard Marsh archdeacon of Richmond and Northumberland, at St. Paul's London, the third of October A.D. 1213, in the fifteenth year of our reign."

This offer and concession so piously and wisely made we regard as acceptable and valid, and we take under the protection of Saint Peter and of ourselves your person and the persons of your heirs together with the said kingdoms and their appurtenances and all other goods which are now reasonably held or may in future be so held: to you and to your heirs, according to the terms set out above and by the general advice of our brethren, we grant the said kingdoms in fief and confirm them by this privilege, on condition that any of your heirs on receiving the crown will publicly acknowledge this as a fief held of the Supreme Pontiff and of the Roman Church, and will take an oath of fealty to them. Let no man, therefore, have power to infringe this document of our concession and confirmation, or presume to oppose it. If any man dare to do so, let him know that he will incur the anger of Almighty God and of SS Peter and Paul, His apostles. AMEN, amen, AMEN.

(Rota)[4] I, Innocent, bishop of the Catholic Church, have signed. Farewell.

✠ I, John, bishop of Sabina, have signed.

✠ I, Hugh, bishop of Ostia and Velletri, have signed.

✠ I, Benedict, bishop of Porto and S. Rufina, have signed.

✠ I, Cinthius, cardinal priest of the title of S. Lorenzo in Lucina, have signed.

✠ I, Cencius, cardinal priest of SS Giovanni e Paolo of the title of Pammachius, have signed.

✠ I, Peter, cardinal priest of the title of S. Marcello, have signed.

✠ I, Leo, cardinal priest of the title of Santa Croce in Gerusalemme, have signed.

✠ I, Peter, cardinal priest of Santa Pudenziana of the title of the pastor, have signed.

✠ I, Guala, cardinal priest of S. Martino of the title of Equitius, have signed.

✠ I, John, cardinal priest of the title of Santa Prassede, have signed.

✠ I, Guy, cardinal deacon of S. Nicola in Carcere Tulliano, have signed.

✠ I, Octavian, cardinal deacon of Santi Sergio e Bacco, have signed.

✠ I, John, cardinal deacon of Santi Cosma e Damiano, have signed.

✠ I, Angelus, cardinal deacon of S. Adriano, have signed.

Rome, St. Peter's, by the hand of Master Raynaldus, acolyte and chaplain to the lord Pope Innocent III, the 21st of April, indiction 2, A.D. 1214, in the 17th year of the Pontificate of the lord Innocent.

I The Bull Unam Sanctam of Pope Boniface VIII (1302)

We are obliged by the faith to believe and hold — and we do firmly believe and sincerely confess — that there is one Holy Catholic and Apostolic Church, and that outside this Church there is neither salvation nor remission of sins. . . . In which Church there is one Lord, one faith, one baptism. At the time of the flood there was one ark of Noah, symbolizing the one Church; this was completed in one cubit and had one, namely Noah, as helmsman and captain; outside which all things on earth, we read, were destroyed. . . . Of this one and only Church there is one body and one head — not two heads, like a monster — namely Christ, and Christ's vicar is Peter, and Peter's successor, for the Lord said to Peter himself, "Feed My sheep."[1] "My sheep" He said in general, not these or those sheep; wherefore He is understood to have committed them all to him. Therefore, if the Greeks or others say that they were not committed to Peter and his successors, they necessarily confess that they

From Henry Bettenson, DOCUMENTS OF THE CHRISTIAN CHURCH (London, 1950), pp. 159–161. Reprinted by permission of the Oxford University Press.

are not of Christ's sheep, for the Lord says in John, "There is one fold and one shepherd."[2]

And we learn from the words of the Gospel that in this Church and in her power are two swords, the spiritual and the temporal. For when the apostles said, "Behold, here" (that is, in the Church, since it was the apostles who spoke) "are two swords" — the Lord did not reply, "It is too much," but "It is enough."[3] Truly he who denies that the temporal sword is in the power of Peter, misunderstands the words of the Lord, "Put up thy sword into the sheath."[4] Both are in the power of the Church, the spiritual sword and the material. But the latter is to be used for the Church, the former by her; the former by the priest, the latter by kings and captains but at the will and by the permission of the priest. The one sword, then, should be under the other, and temporal authority subject to spiritual. For when the apostle says "there is no power but of God, and the powers that be are ordained of God"[5] they would not be so ordained were not one sword made subject to the other. . . .

Thus, concerning the Church and her power, is the prophecy of Jeremiah fulfilled, "See, I have this day set thee over the nations and over the kingdoms," etc.[6] If, therefore, the earthly power err, it shall be judged by the spiritual power; and if a lesser power err, it shall be judged by a greater. But if the supreme power err, it can only be judged by God, not by man; for the testimony of the apostle is "The spiritual man judgeth all things, yet he himself is judged of no man."[7] For this authority, although given to a man and exercised by a man, is not human, but rather divine, given at God's mouth to Peter and established on a rock for him and his successors in Him whom he confessed, the Lord saying to Peter himself, "Whatsoever thou shalt bind," etc.[8] Whoever therefore resists this power thus ordained of God, resists the ordinance of God. . . . Furthermore we declare, state, define and pronounce that it is altogether necessary to salvation for every human creature to be subject to the Roman pontiff.

NOTES

Selection a

1. The cardinal bishops, priests, and deacons were those who lived at Rome and were thus closest to the hinge (*cardo*) of Christendom.

   2. An early pope of the fifth century.

   3. Henry IV (1056–1106).

Selection c

   1. Henry III (1039–1056).

   2. A reference to the decree on papal elections in 1059.

Selection e

   1. Reference to oath taken by Henry IV at Canossa.

Selection f

   1. Job, xli. 34.

   2. In 390 the Roman emperor Theodosius permitted the massacre of the people of Thessalonica to punish them for rioting.

   3. Psalms, xciii. 4.

   4. Roman emperors.

   5. The Carolingian emperors Charlemagne and Louis the Pious.

   6. *Wisdom*, vi. 6.

   7. *Pastoral Rule.*

   8. I Samuel, xv. 17.

Selection g

   1. The four knights Reginald fitz Urse, William de Traci, Hugh of Morville, and Richard Brito, who came from Normandy and killed Becket.

   2. December 26, 1170.

   3. Reginald fitz Urse.

   4. The archbishop's palace.

   5. Evil clerk.

   6. John, xviii. 8.

   7. Edward Grim.

   8. Richard Brito.

   9. Hugh of Morville.

  10. Hugh Mauclerc.

  11. An allusion to the five wounds of Christ.

Selection h

   1. Hebrews, v. 6.

   2. I Peter, ii. 9.

   3. An annual tax paid by England to the papacy.

   4. The rota was formed by two concentric circles, the inner one being intersected by a cross.

Selection i

   1. John, xxi. 17.

   2. John, x. 16.

3. Luke, xxii. 38.
4. John, xviii. 11.
5. Romans, x. 1.
6. Jeremiah, i. 10.
7. I Corinthians, ii. 15.
8. Matthew, xvi. 19.

8

Dissension Among the Crusaders

THE First Crusade (1096–1099), the most successful of all the crusades, was undertaken by men inspired by greater Christian faith and zeal than their successors of the later crusades. The First Crusade was born out of the intense pitch of religious fervor in the late eleventh century and the respected position of the papacy, which proclaimed and directed this first great offensive of Christian Europe against the Islamic world. Despite the sincere faith that motivated the majority of crusaders, there were those who took the cross largely for economic and political reasons. In this category were some of the Norman leaders who hoped to secure lands in Syria. Besides being more materialistic in their objectives, the Normans were also more skeptical and questioned the Christian idealism of the other crusaders. This led to tension and quarrels among the crusaders, a situation best illustrated by the famous incident of Peter Bartholomew and the Holy Lance. The selections below are from two accounts of this affair. The first is by an anonymous writer who fought throughout the crusade in the Norman forces and therefore witnessed much that he describes. He undoubtedly wrote most of the account while on the campaign, because it was completed by 1101. The second account is by Raymond of Aguilers and the Provençal knight Pontius of Balazun. The greater portion of this composition was written by Raymond, who as the chaplain of Count Raymond of Toulouse had easy access to vital information and to the person of the count. Raymond's account is therefore strongly partisan, being actually a defense of Peter Bartholomew and his discovery of the Holy Lance. It was completed by 1102.

A Account by an Anonymous Writer: Anonymi Gesta Francorum et Aliorum Hierosolymitanorum ("The Deeds of the Franks and the Men of Jerusalem by an Anonymous Author")

There was a certain pilgrim of our army, whose name was Peter,[1] to whom before we entered the city St. Andrew, the apostle, appeared and said: "What art thou doing, good man?"

Peter answered, "Who art thou?"

The apostle said to him: "I am St. Andrew, the apostle. Know, my son, that when thou shalt enter the town, go to the church of St. Peter. There thou wilt find the Lance of our Saviour, Jesus Christ, with which He was wounded as He hung on the arm of the cross." Having said all this, the apostle straightway withdrew.

But Peter, afraid to reveal the advice of the apostle, was unwilling to make it known to the pilgrims. However, he thought that he had seen a vision, and said: "Lord, who would believe this?" But at that hour St. Andrew took him and carried him to the place where the Lance was hidden in the ground. When we were a second time situated in such (straits) as we have stated above, St. Andrew came again, saying to him: "Wherefore hast thou not yet taken the Lance from the earth as I commanded thee? Know, verily, that whoever shall bear this lance in battle shall never be overcome by an enemy." Peter, indeed, straightway made known to our men the mystery of the apostle.

The people, however, did not believe (it), but refused, saying: "How can we believe this?" For they were utterly terrified and thought that they were to die forthwith. Thereupon, this man came forth and swore that it was all most true, since St. Andrew had twice appeared to him in a vision and had said to him: "Rise, go and tell the people of God not to fear, but to trust firmly with whole heart in the one true God and they will be everywhere victorious. Within five days the Lord will send them such a token

From A. C. Krey, THE FIRST CRUSADE. THE ACCOUNTS OF EYE-WITNESSES AND PARTICIPANTS (Princeton, 1921), pp. 175–176, 225–229. Reprinted by permission of the Princeton University Press.

that they will remain happy and joyful, and if they wish to fight, let them go out immediately to battle, all together, and all their enemies will be conquered, and no one will stand against them." Thereupon, when they heard that their enemies were to be overcome by them, they began straightway to revive and to encourage one another, saying: "Bestir yourselves, and be everywhere brave and alert, since the Lord will come to our aid in the next battle and will be the greatest refuge to His people whom He beholds lingering in sorrow."

Accordingly, upon hearing the statements of that man who reported to us the revelation of Christ through the words of the apostle, we went in haste immediately to the place in the church of St. Peter which he had pointed out. Thirteen men dug there from morning until vespers. And so that man found the Lance, just as he had indicated. They received it with great gladness and fear, and a joy beyond measure arose in the whole city.

Many revelations were made known to us at this time, which were sent to us from God. The following is one of these, which is written under the name of him who saw it.

"In the year of the Lord 1099, in the seventh Indiction, twenty-sixth Epact, fifth Concurrence, on the night of the Nones of April,[2] when I, Peter Bartholomew, lay in the chapel of the Count of St. Gilles at the siege of Archas, I began to meditate on the priest to whom the Lord appeared with the Cross when we were besieged by the Turks in Antioch. And when I marvelled much that He had never appeared to me with the Cross, I saw the Lord entering with His apostles, Peter and Andrew, and a certain other, large and heavy, of dark complexion, nearly bald, and with large eyes.

"And the Lord said to me 'What art thou doing?'

"I replied, 'Lord, I am standing here.'

"And the Lord spoke again, 'Thou hast barely escaped being submerged (in sin) with the rest. But of what art thou now thinking?'

"And I replied, 'Lord, Father, I was thinking about a priest to whom Thou didst appear with the Cross.'

"The Lord answered, 'I know that.' And then: 'Believe that I am the Lord for whom thou hast come hither and who suffered for sinners on the Cross at Jerusalem, just as thou wilt now behold.'

"And at that very hour I saw there a cross made of two black and round planks, neither polished nor fitted, except that in the middle the beams were notched and supported each other in turn.

"The Lord said to me, 'Behold the Cross, since it is the Cross which thou seekest.' And on that Cross was the Lord extended and crucified as at the time of the Passion. Peter, moreover, supported His head from the right; Andrew from the left bore it on his neck; that third person supported it from the rear with his hands.

"And the Lord said to me, 'Say to My people that thou hast seen Me thus. Dost thou see these, My five wounds? Thus do you consist of five ranks. The first rank is the rank of those who do not fear javelins and swords, or any kind of engine. That rank is like unto Me; for I went to Jerusalem and did not fear swords and lances, cudgels and staves, or, in addition, the Cross. They die for Me; and I died for them; and I am in them, and they in Me. When such as these die, they are placed on the right hand of God, where after the resurrection I sat, having ascended to heaven. The second is the rank of those who are a help to the first; but they guard them from the rear, and to them the former also come for refuge; verily, these are like the apostles who followed Me and ate with Me. The third is the rank of those who bring stones and javelins to the first; they are like those who, when they saw Me placed on the Cross, bemoaning my Passion, beat their breasts, proclaiming that wrong had been done Me. The fourth, indeed, is the rank of those who, upon seeing the battle surge, push themselves into houses and turn to their own affairs, trusting that victory rests not in My might, but in human worth. They are like those who said "He is worthy of death; let Him be crucified; since He makes Himself a king and says that He is the Son of God." The fifth, however, is the rank of those who, when they hear the shout of battle, look on from afar, asking the cause of the outcry, and afford examples of cowardice, not of bravery, and are unwilling to undergo dangers not only for Me, but, likewise, for their brothers. Under the form of avoiding (danger), they want others to fight, or bring arms to the fighters, and they feast at looking on; they are like Judas the Betrayer and Pontius Pilate, the judge.

"Moreover, the Lord was naked upon the Cross, encircled only with a linen cloth from knees to loins, and the linen cloth was of a color midway between red and black. And about His ears He had a white, red, and green head-band. Later, when the Cross had been taken away, the Lord remained in the garb which He wore before.

"And I said to Him, 'Lord, God, if I say this, they will not believe me.'

"The Lord replied to me, 'Dost thou want to recognize those who will not believe this?'

"And I said, 'Yea, Lord.'

"And the Lord answered, 'Let the Count assemble the princes and people, and let them make arrangements about the battles, or when it shall be time for the siege of the fortress. Let the most renowned herald proclaim "God help us!" thrice, and let him strive to carry out the arrangements. Then as I have told thee, thou wilt see these ranks: and together with the others who believe this thou wilt distinguish the unbelievers.'

"And I said, 'What are we to do about the incredulous?'

"The Lord answered, 'Spare them not, kill them; for they are my betrayers, brothers of Judas Iscariot. But give their possessions to those who are of the first rank, according to their needs. If you do this, you will find the right way, which you have thus far gone around. And just as the other things which thou hast prophesied happened unchanged in the future, this also will occur. Dost thou know which people I love especially?'

"And I replied, 'The race of the Jews.'

"The Lord said, 'These people I hold in hate, because they were unbelievers and I have placed them below all peoples. See, therefore, that you are not unbelievers. Otherwise I will take up other peoples, while you remain with the Jews; and through them I will fulfil what I promised you. Say this also to them (the army): "Why do you fear to do justice? And what is better than justice?" I want them to keep the following justice. Let them place judges by families and relatives. When, moreover, anyone shall offend another, let him who suffered the wrong say: "Brother, dost thou wish it to be done thus with thee?" After this, unless the offender shall desist, let the other oppose him in the name of his authority. Then let the judge freely take all his goods from the malefactor, and the half of all that has been taken let him give to the one who suffered this wrong, the remaining part to the authorities. If, however, the judge should defer this for any reason, go to him and say that if he does not correct himself, he will not be absolved even at the last day, unless thou dost release him. Dost thou know how serious a matter it is to be forbidden? For I forbade Adam to touch the tree of good and evil knowledge; he transgressed my prohibition and both he and his posterity were in wretched captivity until I came in the flesh and redeemed them by dying the death of the Cross. Verily, some have done well about the tithe, because they gave it as I commanded. Therefore, I will multiply them, and I will make them known among the others.'

"Moreover, when the Lord had said this, I began to ask Him out of His kindness to give back the knowledge of letters which He had recently taken from me.

"And the Lord said to me, 'Are the things that thou knowest not enough to tell this? And yet thou desirest to know as much as possible!'

"And forthwith I seemed to myself so wise that I would ask nothing further.

"Then the Lord said, 'Is what thou knowest enough for this?'

"I replied, 'It is.'

"The Lord again said, 'What have I said to thee? Answer.'

"And I knew nothing. When He pressed me to answer some of the things which He had said, I replied, 'Lord, I know nothing.'

"And the Lord said, 'Go and tell what thou knowest, and what thou knowest will be sufficient for thee.'

When, however, I would have made this known to the brethren, some began to say that they would never believe that God spoke to such a man, that He passed our princes and bishops and revealed Himself to a peasant man; whence they likewise doubted about the Lance. Wherefore we called together those brethren to whom the Lance had been revealed at one time and another, and after this, Arnulf, chaplain of the Count of Normandy who was, as it were, the head of the unbelievers; and we asked him why he doubted.

When he said that the Bishop of Puy had doubted it, a certain priest by the name of Peter Desiderius replied, "I saw the Bishop of Puy after his death and St. Nicholas with him. After many other things the Bishop said this to me, 'I am in the choir with St. Nicholas, but because I, who should have believed most, doubted the Lance of the Lord, I was led into hell where my hair from the right side of my head and my beard were burned; and though I am not in punishment, yet I will not clearly see the Lord until my hair and beard grow out as they were before.' " This and many other things that priest told us, which afterwards occurred; but these things can be told in their place.

A certain other priest, Ebrard by name, came and said: "At the time when the Turks were besieging our army in Antioch, I was at Tripoli. For before Antioch was taken I had come there for the necessaries of life. When I heard that Antioch had been taken, and that our men in the city were held in such a stage of siege that none of them dared to go in or out, except by stealth, and that many other evils threatened the besieged (mostly false reports which the Saracens and Turks added to the true evils), I was doubtful of my secular life, and fled to a certain church where I knelt before the majesty of the Mother of God. With tears and prayers I began to appeal through her for the mercy of God; and I did this for some days, remaining without food and saying to her: 'O dearest Lady, these are pilgrims who have left all their little ones, their wives, and all their dear ones for the name of thy Son and for thee. They have come hither from distant regions and are fighting for thy Son; have pity on them! And, O Lady, what will be said of thy Son and of thee in their lands, if thou givest them over into the hands of the Turks?'

"And when I had in anger and lament too often repeated this and other statements like it, a certain Syrian, who was a Christian, said to me 'Be of good spirit, and see that you weep no longer. Recently I was before the doors of the church of the Blessed Mary, Mother of the Lord, and a cleric, clothed in white garments, appeared to me. When I asked him who he was, or whence he came, he replied, "I am Mark, the evangelist, and I come from Alexandria; and I turned hither because of the Church of the Blessed Mary." And again when I asked him where he was going, he said, "Our Lord is at Antioch and has sent word to all His disciples to come there, since the Franks are due to fight with the Turks, and we will be their protection." ' And when he had said this, he went away!

"But since I would place little faith in these words, nor cease from grief or tears, the same Syrian said to me, 'Know, in the Gospel of the blessed Peter it is written that the Christian host which shall take Jerusalem shall first have been shut up in Antioch. Nor can they thence go forth until they shall have found the Lance of the Lord.' "

And the priest added, "If you doubt any of this, let the fire be built; and in the name of God and with the witness of these people, I will go through the midst of it."

Then another priest, Stephen, surnamed Valentine, a man of great integrity and good life, came forth and said, "The Lord Jesus Himself spoke to me in the very midst of the suffering which was at Antioch, and promised in the presence of His most Blessed Mother, the Virgin Mary, that on the fifth day to come He would be merciful to His people and complete their different undertakings, if they would return to Him with their whole heart. And on that day the Holy Lance was found; therefore I believe that the promises of the Lord were fulfilled. If you doubt any of this, as soon as I saw this vision I offered the Bishop of Puy as proof of it to go through fire in the presence of the whole multitude, if he wished, or to throw myself from the highest tower. And I still make this very offer to you."

Moreover the Bishop of Agde, came forth and said, "Whether I saw this in my sleep or not, I know not for certain; God knows. A man, dressed in white, and holding the Lance of the Lord, this Lance, I say, in his hands, came and stood before me and said to me, 'Dost thou believe this to be the Lance of the Lord?'

"And I replied: 'I do, Lord.'

"I had hesitated somewhat about it, but after he had sternly exacted this (answer) from me a second and a third time, I said to him: 'I believe, Lord, that this is the Lance of my Lord Jesus Christ.' And after this he left me."

B   *Account by Raymond of Aguilers, Historia Francorum Qui Ceperunt Jerusalem ("History of the Franks Who Captured Jerusalem")*

And I who have written this, in the presence of the brethren and the Bishop said this there: "I was present while the digging took place; and before all of the Lance appeared above the ground, I kissed the point. And there are several in the army who were with me." And I added, "There is a certain other priest, Bertrand of Puy by name, who was a servant of the Bishop of Puy during his life. Moreover, this priest was sick unto death in Antioch; and when he had already given up hope of his life, there came before him the Bishop of Puy with his standard bearer, Heraclius, who, in the greatest fight made at Antioch was wounded in the face by an arrow while he was fearlessly launching forth against the lines of the Turks, and as a consequence ended his life.

"And Heraclius said, 'Lord, he is ill.'

"The Bishop replied, 'He is ill because of his unbelief.'

"And the priest thereupon said: 'Lord, do I not believe in the Lance of the Lord, just as also the Passion of the Lord?'

"Then the Bishop said to him, 'And thou must yet believe many other things.'"

And though this does not pertain to this matter, nevertheless, since it is worthy, I will add something for the sake of good men. When the priest had reseated himself before the Bishop and his lord Heraclius, for he was sick and could not stand, he beheld in the face of his lord the wound from which he had ended the labors of his mortal life. And the priest said to him, "Sire, we believed that thy wound had already healed. Why is this?"

Heraclius answered, "Well hast thou asked this question. When I came before my Lord, I begged him that this wound might never be closed, since because of it I ended my life. And this the Lord

From A. C. Krey, THE FIRST CRUSADE. THE ACCOUNTS OF EYE-WITNESSES AND PARTICIPANTS (Princeton, 1921), pp. 230–233. Reprinted by permission of the Princeton University Press.

granted me." This and much else the Bishop and Heraclius said to the priest, which are not now necessary (to relate).

When he had listened to these and many other men, Arnulf believed and confessed; and he promised the Bishop of Albara that he would do penance in the presence of all the people for his unbelief. However, on the appointed day when Arnulf had come, summoned to council, he began to say that he would place full faith in it (the Lance), but that he wished to speak with his lord before doing penance. But when Peter Bartholomew heard this, he was exceedingly angry, and like a plain man, and one who has well known the truth, he said, "I wish and beg that a very large fire be built; and I will pass through the midst of it with the Lance of the Lord. If it is the Lance of the Lord, I will pass through the fire unhurt, but if it is not, I will be burned in the fire. For I see that neither signs nor witnesses are believed."

All this pleased us; and having commanded him to fast, we said that the fire would be built on the day on which the Lord was wounded on the Cross with it (the Lance) for our salvation. And after the fourth day, then was the day of preparation. So when the appointed day shone, the fire was made ready after midday. Princes and people to the number of sixty thousand men assembled there; priests were there in bare feet and dressed in their priestly vestments. The fire was made of dry olive branches and had a length of thirty feet; and there were four feet in the height of the piles. After the fire had burned violently, I, Raymond, said before the whole multitude, "If Almighty God spoke face to face with this man, and St. Andrew showed him the Lance when he was on watch, let him pass through the fire unhurt. If, however, it is a falsehood, may he be burned, together with the Lance which he will carry in his hand!" And all upon bended knees responded, "Amen!"

The fire was so hot that it filled the air for thirty cubits. Verily, no one could go near it. Then Peter Bartholomew, dressed only in an undergarment, knelt down before the Bishop of Albara and called God as his witness that he had seen Him face to face upon the Cross, and had heard from Him what has been written above, and also from St. Peter and Andrew; and that he had not made up any of the things which he had reported in the name of St. Peter, or St. Andrew, or of the Lord Himself; and that if he had told any lie, he should never pass through the present fire. (He prayed) that God would forgive him the other (sins) which he had committed, both against God and his neighbor, and that the Bishop and all the other priests and the people who had gathered to witness the test would pray for him. After this, when the Bishop had placed the Lance in his hand, he knelt and, after invoking the sign of the cross upon himself, went forth boldly and without fear into the fire. He stopped for a brief moment in the midst of the fire, and thus by the grace of God passed through.

There are, moreover, to this day some who saw this miracle there, that, before he had escaped destruction, a bird flew over head and, after encircling the fire, plunged into it. Ebrard the priest, he of whom we made mention above, and who later remained at Jerusalem for the sake of the Lord, saw this; and William, son of William the Good, an excellent knight, of good reputation, from the region of Arles, bears witness that he saw this. A certain other honorable knight of the people of Beziers, William *Maluspuer* by name, saw a man dressed in priestly garb, except that he had a robe folded back over his head, advance into the fire before Peter went into the flames. When he saw that (this man) did not come forth, thinking that it was Peter Bartholomew, he began to weep, believing that he had been destroyed in the fire. There was a multitude of men there and they could not see everything. And many other things were revealed to us and done which we do not wish to write for fear of tiring the readers — since three suitable witnesses are sufficient for any question. Let us not pass over this one occurrence. After Peter Bartholomew had passed through the fire, though much fire was still burning, yet the people so eagerly gathered brands and coals, together with ashes, that in a short space of time none of it remained. In the faith of those people the Lord afterwards worked many good deeds through these relics.

But as Peter came forth from the fire, with his shirt unburned and with no sign of any hurt on that very fine cloth with which the Lance of the Lord was wound, all the people welcomed him when he had signalled to them, holding the Lance in his hand, and had shouted at the top of his voice, "God help us!" They welcomed him, I say, and dragged him along the ground and almost that whole multitude stepped upon him, each one wishing to touch him, or to take some piece of his garment, and each one believing him near someone else. And thus they made three or four wounds on his legs, cutting off the flesh; and trampling upon his back-bone, they broke it. And there Peter would have breathed out his soul, as we believe, had not Raymond Piletus, a most noble and brave knight, supported by a crowd of companions, rushed into the mass of the confused mob and freed him by fighting even to death. But now from concern and anguish we cannot write more about this.

When Raymond Piletus had brought Peter to our house and his wounds had been bound up, we asked him why he had stopped in the fire. To this he replied, "The Lord met me in the midst of the flames and, taking me by the hand, said to me, 'Since thou didst doubt the finding of the Lance when St. Andrew showed it to thee, thou shalt not pass through unhurt, but thou shalt not see hell.' And having said this, He left me. Look, therefore, if you wish, at my burns." And there was a slight burn on his legs but not much; the wounds, however, were large.

After this we called together all who had doubted the Lance to come and see his face, head, hair, and other members. They would find out that what he said of the Lance and other matters was true, since for proof of these things he had not feared to enter such a fire. Therefore many looked, and, upon seeing his face and whole body, they glorified God, saying, "Well can the Lord, who delivered this man from such a flaming fire, protect us amidst the swords of our enemies! Indeed, we did not believe that any arrow could pass unhurt through the fire, as this man passed through!"

After this Peter called the chaplain of the Count, Raymond,[1] by name, to him and said, "Why did you wish me to pass through fire for proof of the Lance of the Lord and other things that I reported as from God? I know well that you have thought this way and that."

And he told me what he had thought. But when Raymond denied that he had so thought, Peter Bartholomew replied, "You can not deny it to me, since I know it for certain, because the other night the most Blessed Virgin Mary was here and the Bishop of Puy, through whom I learned the things which you deny. Since you did not doubt the words of the Lord and His apostles, I wonder, indeed, why you should wish, at my risk, to hold trial about these matters alone."

Then Raymond, seeing his thought detected and himself culpable before God, broke forth most bitterly in tears. And Peter thereupon said: "Do not despair for the most Blessed Virgin Mary and St. Andrew will obtain pardon for you with God. But you must be more zealous in beseeching them."

NOTES

Selection a
   1. Peter Bartholomew.
   2. April 3.

Selection b
   1. Count of Toulouse.

9

Twelfth-Century Monasticism

LARGELY responsible for the reform and revival of the church in the eleventh century was the zeal with which the Cluniac monastic order revitalized Benedictine monasticism. The first monastery of this order was established at Cluny in Burgundy in 910. By the late eleventh and twelfth centuries, however, the reforming spirit of the Cluniac order had so flagged that much of the clergy felt it essential to return to the primitive ideals and practices of Christianity. This led to the founding of new monastic orders, among which the most celebrated was the Cistercian founded at Cîteaux in Burgundy in 1908. This order grew and spread so rapidly throughout western Europe that by the middle of the twelfth century it numbered almost three hundred fifty houses. The success of the Cistercian order was due to St. Bernard and to its efficient organization, created by the so-called Charter of Love drawn up about 1117 by Stephen Harding, second abbot of Cîteaux. In the Charter of Love, reprinted below, is found the complete plan for the organization of the Cistercian order. The second of the following selections concerns the career of Samson, abbot of the Benedictine monastery of Bury St. Edmunds in England from 1182 to 1211. Thanks to the monk Jocelin of Brakelond we have here not only a fine portrait of Samson but an intimate sketch of life within a twelfth-century monastery and of the problems that confronted the abbot.

A The Charter of Love

Before the Cistercian abbeys began to flourish, the lord abbot, Stephen, and his monks ordained that abbeys were on no account to be established in the diocese of any bishop prior to his ratification and confirmation of the decree drawn up in writing between the abbey of Cîteaux and its daughter-houses, in order to avoid occasion of offence between the bishop and the monks. In this

CARTA CARITATIS, in D. C. Douglas and G. W. Greenaway, ENGLISH HISTORICAL DOCUMENTS, 1042–1189 (New York, 1953), pp. 687–691. Reprinted by permission of the Oxford University Press.

decree, therefore, the aforesaid brethren, guarding against possible dangers to their mutual peace, have made clear and established and handed down to later generations in what manner and by what agreement, nay rather, with what *love* the monks of their Order, though separated in body in abbeys and divers parts of the world, might be knit together inseparably in spirit. Moreover, they were of opinion that this decree should be called the "Charter of Love," because it casts off the burden of all exactions, pursues love alone and promotes the welfare of souls in things human and divine.

I] Inasmuch as we are known to be servants of the One True King, Lord and Master, albeit unprofitable, we therefore make no claim for worldly advantage or temporal gain on our abbots and brother monks, whom in divers places devotion to God shall call through us, the most wretched of men, to live under regular discipline. For, in our desire for their profit and that of all sons of holy Church, we are not disposed to lay any burden upon them or to effect anything calculated to diminish their substance, lest in striving to grow rich at their expense, we may not escape the sin of avarice, which is declared by the apostle to be servitude to idols.

II] Nevertheless we desire for love's sake to retain the cure of their souls, so that if they shall essay to swerve from their sacred purpose and the observance of the holy Rule — which God forbid — they may through our solicitude return to righteousness of life.

III] We will therefore and command them to observe the Rule of St. Benedict in all things as it is observed in the new monastery.[1] Let the monks put no other interpretation upon the holy Rule but what the holy fathers, our predecessors, namely the monks of the new minster, have understood and maintained; and as we today understand and uphold it, so let them do also.

IV] And inasmuch as we receive in our cloister all the monks of their houses who come to us, and they likewise receive ours in theirs, so it seems good to us and in accordance with our will that they should maintain the customary ceremonial, chants and all books necessary for the canonical offices, both by day and by night, and for the Mass, after the form of the customs and books of the new minster, so that there be no discord in our worship, but that we may all dwell in one love and under one rule and with like customs.

V] No church or person of our Order shall presume to solicit from anyone a privilege contrary to the common customs of the Order, or in any wise retain it, if it has been granted.

VI] When the abbot of the new minster shall come on a visitation to one of these houses, let the abbot of the place recognize the church of the new minster as his mother-church and give place to him in all the precincts of the monastery, and let the visiting abbot take the place of the abbot of that house, so long as he remains there.

VII] Except that he shall not take his meals in the guest-room, but in the refectory with the brethren, that discipline may be preserved, unless the abbot of the house be absent. Likewise let it be done in the case of all abbots of our Order who may chance to come on a visit. But if several shall come at the same time, and the abbot of the house be absent, let the abbot senior in rank take his meals in the guest-room. An exception shall also be made that the abbot of the house shall, even when a greater abbot is present, bless his own novices after the regular term of probation.

VIII] But let the abbot of the new minster be careful not to presume in any wise to conduct or order the affairs of the house he is visiting, or meddle in them, against the will of the abbot or the brethren.

IX] But if he learn that the precepts of the Rule or of our Order are transgressed in the said house, let him be diligent to correct the brethren lovingly, and with the advice and in the presence of the abbot. Even if the abbot be absent, he shall nevertheless correct what he has found wrong therein.

X] Once a year let the abbot of the mother-church[2] visit all the houses of his foundation either in person or through one of his co-abbots. And if he shall visit the brethren more often, let them the more rejoice.

XI] Moreover, let the abbey of Cîteaux be visited by the four primary abbots, namely of La Ferté, Pontigny, Clairvaux and Morimond, together in person on such a day as they may choose, except that appointed for the holding of the annual chapter, unless perchance one of them be prevented by grievous sickness.

XII] When any abbot of our Order shall come to the new minster, let fitting reverence be shown to him; let him occupy the abbot's stall and take his meals in the guest-room if the abbot be absent. But if the abbot be present, let him do none of these things, but let him dine in the refectory. Let the prior of the abbey take charge of its affairs.

XIII] Between abbeys having no direct relationship with each other, this shall be the rule. Let every abbot give place to his co-abbot within the precincts of his monastery, that the saying may be fulfilled, "in honour preferring one another." If two or more abbots shall come to the monastery, the superior in rank shall take precedence of the others. But let them all take their meals together in the refectory, except the abbot of the house, as stated above. But whenever they meet on other occasions, they shall maintain their rank in accordance with the seniority of their abbeys so that he whose church is of older foundation, shall take precedence of the others. Whenever they take their seats together, let each humble himself before the others.

XIV] But when any of our churches has by God's grace so increased that it is able to establish a new house, let the two houses maintain the same relationship between them as obtains between us and our brethren, except that they shall not hold an annual chapter among themselves.

XV] But all the abbots of our Order shall without fail attend each year the general chapter at Cîteaux, with the sole exception of those detained by bodily infirmity. The latter, however, ought to appoint a suitable delegate, by whom the reason for their absence may be reported to the chapter. An exception may also be made for those who dwell in distant lands; let them attend at the intervals appointed for them in the chapter. But if, and when, on any other occasion any abbot shall presume to absent himself from our general chapter, let him crave pardon for his fault at the chapter held in the following year; let his absence not be passed over without serious attention being paid to it.

XVI] In this general chapter let the abbots take measures for the salvation of their souls, and if anything in the observance of the holy Rule or of the Order ought to be amended or supplemented, let them ordain it and re-establish the bond of peace and charity among themselves.

XVII] But if any abbot be found remiss in keeping the Rule, or too intent upon worldly affairs or in any way corrupt or wicked, let him be charged with the offence in the chapter, albeit in all charity. Let the accused crave pardon and perform the penance laid on him for his fault. Such a charge, however, may not be brought except by an abbot.

XVIII] If perchance any dispute shall arise between certain abbots, or an offence be charged against one of them so grave as to merit suspension or deposition, the decision of the chapter shall be observed without question.

XIX] But if, by reason of a difference of opinion, the case shall result in discord, the judgment of the abbot of Cîteaux and of those of sounder and more appropriate counsel shall be inflexibly upheld, precaution being taken that none of those personally involved in the case shall take part in the judgment.

XX] Should any church fall into extreme poverty, let the abbot of that house take pains to inform the whole chapter of the fact. Thereupon the abbots, one and all inflamed with an ardent fire of love, shall hasten to relieve that church from its poverty, so far as they are able, out of the resources bestowed upon them by God.

XXI] If any house of our Order become bereft of its abbot, let the abbot of the house from which it sprung, take every care for its governance, until a new abbot shall be elected. Moreover, on the day appointed for the election, let the abbots of the daughter-houses of that house be summoned, and let them and the monks of that house elect an abbot with the advice and assent of the abbot of the mother-house.

XXII] When the house of Cîteaux, the mother of us all, shall be bereft of its abbot, let the four primary abbots, namely those of La Ferté, Pontigny, Clairvaux and Morimond, make provision for it, and let the responsibility for the abbey rest upon them, until a new abbot be elected and appointed.

XXIII] A day having been fixed and named for the election of an abbot of Cîteaux, let a summons be conveyed with at least fifteen days' notice to the abbots of the houses sprung from Cîteaux and to such others as the aforesaid abbots and the monks of Cîteaux shall deem suitable and, being assembled in the name of the Lord, let the abbots and the monks of Cîteaux elect an abbot.

XXIV] It is permissible for any monk to be raised to the office of abbot of the mother-church of our Order, not only those of her daughter-churches, but also, in case of necessity for their abbots to be free to do so. But no member of another Order may be elected abbot, even as it is not permissible for one of us to be appointed to another monastery which is not of our Order.

xxv] Should any abbot beg leave of his father, the abbot of the house from which his own has sprung, to be relieved of the burden of his office on the pretext of his incapacity or through faint-heartedness, let the father-abbot have a care lest he assent to his request too readily and without a reasonable cause and urgent need. But if the necessity be very great, let the father-abbot do nothing in the matter of his own initiative, but let him summon certain other abbots of our Order and by their advice act in the way they have agreed upon.

xxvi] If any abbot become notorious for contempt of the holy Rule or as a transgressor of the Order or an accessory to the faults of the brethren committed to his charge, let the abbot of the mother-church, either in person or through his prior, or in whatever way is more convenient, exhort him on four occasions to mend his ways. But if he will neither suffer correction nor yield of his own accord, let a sufficient number of the abbots of our congregation be gathered together, and let them remove the transgressor of the holy Rule from his office; after which another more worthy of it may be elected by the monks of that church with the advice and goodwill of the greater abbot and in co-operation with the abbots and those who are related to it, as stated above.

xxvii] But if — which God forbid — the deposed abbot or his monks shall be contumacious and rebellious, and will not acquiesce in the sentence, let them be subject to excommunication by the abbot of the mother-church and his co-abbots, and thereafter coerced by him according as he thinks fit and is able.

xxviii] Arising out of this, should any one of those so condemned come to himself again and desire to arise from the death of the soul and return to his mother, let him be received as a penitent son. For except for this occasion, which should always be avoided as far as possible, let no abbot retain a monk belonging to any other abbot of our Order without his assent; also let none bring his monks to dwell in the house of any other without his permission.

xxix] In like manner if — which God forbid — the abbots of our Order shall discover that our mother-church of Cîteaux is becoming lukewarm in its sacred purpose, or is departing from the observance of the holy Rule, let them admonish the abbot of that house four times through the four primary abbots, namely those of La Ferté,

Pontigny, Clairvaux and Morimond, in the name of the other abbots of the Order, to amend his life and take pains to amend that of others, and let them diligently fulfil in his case the remaining precepts prescribed for the other abbots, when they are intolerant of correction. But if he will not yield of his own accord, they may neither depose him nor condemn him as contumacious, until they come to depose him from his office as an unprofitable steward, either in the general chapter or — if perchance it be already known that the chapter is not due for summons — in another assembly specially convened for the abbots of the daughter-houses of Cîteaux and some of the others; whereupon both the said abbots and the monks of Cîteaux shall take care to elect a suitable abbot in his place. But if the former abbot and the monks of Cîteaux shall contumaciously resist, let them not forbear to strike them with the sword of excommunication.

xxx] Should any such transgressor afterwards come to his senses and, in the desire to save his soul, take refuge in one of our four primary churches, whether at La Ferté, or Pontigny, or Clairvaux, or Morimond, let him be received as an inmate and co-partner in the abbey in accordance with the Rule, until such time as he be justly reconciled with his own church, whereupon he may be restored thither. In the meantime the annual chapter of the abbots shall not be held at Cîteaux, but wheresoever the above-named four abbots shall previously have appointed.

B   *Abbot Samson of Bury St. Edmunds,* Cronica Jocelini de Brakelonda ("*The Chronicle of Jocelin of Brakelond*")

SEVEN months had not passed since his election,[1] when lo and behold! letters of the Lord Pope were brought to him, offering to appoint him judge delegate for the hearing of causes, a task of which he had neither knowledge nor experience, though he was learned in the liberal arts and in the Holy Scriptures, being a literate man, brought up in the schools and once a schoolmaster, well known and approved in his country. He forthwith called to him two clerks skilled in the law and associated them with himself, making use of their counsel in ecclesiastical business, and studying the decrees and decretal letters, whenever he had time, so that within a short time by reading of books and practice in causes he came to be regarded as a wise judge, proceeding in court according to the form of law. Wherefore one said, "A curse upon the court of this Abbot, where neither gold or silver may help me for the confounding of my adversary!" In process of time when he had acquired some practice in secular cases, being guided by his native power of reasoning, he showed himself so subtle of understanding, that all marvelled, and the Undersheriff Osbert FitzHervey said of him, "This Abbot is a fine disputer: if he goes on as he has begun, he will blind us all, every one." And having approved himself in causes of this kind, he was made a justice errant,[2] though he erred not, but was careful not to wander from the right way. But "Envy assails earth's highest!" When his men complained to him in the court of St. Edmund, because he would not give judgment hastily nor "believe every spirit," but proceeded in the order prescribed by law, knowing that the merits of causes are revealed by the statements of the parties, it was said that he was unwilling to do justice to any complainant, unless money were first given or promised; and because his glance was sharp and penetrating, and his brow worthy of

From H. E. Butler, THE CHRONICLE OF JOCELIN OF BRAKELOND CONCERNING THE ACTS OF SAMSON ABBOT OF THE MONASTERY OF ST. EDMUND (*Edinburgh,* 1949), *pp.* 33–45, 87–89. *Reprinted by permission of Thomas Nelson and Sons Ltd.*

Cato and rarely relaxed into a smile, he was said to be more inclined to severity than kindness. And when he took amercements for any offence, he was said to exalt justice above mercy, because, as it seemed to many, when it was a matter of getting money, he rarely remitted what he might justly receive. As his wisdom grew, so also did his prudence in managing his property and increasing it, and in all honourable expenditure. But in this also his detractors used to bring charges against him, saying that he took from the sacristy whatever he wanted, sparing his own money, allowing his corn to lie until the time came when it sold dear, and in lodging at his manors as his predecessors had never done, thereby burdening the Cellarer with guests who ought rather to have been entertained by the Abbot, so that at the end of the year he might be called a wise Abbot, well-stocked and full of forethought, while the Convent and obedientiaries were deemed both ignorant and improvident. To these detractions I used to reply that, if he took anything from the sacristy, he employed it for the profit of the church; and this no jealous critic could deny. And to confess the truth, much greater and more frequent good was done with the oblations of the sacristy during the fifteen years after his election than in the forty years before. To other objections, that the Abbot lay at his manors, I was wont to answer and excuse him, saying that the Abbot was happier and more cheerful elsewhere than at home; and this was very true, either because of the multitude of persons who came to lay their complaints before him, or on account of tale-bearers; whence it often happened that, because he showed them a stern face, he lost much favour and gratitude with his guests, although he satisfied them in respect of their food and drink. Now I, noting this, once when I found the opportunity, for I was standing by him, being then his secretary, said to him, "There are two things about you whereat I marvel much." And when he asked, "What two?" I made answer, "One is that, being in such a position as you now hold, you still cherish the maxim of the men of Melun[3] who say that from false premises no conclusion can be drawn, and such trifles as these." And when he had answered this as pleased him, I proceeded, "The other is that at home you do not show as kind a face as elsewhere, not even among the brethren who love you still and loved you of old and chose you to be their lord, but you are rarely among them, nor do you rejoice with them, as they say." When he heard this he changed countenance and hung his head and thus made answer, "You are a fool and speak like a fool. You should know what Solomon says, 'Thou has many daughters. Show not thy face cheerful towards them.'" At that I was silent, and thenceforth set a guard upon my tongue. Yet on another occasion I said, "My lord, last night I heard you after matins lying awake and sighing deeply, as is not your common custom." And he replied, "No wonder that I sigh; you share my food and drink, my horses, and the like! but you little think of the ordering of my house and household, or concerning the many troubles of my pastoral care, that vex me and cause my spirit to groan and to be filled with anxiety." To which I made answer, raising my hands to heaven, "Almighty God, grant that such anxiety may never be mine!" I heard the Abbot say that, if he had been in that state of life in which he was before he became a monk, and had had five or six marks of income wherewith he might have maintained himself in the schools, he would never have become monk or Abbot. On another occasion he said with an oath, that if he had sooner known what and how great the cares of his abbacy would be, he had sooner have been the master of the aumbrey[4] and custodian of the books, than Abbot and lord; for he said that of all offices this was the one which he had ever most desired. Who would believe it? I found it hard; nor indeed would I have believed it, had I not, by living with him six years, night and day, come to know the merits of his life and the depths of his wisdom in all their fullness. He told me once that when he was a boy nine years old, he dreamed that he was standing before the cemetery gates of the church of St. Edmund, and that the devil sought to catch him with outstretched arms; but St. Edmund stood by and received him in his arms; and when he cried out in his dream, "St. Edmund, help me!" though he had never so much as heard his name, he suddenly awoke. But his mother was amazed at the loudness and the nature of his cry and, when she had heard his dream, she took him to St. Edmund's that he might pray there, and when they came to the cemetery gate, he said, "Mother, behold the place, the selfsame gate which I saw in my dream, when the devil wished to catch me!" And he said that he recognised the place as clearly as if he had seen it with his fleshly eyes. The Abbot himself expounded his dream, interpreting the devil as being the pleasure of this world which sought to entice him, but St. Edmund embraced him because he desired him to become a monk of his Church.

Once when he was told that certain of the Convent murmured at something which he had done, he said to me as I sat beside him, "God, God, it is most expedient that I should remember the dream that was dreamed before I became Abbot, to wit, that I should raven like a wolf. For assuredly this is what I fear most above all earthly things, namely that my Convent may say or do something that will make it my duty so to raven. But thus it is, when they say or do something contrary to my desire, I remember that dream and, though I raven in my heart, secretly roaring and gnashing my teeth, I force myself not to raven in word or deed; and

> my pent-up grief
> Doth choke me and my heart within me boils."

But though he was naturally quick to anger and easily kindled to wrath, yet more often, remembering his position, with a great struggle he curbed his wrath. And of this at times he boasted, saying, "I have seen this thing and that, I have heard this and that, and yet have patiently endured it."

The Abbot once, as he sat in Chapter, uttered certain words, in which he seemed to court the favour of the Convent. "I do not desire," he said, "that anyone should come to me to accuse another, unless he is ready to say the same thing in public; but if any should do otherwise, I shall make known the name of the accuser. I desire also that every cloister monk should have free access to me to speak with me concerning his need, whenever he wishes." Now he said this because our chief men in the time of Abbot Hugh, wishing that nothing should be done in the monastery save through themselves, decreed that no cloister monk should speak with the Abbot, unless he first made known to the Abbot's chaplain what he desired to say to the Abbot and why.

One day he gave orders in the Chapter that anyone who possessed a seal of his own should deliver it up to him. His command was obeyed, and thirty-three seals were found. He himself revealed the reason for this command, and forbade any obedientiary to borrow more than twenty shillings, as was often done, without the assent of the Prior and Convent. But he gave back their seals to the Prior and the Sacrist, and kept the rest. On another occasion he ordered that all the keys of chests, aumbries and baskets should be given up to him, forbidding anyone in future to possess a chest or anything else under lock and key, save by his leave, or to own anything save what the Rule permitted. But he gave general permission to all of us to possess money to the amount of two shillings, if it were given to us out of charity, yet on this condition that it should be expended on poor kinsfolk or pious purposes. At another time the Abbot said that he desired to keep our ancient customs concerning the entertainment of guests, to wit, that when the Abbot was at home, he should receive all guests of every kind saving the religious and secular priests, and their men who invited themselves to the court-gate under cover of their masters; but if the Abbot should be away from home, then all guests of every condition should be received by the Cellarer, up to the number of thirteen horses. But if a layman or a clerk should come with more than thirteen horses, he should be received by the serv-ants of the Abbot, either within the court or without, at the Abbot's expense. All religious, even Bishops, should they chance to be monks, fall to the care of the Cellarer at the Convent's expense, un-less the Abbot should desire to do them honour and to receive them in his hall at his own expense.

Abbot Samson was of middle height, and almost entirely bald; his face was neither round nor long, his nose prominent, his lips thick, his eyes clear as crystal and of penetrating glance; his hearing of the sharpest; his eyebrows grew long and were often clipped; a slight cold made him soon grow hoarse. On the day of his election he was forty-seven years old, and had been a monk for seventeen. He had a few white hairs in a red beard and a very few in the hair of his head, which was black and rather curly; but within fourteen years of his election he was white as snow. He was a man of extreme sobriety, never given to sloth, extremely strong and ever ready to go either on horseback or on foot, until old age prevailed and tempered his eager-ness. When he heard of the capture of the Cross and the fall of Jerusalem, he began to wear drawers of haircloth, and a shirt of hair instead of wool, and to abstain from flesh and meat; none the less he desired that meat should be placed before him when he sat at table, that so our alms might be increased. He preferred fresh milk and honey and the like to any other food. He hated liars and drunkards and wordy fellows, since virtue loves itself and hates its opposite. He condemned those who murmur at their food and drink, especially if they were monks, and preserved the old way of life that he had fol-lowed as a cloister monk; but he had this virtue, that he never liked to have a dish changed when it had once been placed before him. When I was a novice, I wished to try if this were true and, chancing to be a server in the refectory, I thought in my heart that I would place before him a dish, which displeased all the rest, on a platter that was very black and broken. And when he saw this, he was as one that saw not. But after a time I repented that I had done this, and forthwith seizing the platter, I changed both dish and platter for the better and carried them away; but he was angry and vexed and took the improvement ill. He was eloquent both in French and Latin, having regard rather to the sense of what he had to say than to ornaments of speech. He read English perfectly, and used to preach in English to the people, but in the speech of Norfolk, where he was born and bred, and to this end he ordered a pulpit to be set up in the church for the benefit of his hearers and as an ornament to the church. The Abbot seemed also to love the active life better than the contemplative; he had more praise for good obedientiaries than for good cloister monks; and rarely did he approve of any man solely for his knowledge of literature, unless he were also wise in worldly affairs. And when he heard of any prelate that he grew faint beneath the burden of his pastoral cares and turned anchorite, he did not praise him for so doing. He was loth to bestow much praise on kindly men, for he said, "He that seeks to please everyone, ought to please nobody." So in the first year of his abbacy he regarded all flatterers with hatred, especially if they were monks. But in process of time he seemed more ready to give ear to them and to be more friendly toward them. Wherefore it came to pass that, when a certain brother skilled in this art kneeled before him, and under pretence of giving him some advice had poured the oil of flattery into his ears, I laughed softly as I stood afar off: but when the monk retired, he called me and asked me why I laughed, and I replied that it was because the world was full of flatterers. To which the Abbot made answer, "My son, it is long since I have been acquainted with flatterers, and it is therefore that I cannot help listening to them. In many things I must feign, and in many I must dissemble, to maintain peace in the Convent. I shall not cease to listen to their words, but they will not deceive me, as they deceived my predecessor who was so foolish as to put faith in their counsels, so that long before his death neither he nor his household had aught to eat save what was borrowed from their creditors; nor on the day of his burial was there anything that could be given to the poor save only fifty shillings, which were received from Richard the tenant of Palgrave because it was that very day when he entered on his tenancy at Palgrave; and the said Richard afterwards repaid this sum to the King's bailiffs, who demanded the rent in its entirety on the King's behalf." I was comforted by these words. And in truth the Abbot was at pains to have his house well-disciplined and a household that, although large, was all of it necessary, and he made provision for himself so that the weekly sum, which had served his predecessor only for the expenses of five days, served him for eight, or nine, or ten, if he was away at his manors and there was no large arrival of guests. And every week he heard the account of his expenditure, not by deputy, but in person, which had never been the custom of his predecessor. During the first seven years of his abbacy four dishes were served to him, but afterwards only three, except when he had received presents or venison from his parks or fish from his ponds. And if perchance he kept any man in his household at the request of some person of importance or of some familiar friend, or maintained messengers or harpers or any such persons, as soon as he had an opportunity to go overseas or on a long journey, he prudently discarded such burdensome superfluities. As for the monks who had been his comrades before he succeeded to the abbacy, and had stood high in his love and regard, he rarely promoted them to office on the strength of his former affection, unless they were fit; wherefore some of our brethren, who had favoured his election as Abbot, said that he showed less regard than was seemly toward those who had loved him before he was Abbot, and that he loved those better who had both openly and in secret disparaged him, and had publicly and even in the hearing of many called him an angry and unsociable man, a haughty fellow and a barrator from Norfolk. But as after his succession to the abbacy he vouchsafed no indiscreet affection or honour to those who had once been his friends, even so he showed no sign of rancour or hatred to others, such as their conduct might seem to deserve, sometimes rendering good for evil and doing good to those who had persecuted him. He also had a habit, which I have never marked in any other man, namely, that he warmly loved many towards whom he never or rarely showed a loving countenance, nor conformed to the proverb "where your love is, there you eye is also." And he had another characteristic that calls for wonder, namely, that he wittingly put up with losses in temporal matters at the hands of his servants, and acknowledged that he did so; but to my thinking the reason was this, that he might wait for a suitable occasion to set matters right with greater prudence or that by shutting his eyes to the offence he might avoid great loss.

He loved his kin in moderation, and not over tenderly, as others are wont to do. For he had no kin within the third degree or at any rate pretended that this was so. But I have heard him say that he had kinsfolk of high birth and noble blood, whom he would never recognise as kindred at any time, because, as he said, they would be more of an onus than an honour to him, if they were aware of it. But he desired to treat those as being of his blood, who had treated him as their kinsman when he was a poor cloister monk. Some of them, according as he thought them suitable and like to be of use to himself, he appointed to sundry offices in his house or to have charge of townships. But those whom he found untrustworthy he banished far from him without hope of return. A certain man of no high birth, who had faithfully preserved his patrimony and had served him devotedly in his youth, he treated as a dear kinsman and gave his son, a clerk, the first church that fell vacant after the abbey had been committed to his charge; and to all his other sons he gave advancement. A certain chaplain, who had maintained him by the profits made from the sale of holy water, in the days when he was a poor student in the schools of Paris, he caused to be summoned to him, and as a token of his affectionate gratitude conferred upon him an ecclesiastical benefice sufficient to maintain him. To a certain servant of his predecessor, who had at the bidding of his lord fettered his feet when he was put in prison, he gave food and clothing for all the days of his life. To the son of Elias, the butler of Abbot Hugh, when he did homage to him for his father's land, he said in full court; "For seven years have I put off your homage for the land which Abbot Hugh gave your father, because the gift of that land was to the detriment of the hall of Elmswell, but now I give way, for I remember the kindness which your father showed me when I was in chains; for he sent me a portion of that very same wine which his lord was used to drink, bidding me to be comforted in God." To Master Walter, the son of Master William of Diss, when he besought him of his charity that he might have the vicarage of the church of Chevington, he replied; "Your father was master of the schools: and when I was a poor clerk, he, out of pure charity and making no conditions, gave me admission to his school and the opportunity of learning; and I now for God's sake grant your desire." When it chanced that two knights of Risby, William and Norman were amerced in his court, he thus addressed them in the presence of all, "When I was a cloister monk and having been sent to Durham on business of our Church, I was returning home by Risby, I was benighted and asked Lord Norman to give me lodging; but he utterly refused to take me in; but when I approached the house of Lord William and asked for lodging, I was received by him with honour. Wherefore from Norman I will recover twenty shillings, to wit, the full amercement without mercy. But to William I offer my thanks and gratefully remit the amercement of twenty shillings which he owes me."

In the year of grace 1197 certain innovations and changes were made in our Church which must not be passed over in silence. Since his former revenues did not suffice the Cellarer, Abbot Samson ordered that a yearly increment of fifty pounds from Mildenhall should be given to the Cellarer by the hand of the Prior, not however all at once, but by monthly instalments, so that every month he might have something to spend, and that the whole sum should not be squandered all at once in one portion of the year: and this was done for one year. But the Cellarer and his accomplices complained of this, saying that, if he had the whole sum, he would make provision for the future and stock himself. The Abbot, though unwillingly, granted his request; and by the beginning of August the Cellarer had spent all, and in addition already owed twenty-six pounds and was like to owe fifty before Michaelmas. Hearing this, the Abbot took it very ill and said in Chapter, "I have often threatened that I would take our cellary into my own hands on account of your default and improvidence, for you encumber yourselves with a great load of debt every year. I placed my clerk with your Cellarer as a witness, that the business might be carried on with greater wisdom. But there is neither clerk nor monk that dare tell me the cause of the debt. It is said nevertheless that the cause is to be found in the immoderate feasting that takes place in the Prior's lodging with the assent of the Prior and the Cellarer, and in superfluous extravagance in the guest-house owing to the carelessness of the Guest-master. "You see," he said, "the great debt that weighs upon us. Tell me how the matter may be set right." Many cloister monks almost smiled at this, and were pleased with what had been said, saying that the Abbot's words were true. The Prior put the blame on the Cellarer, the Cellarer on the Guest-master. Everybody excused himself. We did indeed know the truth, but we were silent because we were afraid. On the morrow the Abbot came and spoke again to the Convent. "Give your advice as to how your cellery may be better managed." Nobody replied save one, who said that there was certainly no superfluity in the Refectory that could account for that debt or burden. On the third day the Abbot said the same; and one replied, "This advice should proceed from you as being our head." And the Abbot made answer, "Since you will not give your advice, and do not know how to govern your house, the management of the monastery falls upon me as your father and supreme guardian. I take into my hand your cellary and all expenses in respect of guests, and the management of all things both within and without." This said, he deposed the Cellarer and Guest-master, and set in their places two other monks, entitled sub-cellarer and guest-master, associating with them a clerk from his own table, Master G., without whose assent nothing might be done in respect of food or drink, expenditure and receipts. The old buyers were removed from buying in the market, and food was bought by the Abbot's clerk, and our deficits were made good from the Abbot's purse. Guests who had a claim to be received were received, and those who deserved honour were given it; officials and cloister monks all alike fed in the refectory, and superfluous expenses were everywhere cut down. But some cloister monks said among themselves, "There were seven, aye seven, who devoured our goods, and if anyone spoke of those devourings he was held guilty of lese-majesty." Another said, holding up his hands to heaven, "Blessed be God, who has inspired the Abbot with such desire to set these things right." And many said that it was well done. But others said, "No!" thinking such a reform to be degrading to the honour of their Church, and styling the Abbot's prudence the ravening of a wolf; for they called to mind the ancient dream that the Abbot would raven like a wolf. The knights wondered and the people wondered at the things that were done; and one of the common folk said, "It is a wonder that the monks, being so many and with such knowledge of letters, suffer their property and revenues to be confounded and mingled with the property of the Abbot; for these things used always to be distinguished and kept apart. It is a wonder that they do not beware of the danger that will arise after the Abbot's death, if our lord the King finds matters in such a state." Another said that the Abbot alone was wise in matters outside the monastery, and that he who knew how to govern the whole, should rule the whole. And there was one that said, "If there were at least one wise monk in so large a Convent who knew how to rule the house, the Abbot would not have done such things." And so we were made "a mockery and a laughing-stock to those that dwell round about us."

Such being the state of affairs, it chanced that the service for the anniversary of Abbot Robert was being read in the Chapter, and orders were given that the Placebo and Dirige[5] should be sung with greater solemnity than usual, that is, to the ringing of the great bells, as is done on the anniversaries of Abbot Ording and Abbot Hugh, because of the great deed of the said Abbot Robert, who separated our property and revenues from those of the Abbot. Now this solemn celebration was due to the design of a few, that thus at least the Lord Abbot's heart might be moved to do good. But there were those who thought that this was done for the confusion of the Abbot who, because he had seized our cellary into his own hand, was said to desire to confound and mingle our property and revenues with his. But the Abbot on hearing the unwonted sound of bells and knowing well and noting that this was done contrary to custom, wisely ignored the reason for the deed and sang mass solemnly. On the following Michaelmas day, wishing in part to silence the murmurings of certain persons, he gave the office of Cellarer to him who before was sub-cellarer, and ordered another monk to be nominated as sub-cellarer, the aforesaid clerk being still associated with them and managing everything as before. But when that clerk exceeded the bounds of temperance, saying, "I am Bu" (that is to say, when the Cellarer had exceeded the bounds of temperance in drinking) and, without consulting the Abbot, held the Cellarer's court and took gage and pledge, and received the yearly revenues and himself expended the moneys, he was openly called the Chief Cellarer by the people. And since he often strolled about the court and as being master and chief manager was followed by many debtors rich and poor, and by claimants, all of different quality and bent on differing business, one of our obedientiaries chanced to be standing by in the court and, seeing this, he wept for confusion and shame, thinking it a disgrace to our Church, and thinking too of the peril that would ensue, and that a clerk was preferred over a monk to the prejudice of the whole Convent. He therefore, whoever he may have been, took steps through a third person that these things should be suitably and reasonably brought to the notice of the Abbot, who was thus led to understand that such arrogance in a clerk, displayed to the disgrace and abasement of the whole community, might be a cause of great disturbance and discord in the Convent. The Abbot, therefore, when he heard of it, at once sent for the Cellarer and the aforesaid clerk, and gave orders that for the future the Cellarer should act as Cellarer in respect of receiving money, holding pleas, and all else, saving always this, that the aforesaid clerk should assist him not as his equal, but only as a witness and an adviser.

NOTES

Selection a
1. A reference to the monastery of Cîteaux.
2. Cîteaux.

Selection b
1. A reference to the recently elected Abbot Samson.
2. An itinerant justice of the king.
3. A reference to the school of dialectic at Melun founded by Peter Abelard.
4. A book cupboard.
5. These were responses from the Office for the Dead.

10

St. Francis of Assisi and the Friars

THE monastic orders founded in the eleventh and twelfth centuries, attuned to the feudal and seignorial mentality of western Europe, located their monasteries in the countryside or in the solitude of forests and mountains. But with the development of trade and industry, the return of a money economy, and the swell in the urban population, the old monastic orders lost touch with the new social and economic currents. By the thirteenth century it became obvious to some men that the church must reach the great populations of the towns if it was to remain dynamic and to retain its exalted position. Early in the thirteenth century, therefore, St. Francis and St. Dominic founded their orders of friars which were to play a dominant role in the Christian life of Europe. Best known and most beloved of religious figures in the thirteenth century was St. Francis of Assisi (1182–1226), whose followers celebrated his holy life with written anecdotes and biographies. Of the latter one of the best was by the friar Thomas of Celano who, under commission of the pope, wrote his first life of St. Francis in 1228–1229. Here one gets a good picture of the character of St. Francis and of the friars who became his followers. The first of the following selections comes from this life rather than from the second life completed by Thomas in 1247, which incorporated material supplied by friars who had been personally associated with St. Francis. The second selection is the Rule of St. Francis, which was approved by Pope Honorius III in 1223. Although St. Francis formulated a number of the rules, we know that many of the more practical ones were added at the request of Honorius III in order to provide for the efficient organization of the growing Franciscan Order.

A St. Francis and His Friars, Thomas of Celano, Vita Prima ("The First Life")

xv] *Of the fame of St. Francis, and of the conversion of many to God. How the Order was called that of the Lesser Brethren (Friars Minor); and how blessed Francis fashioned those entering the Religion*

36] FRANCIS, therefore, Christ's valiant knight, went round the cities and fortresses proclaiming the Kingdom of God, preaching peace, teaching salvation and repentance for the remission of sins, not with plausible words of human wisdom, but with the learning and power of the Spirit. The Apostolic authority which had been granted him enabled him to act in all things with greater confidence, without using flattery or seducing blandishments. Incapable of caressing the faults of certain men, he could pierce them; incapable of showing favour to the lives of sinners, he could smite them with sharp reproof because he had first persuaded himself by practice of that which he endeavoured to commend to others by his words; and without fear of any reprover he uttered the truth most confidently, so that even the most learned men, mighty in renown and dignity, wondered at his discourses and were smitten by his presence with wholesome fear. Men ran, women too ran, clerks hastened, and Religious made speed to see and hear the Saint of God who seemed to all to be a man of another world. People of every age and either sex hastened to behold the wonders which the Lord was newly working in the world by His servant. Surely at that time, whether by holy Francis' presence or by the fame [of him], it seemed that, as it were, a new light had been sent from heaven on earth, scattering the universal blackness of darkness which had so seized on well-nigh the whole of that region, that scarce any one knew whither he must go. For such depth of forgetfulness of God and such slumber of neglect of His commandments had oppressed almost all that they could scarce endure to be roused, even slightly, from their old and inveterate sins.

From A. G. Ferrers Howell, THE LIVES OF S. FRANCIS OF ASSISI BY BROTHER THOMAS OF CELANO (London, 1908), pp. 36–42, 57–63, 78–81. Reprinted by permission of Methuen and Co.

37] He darted his beams like a star shining in the gloom of night, and as it were the morning spread over the darkness; and thus it came to pass that in a short time the face of the whole province was changed, and she appeared of more cheerful countenance, the former foulness having everywhere been laid aside. The former dryness was done away and in the field erstwhile hard the crops sprang up quickly; the untended vine began moreover to put forth shoots of divine fragrance, and, after bearing blossoms of sweetness, yielded fruits of honour and virtue together. Everywhere thanksgiving and the voice of praise were resounding in such wise that many cast away the cares of the world, and in the life and teaching of the most blessed father Francis gained knowledge of themselves, and aspired to love of their Creator and reverence for Him. Many among the people, nobles and plebeians, clerks and lay-folk, pierced by God's inspiration, began to come to holy Francis, longing evermore to fight under his discipline and leadership: all of whom the Saint of God like a plenteous stream of heavenly grace watered with anointing showers, and beautified the field of their hearts with flowers of virtue. Truly an excellent craftsman; after whose pattern, rule and teaching, heralded with noteworthy proclamation, Christ's Church is being renewed in either sex, and is triumphing in a threefold army of men who are to be saved. For he assigned to all their rule of life, and pointed out truly the way to be saved in every station.

38] But the chief matter of our discourse is the Order which as well from charity as by profession he took upon him and maintained. What then shall we say of it? He himself first planted the Order of Friars Minor (Lesser Brethren) and on that very occasion gave it that name; since (as is well known) it was written in the Rule: "And be they lesser": and in that hour, when those words were uttered, he said: "I will that this brotherhood be called the Order of Lesser Brethren" (Friars Minor). And truly they were "lesser," for, being subject to all, they ever sought for lowly dwellings, and for occupations in the discharge of which they might appear in some sort to suffer wrong, that they might deserve to be so founded on the solid basis of true humility that in happy disposition the spiritual building of all the virtues might arise in them. Verily on the foundation of stedfastness a noble structure of charity arose, wherein living stones heaped together from all parts of the world were built up into an habitation of the Holy Spirit. Oh, with what ardour of charity did Christ's new disciples burn! What love of their pious fellowship flourished among them! For whenever they came together in any place or met one another in the way, (as is usual) there sprang up a shoot of spiritual love scattering over all love the seeds of true affection. What can I say more? Their embraces were chaste, their feelings gentle, their kisses holy, their intercourse sweet, their laughter modest, their look cheerful, their eye single, their spirit submissive, their tongue peaceable, their answer soft, their purpose identical, their obedience ready, their hand untiring.

39] And for that they despised all earthly things, and never loved one another with private love, but poured forth their whole affection in common, the business of all alike was to give up themselves as the price of supplying their brethren's need. They came together with longing, they dwelt together with delight; but the parting of companions was grievous on both sides, a bitter divorce, a cruel separation. But these obedient knights durst put nothing before the orders of holy Obedience, and before the word of command was finished they were preparing to fulfil the order; not knowing how to distinguish between precept and precept, they ran, as it were, headlong to perform whatever was enjoined, all contradiction being put aside.

The followers of most holy Poverty, having nothing, loved nothing, and therefore had no fear of losing anything. They were content with a tunic only, patched sometimes within and without; no elegance was seen in it, but great abjectness and vileness, to the end they might wholly appear therein as crucified to the world. They were girt with a cord, and wore drawers of common stuff; and they were piously purposed to remain in that state, and to have nothing more. Everywhere, therefore, they were secure, nor kept in suspense by any fear; distracted by no care, they awaited the morrow without solicitude, nor, though oftentimes in great straits in their journeyings, were they ever in anxiety about a night's lodging. For when, as often happened, they lacked a lodging in the coldest weather, an oven sheltered them, or, at least, they lay hid by night humbly in underground places or in caves. And by day those who knew how to, worked with their hands, and they stayed in lepers' houses, or in other decent places, serving all with humility and devotion.

40] They would exercise no calling whence scandal might arise, but, by always doing holy, just, virtuous, and useful deeds, they provoked all with whom they lived to copy their humility and patience. The virtue of patience had so compassed them about that they rather sought to be where they might suffer persecution of their bodies than where they might be uplifted by the world's favour, if their holiness was acknowledged or praised. For many times when they were reviled, insulted, stripped naked, scourged, bound or imprisoned, they would not avail themselves of any one's protection, but bore all so bravely that the voice of praise and thanksgiving alone sounded in their mouth. Scarcely, or not at all, did they cease from praising God and from prayer; but, recalling by constant examination what they had done, they rendered thanks to God for what they had done well, and groans and tears for what they had neglected or unadvisedly committed. They deemed themselves forsaken by God unless they knew themselves to be constantly visited in their devotions by their wonted piety. And so when they would apply themselves to prayer they sought the support of certain appliances lest their prayer should be disturbed by sleep stealing over them. Some were held up by hanging ropes, some surrounded themselves with instruments of iron, while others shut themselves up in wooden cages. If ever their sobriety were disturbed (as commonly happens) by abundance of food or drink, or if, tired by a journey, they overpassed, though but a little, the bounds of necessity, they tortured themselves most severely by many days' abstinence. In short they made it their business to keep down the promptings of the flesh with such maceration that they shrank not from often stripping themselves naked in the sharpest frost, and piercing their whole body with thorns so as to draw blood. 41] And so vigorously did they set at naught all earthly things that they scarce submitted to take the barest necessaries of life, and shrank not from any hardships, having been parted from bodily comfort by such long usage. Amid all this they followed peace and gentleness with all men, and, ever behaving themselves modestly and peaceably, were most zealous in avoiding all occasions of scandal. For they scarcely spoke even in time of need, nor did any jesting or idle words proceed out of their mouth, in order that nothing immodest or unseemly might by any means be found in all their behavior and conversation. Their every act was disciplined, their every movement modest, all the senses had been so mortified in them that they scarce submitted to hear or see anything but what their purpose demanded;

their eyes were fixed on the ground, their mind clave to Heaven. No envy, malice, rancour, evil-speaking, suspicion or bitterness had place in them, but great concord, continual quietness, thanksgiving, and the voice of praise were in them. Such were the teachings wherewith the tender father, not by word and tongue only, but above all in deed and truth, was fashioning his new sons.

XXI] *Of his preaching to the birds and of the obedience of the creatures*

58] DURING the time when (as has been said) many joined themselves to the brethren the most blessed father Francis was journeying through the valley of Spoleto, and came to a spot near Bevagna where a very great number of birds of different sorts were gathered together, viz., doves, rooks, and those other birds that are called in the vulgar tongue *monade.* When he saw them, being a man of the most fervent temper and also very tender and affectionate toward all the lower and irrational creatures, Francis the most blessed servant of God left his companions in the way and ran eagerly toward the birds. When he was come close to them and saw that they were awaiting him, he gave them his accustomed greeting. But, not a little surprised that the birds did not fly away (as they are wont to do) he was filled with exceeding joy and humbly begged them to hear the word of God: and, after saying many things to them he added: "My brother birds, much ought ye to praise your Creator, and ever to love Him who has given you feathers for clothing, wings for flight, and all that ye had need of. God has made you noble among His creatures, for He has given you a habitation in the purity of the air, and, whereas ye neither sow nor reap, He Himself doth still protect and govern you without any care of your own." On this (as he himself and the brethren who had been with him used to say) those little birds rejoicing in wondrous fashion, after their nature, began to stretch out their necks, to spread their wings, to open their beaks and to gaze on him. And then he went to and fro amidst them, touching their heads and bodies with his tunic. At length he blessed them, and, having made the sign of the cross, gave them leave to fly away to another place. But the blessed father went on his way with his companions, rejoicing and giving thanks to God Whom all creatures humbly acknowledge and revere. Being now,

by grace, become simple (though he was not so by nature) he
began to charge himself with negligence for not having preached to
the birds before, since they listened so reverently to God's word.
And so it came to pass that from that day he diligently exhorted all
winged creatures, all beasts, all reptiles and even creatures insen-
sible, to praise and love the Creator, since daily, on his calling on
the Saviour's name, he had knowledge of their obedience by his own
experience.

59] One day (for instance) when he was come to the fortress
called Alviano to set forth the word of God, he went up on an
eminence where all could see him, and asked for silence. But though
all the company held their peace and stood reverently by, a great
number of swallows who were building their nests in that same
place were chirping and chattering loudly. And, as Francis could
not be heard by the men for their chirping, he spoke to the birds
and said: "My sisters, the swallows, it is now time for me to speak
too, because you have been saying enough all this time. Listen to
the word of God and be in silence, and quiet, until the sermon is
finished!" And those little birds (to the amazement and wonder of
all the bystanders) kept silence forthwith, and did not move from
that place till the preaching was ended. So those men, when they
had seen that sign, were filled with the greatest admiration, and
said: "Truly this man is a Saint, and a friend of the Most High."
And with the utmost devotion they hastened at least to touch his
clothes, praising and blessing God.

And it is certainly wonderful how even the irrational creatures
recognised his tender affection towards them and perceived beforehand the sweetness of his love.

60] For once when he was staying at the fortress of Greccio, one of
the brethren brought him a live leveret[1] that had been caught in a
snare; and when the blessed man saw it he was moved with compassion and said: "Brother leveret, come to me. Why didst thou let
thyself be so deceived?" And forthwith the leveret, on being released by the brother who was holding him fled to the holy man,
and, without being driven thither by any one, lay down in his bosom
as being the safest place. When he had rested there a little while the
holy father, caressing him with maternal affection, let him go, so
that he might freely return to the woodland. At last, after the leveret
had been put down on the ground many times, and had every

time returned to the holy man's bosom, he bade the brethren carry it into a wood which was hard by. Something of the same kind happened with a rabbit (which is a very wild creature) when he was on the island in the lake of Perugia. He was also moved by the same feeling of pity towards fish, for if they had been caught, and he had the opportunity, he would throw them back alive into the water, bidding them beware of being caught a second time.

61] Once accordingly when he was sitting in a boat near a port on the lake of Rieti a fisherman caught a big fish called a tench, and respectfully offered it to him. He took it up joyfully and kindly, began to call it by the name of brother, and then putting it back out of the boat into the water he began devoutly to bless the name of the Lord. And while he continued thus for some time in prayer, the said fish played about in the water close to the boat, and did not leave the place where Francis had put him, until, having finished his prayer, the holy man of God gave him leave to depart. Even so did the glorious father Francis, walking in the way of obedience, and taking upon him perfectly the yoke of Divine submission, acquire great dignity before God in that the creatures obeyed him. For water was even turned to wine for him when he was once in grievous sickness at the hermitage of Sant' Urbano; and when he had tasted it he got well so easily that all believed it to be a Divine miracle, as indeed it was. And truly he is a Saint whom the creatures thus obey and at whose nod the very elements are transmuted for other uses.

XXII] *Of his preaching at Ascoli; and how the sick were healed in his absence by things that his hand had touched*

62] AT the time when (as has been said) the venerable father Francis preached to the birds, as he went round about the cities and fortresses scattering seeds of blessing everywhere, he came to the city of Ascoli. Here, when according to his wont he was most fervently uttering the word of God, almost all the people, changed by the right hand of the Highest, were filled with such grace and devotion that in their eagerness to see and hear him they trod on one another. And at that time thirty men, clerks and lay-people, received from him the habit of holy Religion. Such was the faith of men and women, such their devotion of mind toward God's Saint that he who could but touch his garment called himself happy. If he entered any city the clergy were joyful, the bells were rung, the men exulted, the women rejoiced together, the children clapped their hands and often took boughs of trees and went in procession to meet him singing Psalms. Heretical wickedness was confounded, the Church's faith was magnified; and while the faithful shouted for joy, the heretics slunk away. For the tokens of holiness that appeared in him were such that no one durst speak against him; seeing that the crowds hung on him alone. Amidst and above all else he pronounced that the faith of the Holy Roman Church, wherein alone consists the salvation of all that are to be saved, must be kept, revered, and imitated. He revered the priests and embraced the whole hierarchy with exceeding affection.

63] The people would offer him loaves to bless, and would keep them for long after, and by tasting them they were healed of divers sicknesses. Many times also in their great faith in him they cut up his tunic so that he was left almost naked; and, what is more wonder, some even recovered their health by means of objects which the holy father had touched with his hand, as happened in the case of a woman who lived in a little village near Arezzo. She was with child, and when the time of her delivery came was in labour for several days and hung between life and death in incredible suffering. Her neighbours and kinsfolk had heard that the blessed Francis was going to a certain hermitage and would pass by that way. But while they were waiting for him it chanced that he went to the place by a different way, for he was riding because he was weak and ill. When he reached the place he sent back the horse to the man who had lent it him out of charity, by a certain brother named Peter. Brother Peter, in bringing the horse back passed through the place where the suffering woman was. The inhabitants on seeing him ran to him in haste, thinking he was the blessed Francis, but were exceedingly disappointed when they found he was not. At length they began to inquire together if anything might be found which the blessed Francis had touched with his hand; and after spending a long time over this they at last hit upon the reins which he had held in his hand when riding: so they took the bit out of the mouth of the horse on which the holy father had sat, and laid the reins which he had touched with his own hands upon the woman: and forthwith her peril was removed and she brought forth her child with joy and in safety.

64] Gualfreduccio, who lived at Castel della Pieve, a religious man fearing and worshipping God with all his house, had by him a cord wherewith the blessed Francis had once been girded. Now it came to pass that in that place many men and not a few women were suffering from various sicknesses and fevers; and this man went through the houses of the sick, and, after dipping the cord in water or mixing with water some of the strands, made the sufferers drink of it, and so, in Christ's name, they all recovered. Now these things were done in blessed Francis' absence, besides many others which we could in nowise unfold in the longest discourse. But a few of those things which the Lord our God deigned to work by means of his presence we will briefly insert in this work.

XXIX] *Of the love which he bore to all creatures for the Creator's sake. Description of his inner and outer man*

80] IT were exceeding long, and indeed impossible, to enumerate and collect all the things which the glorious father Francis did and taught while he lived in the flesh. For who could ever express the height of the affection by which he was carried away as concerning all the things that are God's? Who could tell the sweetness which he enjoyed in contemplating in His creatures the wisdom, power and goodness of the Creator? Truly such thoughts often filled him with wondrous and unspeakable joy as he beheld the sun, or raised his eyes to the moon, or gazed on the stars, and the firmament. O simple piety! O pious simplicity! Even towards little worms he glowed with exceeding love, because he had read that word concerning the Saviour: "I am a worm, and no man." Wherefore he used to pick them up in the way and put them in a safe place, that they might not be crushed by the feet of passers-by. What shall I say of other lower creatures, when in winter he would cause honey or the best wine to be provided for bees, that they might not perish from cold? And he used to extol, to the glory of the Lord, the efficacy of their works and the excellence of their skill with such abundant utterance that many times he would pass a day in praise of them and of the other creatures. For as of old the three children placed in the burning fiery furnace invited all the elements to praise and glorify the Creator of the universe, so this man also, full of the spirit of God, ceased not to glorify, praise, and bless in all the elements and creatures the Creator and Governor of them all.

81] What gladness thinkest thou the beauty of flowers afforded to his mind as he observed the grace of their form and perceived the sweetness of their perfume? For he turned forthwith the eye of consideration to the beauty of that Flower which, brightly coming forth in springtime from the root of Jesse, has by its perfume raised up countless thousands of the dead. And when he came upon a great quantity of flowers he would preach to them and invite them to praise the Lord, just as if they had been gifted with reason. So also cornfields and vineyards, stones, woods, and all the beauties of the field, fountains of waters, all the verdure of gardens, earth and fire, air and wind would he with sincerest purity exhort to the love and willing service of God. In short he called all creatures by the name of brother, and in a surpassing manner, of which other men had no experience, he discerned the hidden things of creation with the eye of the heart, as one who had already escaped into the glorious liberty of the children of God.

Now, O good Jesus, in the heavens with the angels he is praising Thee as admirable who when on earth did surely preach Thee to all creatures as lovable.

82] For when he named Thy name, O holy Lord, his emotion passed man's understanding: he was all joy, filled with the purest gladness, and seemed in truth to be a new man and one of the other world. Accordingly wherever he found any writing, Divine or human, whether by the way, in a house, or on the floor, he picked it up most reverently and placed it in some sacred or decent place, in case the name of the Lord or anything pertaining thereto should have been written on it. And one day, when one of the brethren asked him why he so diligently picked up even writings of pagans, and writings in which the name of the Lord was not traced, he gave this answer: "My son, it is because the letters are there whereof the most glorious name of the Lord God is composed. The good, therefore, that is in the writing belongs not to the pagans nor to any men, but to God alone, of whom is all good." And, what is not less to be wondered at, when he caused any letters of greeting or admonition to be written, he would not suffer a single letter or syllable to be cancelled, even though (as often happened) it were superfluous or misplaced.

83] O how fair, how bright, how glorious did he appear in in-
nocency of life, in simplicity of word, in purity of heart, in the love
of God, in charity to the brethren, in ardent obedience, in willing
submission, in angelic aspect! He was charming in his manners, of
gentle disposition, easy in his talk; most apt in exhortation, most
faithful in what he was put in trust with, far-seeing in counsel, effec-
tual in business, gracious in all things; calm in mind, sweet in temper, sober in spirit, uplifted in contemplation, assiduous in prayer,
and fervent in all things. He was stedfast in purpose, firm in virtue,
persevering in grace, and in all things the same. He was swift to
pardon and slow to be angry. He was of ready wit, and had an excellent memory, he was subtle in discussion, circumspect in choice,
and simple in all things; stern to himself, tender to others, in all
things discreet. He was a man most eloquent, of cheerful countenance, of kindly aspect, free from cowardice, and destitute of arrogance. He was of middle height, inclining to shortness; his head was
of moderate size, and round; his face somewhat long and prominent,
his forehead smooth and small; his eyes were black, of moderate size,
and with a candid look; his hair was dark, his eyebrows straight; his
nose symmetrical, thin, and straight; his ears upright, but small; his
temples smooth. His words were kindly, [but] fiery and penetrating;
his voice was powerful, sweet-toned, clear and sonorous. His teeth
were set close together, white, and even; his lips thin and fine, his
beard black and rather scanty, his neck slender; his shoulders straight,
his arms short, his hands attenuated, with long fingers and nails; his
legs slight, his feet small, his skin fine, and his flesh very spare. His
clothing was rough, his sleep very brief, his hand most bountiful.
And, for that he was most humble, he showed all meekness to all
men, adapting himself in profitable fashion to the behaviour of all.
Among the saints, holier [than they], among the sinners he was like
one of themselves. Help therefore the sinners, most holy father, thou
lover of sinners, and deign, we pray thee, of thine abundant mercy, to
raise up by thy most glorious advocacy those whom thou seest miserably lying in the defilement of their misdeeds.

B St. Francis, Regula ("The Rule of St. Francis," 1223)

1] THIS is the Rule and way of life of the brothers minor; to observe the holy Gospel of our Lord Jesus Christ, living in obedience, without personal possessions, and in chastity. Brother Francis promises obedience and reverence to our Lord Pope Honorius, and to his canonical successors, and to the Roman Church. And the other brothers shall be bound to obey brother Francis and his successors.

2] If any wish to adopt this way of life, and shall come to our brothers, they shall send them to their provincial ministers;[1] to whom alone, and to no others, permission is given to receive brothers. And the ministers shall carefully examine them in the Catholic faith and the sacraments of the Church. And if they believe all these, and will confess them faithfully and observe them steadfastly to the end; and if they have no wives, or if they have them and the wives have already entered a convent, or if with permission of the diocesan bishop they shall have given them permission to do so — they themselves having already taken a vow of continence, and their wives being of such age that no suspicion can arise in connection with them: the ministers shall tell them, in the words of the holy Gospel, to go and sell all that they have and carefully give it to the poor. But if they shall not be able to do this, their good will is enough. And the brothers and their ministers shall be careful not to concern themselves about their temporal goods; so that they may freely do with those goods exactly as God inspires them. But if advice is required, the ministers shall be allowed to send them to some God-fearing men by whose counsel they shall dispense their goods to the poor. After that they shall be given the garments of probation: namely two gowns without cowls and a belt, and hose and a cape down to the belt: unless to these same ministers something else may at some time seem to be preferable in the sight of God. And, when the year of probation is over, they shall be received into obedience; promising always to observe this way of life and Rule. And, according to the

From Henry Bettenson, DOCUMENTS OF THE CHRISTIAN CHURCH (London, 1950), pp. 344–349. Reprinted by permission of the Oxford University Press.

mandate of the lord pope, they shall never be allowed to break these bonds. For according to the holy Gospel, no one putting his hand to the plough and looking back is fit for the kingdom of God. And those who have now promised obedience shall have one gown with a cowl, and another, if they wish it, without a cowl. And those who really need them may wear shoes. And all the brothers shall wear humble garments, and may repair them with sack cloth and other remnants, with God's blessing. And I warn and exhort them lest they despise or judge men whom they shall see clad in soft garments and in colours, enjoying delicate food and drink; but each one shall rather judge and despise himself.

3] The clerical brothers shall perform the divine service according to the order of the holy Roman Church; excepting the psalter, of which they may have extracts. But the lay brothers shall say twenty-four Paternosters at matins, five at lauds, seven each at Prime, Terce, Sext and None, twelve at Vespers, seven at the Completorium;[2] and they shall pray for the dead. And they shall fast from the feast of All Saints to the Nativity of the Lord; but as to the holy season of Lent, which begins after the Epiphany of the Lord and continues forty days, a season the Lord consecrated by his holy fast — those who fast during this time shall be blessed of the Lord, and those who do not wish to fast shall not be bound to do so; but otherwise they shall fast until the Resurrection of the Lord. At other times the brothers shall not be bound to fast save on the sixth day (Friday); but when there is a compelling reason the brothers shall not be bound to observe a physical fast. But I advise, warn and exhort my brothers in the Lord Jesus Christ, that, when they go into the world, they shall not quarrel, nor contend with words, nor judge others. But let them be gentle, peaceable, modest, merciful and humble, with honourable conversation towards all, as is fitting. They ought not to ride, save when necessity or infirmity clearly compels them so to do. Into whatsoever house they enter let them first say, "Peace be to this house." And according to the holy Gospel it is lawful for them to partake of all dishes placed before them.

4] I strictly command all the brothers never to receive coin or money either directly or through an intermediary. The ministers[3] and guardians alone shall make provision, through spiritual friends, for the needs of the infirm and for other brothers who need clothing, according to the locality, season or cold climate, at their discretion. . . .

5] Those brothers, to whom God has given the ability to work, shall work faithfully and devotedly and in such a way that, avoiding idleness, the enemy of the soul, they do not quench the spirit of holy prayer and devotion, to which other and temporal activities should be subordinate. As the wages of their labour they may receive corporal necessities for themselves and their brothers but not coin nor money, and this with humility, as is fitting for servants of God, and followers of holy poverty.

6] The brothers shall possess nothing, neither a house, nor a place, nor anything. But, as pilgrims and strangers in this world, serving God in poverty and humility, they shall confidently seek alms, and not be ashamed, for the Lord made Himself poor in this world for us. This is the highest degree of that sublime poverty, which has made you, my dearly beloved brethren, heirs and kings of the Kingdom of Heaven; which has made you poor in goods but exalted in virtues. Let this be "your portion," which leads you to "the land of the living" [Ps. cxlii. 5]. If you cleave wholly to this, beloved, you will wish to have for ever in Heaven nothing save the name of Our Lord Jesus Christ. Wherever the brethren are, and shall meet together, they shall shew themselves as members of one family; each shall with confidence unfold his needs to his brother. A mother loves and cherishes her son in the flesh; how much more eagerly should a man love and cherish his brother in the Spirit? And if any of them fall sick the other brothers are bound to minister to him as they themselves would wish to be ministered to.

7] But if any of the brethren shall commit mortal sin at the prompting of the adversary: in the case of those sins concerning which it has been laid down that recourse must be had to the provincial ministers, the aforesaid brethren must have recourse to them without delay. Those ministers, if they are priests, shall with mercy enjoin penance: if they are not priests they shall cause it to be enjoined through others, who are priests of the order, as it seems to them most expedient in the sight of God. They must beware lest they become angry and disturbed on account of the sin of any brother; for anger and indignation hinder love in ourselves and others.

8] All the brothers shall be bound always to have one of the brothers of the order as minister general and servant of the whole brotherhood, and shall be strictly bound to obey him. On his death the election of a successor shall be made by the provincial ministers and guardians in the chapter at Pentecost, at which the provincial ministers shall always be bound to assemble, wherever the minister general provides; and this once in three years or at a greater or less interval, according as is ordered by the aforesaid minister. And if at any time it shall be clear to the whole body of provincial ministers and guardians that the said minister does not suffice for the service and common advantage of the brethren, it shall be the duty of the said brethern who have the right of election to elect another as their guardian, in the name of God. But after the chapter held at Pentecost the ministers and guardians may (if they so wish and it seem expedient) call together their brethren, in their several districts, to a chapter, once in that same year.

9] The brothers shall not preach in the diocese of any bishop who has forbidden them to do so. And none of the brothers shall dare to preach at all to the people unless he has been examined and approved by the minister general of this brotherhood and the privilege of preaching has been granted him. I also exhort these same brothers that in all their preaching their language shall be pure and careful, to the advantage and edification of the people; preaching to them of vices and virtues, punishment and glory; and let their discourse be brief; for the words which the Lord spoke upon earth were brief.

10] The brothers who are the ministers and servants of the other brothers shall visit and admonish their brothers and humbly and lovingly correct them; not teaching them anything which is against their conscience and our Rule. But the brothers who are subjected to them shall remember that, before God, they have discarded their own wills. Wherefore I strictly charge them that they obey their ministers in all things which they have promised God to observe, and which are not contrary to their conscience and to our Rule. And wherever there are brothers who are conscious of their inability to observe the Rule in the spirit, they may and should have recourse to their ministers. But the ministers shall receive them lovingly and kindly, and shall exercise such familiarity towards them, that they may speak and act towards them as masters to their servants; for so it ought to be, that the ministers should be the servants of all the brothers. I warn and exhort, moreover, in Christ Jesus the Lord, that the brothers be on their guard against all pride, vainglory, envy, avarice, care and worldly anxiety, detraction and murmuring. And they shall not be concerned to teach those who are ignorant of letters, but shall take care that they desire to have the spirit of God and its holy workings; that they pray always to God with a pure heart; that they have humility, patience, in persecution and infirmity; and that they love those who persecute, revile and attack us. For the Lord saith: "Love your enemies, and pray for those that persecute you and speak evil against you; Blessed are they that suffer persecution for righteousness' sake, for of such is the kingdom of Heaven; He that is steadfast unto the end shall be saved."

11] I strictly charge all the brethren not to hold conversation with women so as to arouse suspicion, nor to take counsel with them. And, with the exception of those to whom special permission has been given by the Apostolic Chair, let them not enter nunneries. Neither may they become fellow god-parents with men or women, lest from this cause a scandal may arise among the brethren or concerning brethren.

12] Whoever of the brothers by divine inspiration may wish to go among the Saracens and other infidels, shall seek permission to do so from their provincial ministers. But to none shall the ministers give permission to go, save to those whom they shall see to be fit for the mission.

Furthermore, I charge the ministers on their obedience that they demand from the lord pope one of the cardinals of the holy Roman Church, who shall be the governor, corrector and protector of the fraternity, so that, always submissive and lying at the feet of that same Holy Church, steadfast in the Catholic faith, we may observe poverty and humility, and the holy Gospel of our Lord Jesus Christ; as we have firmly promised.

NOTES

Selection a
1. A hare.

Selection b
1. The Franciscans were organized into administrative districts called provinces.
2. The times at which divine services were celebrated.
3. The officials of the Franciscan Order.

11

The Life and Love of Peter Abelard

IN the revival of intellectual life during the eleventh century that led to the so-called Renaissance of the twelfth, Peter Abelard (1079–1142) was one of the two or three most influential figures. He took a leading part in the heated battle between nominalists and realists, became the most famous and popular master of the early twelfth century, and through his teaching at Paris helped to make it the intellectual center of western Europe and the home of the University of Paris. More than any other, he was responsible for the development of scholastic thought and for a more systematic and rational study of theological questions. But his fiery, egotistical nature and his often unorthodox opinions made him a controversial figure frequently in trouble with his scholastic colleagues and with authorities of the church. Most people, however, best remember Abelard not for his importance in the history of western thought but for his tragic love affair with Héloise. His tempestuous career and his love for Héloise are recorded in their justly celebrated correspondence. The selection below is from a letter Abelard wrote while abbot of the Breton monastery of St. Gildas to an anonymous friend. It contains the famous account of his intellectual battles, his teaching triumphs, and his violent love for Héloise. Not least important is the impression it creates of Abelard's character.

Historia Calamitatum ("The History of My Calamities")

OFTEN examples serve better than words to excite or to mitigate human passions. Wherefore, after certain comfort offered thee in speech in thy presence, I have decided in absence to write by

Reprinted from THE LETTERS OF ABELARD AND HELOISE by C. K. Scott Moncrieff (New York, 1926), pp. 3–13. By permission of Alfred A. Knopf, Inc. Copyright by Alfred A. Knopf, Inc., renewed, 1954.

way of comfort the experience of my own calamities, that in comparison with mine thou mayest see thy trials to be none at all, or but slight matters, and may be better able to endure them.

I] *Of the birthplace of* Peter Abelard *and of his parentage*

I then was born in a certain town which, situated at the entering into Brittany, distant from the city of Nantes about eight miles, I believe, in an easterly direction, is properly known as Palatium. As by the nature of the soil or of my blood I am light of heart, so also I grew up with an aptitude for the study of letters. A father, moreover, I had who was to no small extent imbued with letters before he girded on himself the soldier's belt. Whence, at a later time, he was seized with so great a love of letters that whatever sons he had he was disposed to instruct in letters rather than in arms. And so it befell us. I too, being the first-born, in so far as I was dearer to him than the rest, so much the more diligently did he care for my education. And I, when I advanced farther and had more facility in the study of letters, so much the more ardently did I adhere to it, and with such love of that study was I consumed that, abandoning the pomp of military glory with the inheritance and the privileges of a first-born son to my brother, I finally relinquished the court of Mars that I might be educated in the lap of Minerva. And inasmuch as I preferred the equipment of dialectic to all the teachings of philosophy, I exchanged those weapons for these and to the trophies of war preferred the conflicts of discussion. Thereafter, perambulating divers provinces in search of discussion, wherever I had heard the study of this art to flourish, I became an emulator of the Peripatetics.

II] *Of the persecution of him by his master* William. *Of his mastership at Melun, at Corbeil and in Paris. Of his retirement from the city of Paris to Melun, his return to Mont Sainte-Genevieve and to his own country*

I came at length to Paris, where this study had long been greatly flourishing, to *William* styled "of Champeau,"[1] my preceptor, a man at that time pre-eminent, rightly and by common repute, in this teaching: with whom I stayed for a while, welcomed by him at first but afterwards a grave burden to him, since I endeavoured to refute certain of his opinions and often ventured to reason with him, and at times shewed myself his superior in debate. Which things indeed those who among our fellow-scholars were esteemed the foremost suffered with all the more indignation in that I was junior to them in age and in length of study. Hence arose the beginnings of my calamities which have continued up to the present time, and the more widely my fame extended, the more the envy of others was kindled against me. At length it came to pass that, presuming upon my talents beyond the capacity of my years, I aspired, boy as I was, to the mastership of a school, and found myself a place in which to practise, namely Melun, at that time a town of note and a royal abode. My master afore-named suspected this plan and, seeking to remove my school as far as possible from his own, secretly employed all the means in his power to contrive that before I left his school he might take from me mine and the place that I had selected. But inasmuch as among the powerful in the land he numbered several there who were jealous of him, relying upon their help I succeeded in obtaining my desire and won the support of many for myself by the manifest display of his envy. And from this beginning of my school, so much did my name in the art of dialectic begin to be magnified that not only the repute of my fellow-scholars but that of the master himself began to decline and was gradually extinguished. Hence it came about that, presuming more largely upon myself, I made haste to transfer my school to the town of Corbeil, which is nearer to the city of Paris, so that there opportunity might furnish more frequent contests of disputation. Not long afterwards, however, being stricken with an infirmity by the immoderate burden of my studies, I was obliged to return home, and for some years, being banished, so to speak, from France, I was sought out more ardently by those to whom the teaching of dialectic appealed.

But a few years having gone by, when for some time I had recovered from my infirmity, that teacher of mine, *William,* Archdeacon of Paris, laying aside his former habit transferred himself to the order of the regular clergy, with the intention, as was said, that being thought to be more religious he might be promoted to a higher grade in the prelacy, as shortly happened, he being made Bishop of Chalons. Nor did this change of habit call him away either from the city of Paris or from his wonted study of philosophy; but in that same monastery to which for religion's sake he had repaired, he at

once opened public classes in his accustomed manner. Then I returning to him that from his lips I might learn rhetoric, among the other
efforts of our disputations, contrived, by the clearest chain of argument, to make him alter, nay shatter, his former opinion with regard
to universals. For he had been of this opinion touching the community of universals, that he maintained a thing as a whole to be
essentially the same in each of its individuals, among which, forsooth,
there was no difference in essence but only variety in the multitude
of their accidents. He now so corrected this opinion that thereafter
he proclaimed the thing to be the same not essentially, but indis-
criminately. And inasmuch as this has always been the main question
among dialecticians concerning universals so much so that even
Porphyry[2] in his Isagoga, when he treats of universals, does not
presume to define it, saying: "For this is a most weighty business,"
after he had corrected and then perforce abandoned his opinion, into
such neglect did his instruction fall that he was scarcely admitted to
be a teacher of dialectic at all; as if in this opinion about universals
consisted the sum total of that art. Hence did my teaching acquire so
great strength and authority that they who formerly adhered most
vehemently to our said master and attacked my doctrine most
strongly now flocked to my school, and he who had succeeded to our
master's chair in the school of Paris offered me his own place, that
there among the rest he might submit himself to my teaching where
formerly his master and mine had flourished.

And so after a few days, I reigning there in the study of dialectic,
with what envy our master began to consume away, with what rage
to boil, is not easily expressed. Nor long sustaining that heat of the
affliction that had seized him, he cunningly attempted to remove me
once again. And because in my conduct there was nothing whereon
he could openly act, he laboured to remove the school from him who
had yielded up his chair to me (charging him with the vilest accusations), and to substitute a certain other, one of my jealous rivals,
in his place. Then I, returning to Melun, established my school there
as before; and the more openly his jealousy pursued me, the more
widely it enlarged my authority, according to the words of the poet:

Envy seeketh the heights, the winds blow on the mountain-tops.

Not long after this, when it came to his knowledge that well-nigh
all his disciples were in the utmost hesitation as to his religion, and

were murmuring vehemently as to his conversion, in that evidently he had not retired from the city, he transferred himself and his conventicle of brethren, with his school, to a certain village at some distance from the city. And immediately I returned from Melun to Paris, hoping that thenceforth I should have peace from him. But seeing that, as I have said, he had caused my place there to be filled by one of my rivals, outside the city on the Mount of Saint Genevieve I pitched the camp of our school, as though to beleaguer him who had occupied my place. Hearing which, our master straightway returning unashamed to the city, brought back such pupils as he might still have, and the conventicle of brethren to their former monastery, as though to deliver his soldier, whom he had abandoned, from our siege. In truth, whereas he intended to advantage him, he greatly harmed him. He, forsooth, had until then retained sundry disciples, principally for the lectures on *Priscian*[3] in which he was considered to excel. But after the master arrived he lost them one and all, and so was compelled to cease from the tenour of his school. And not long after this, as though despairing for the future of any worldly fame, he too was converted to the monastic life. Now after the return of our master to the city, the conflicts of discussion which our scholars waged as well with him as with his disciples, and the results which fortune in these wars gave to my people, nay to myself in them, thou thyself hast long known as matters of fact. But this saying of *Ajax* I may with more modesty than he repeat and more boldly utter:

> Shouldst thou demand the issue of this fight,
> I was not vanquished by mine enemy.

As to which, were I silent, the facts themselves speak and its outcome indicates the whole matter. But while these things were happening my dearest mother *Lucy* obliged me to return home. Who, to wit, after the conversion of *Berenger,* my father, to the monastic profession, was preparing to do likewise. Which being accomplished, I returned to France, principally that I might learn divinity, when our afore-mentioned master *William* attained to the Bishopric of Chalons. In this study, moreover, his own master, *Anselm* of Laon,[4] was of great and long-established authority.

III] *How he came to Laon to the master* Anselm

I came therefore to this old man, who owed his name rather to long familiarity than to his intelligence or his memory. To whom if any came knocking upon his door in uncertainty as to some question, he departed more uncertain still. Indeed, he was admirable in the eyes of his hearers, but of no account in the sight of questioners. His fluency of words was admirable but in sense they were contemptible and devoid of reason. When he kindled a fire he filled his house with smoke, rather than lighted it with the blaze. His tree, in full life, was conspicuous from afar to all beholders, but by those who stood near and diligently examined the same it was found to be barren. To this tree therefore when I had come that I might gather fruit from it, I understood that it was the figtree which the Lord cursed, or that old oak to which *Lucan* compares *Pompey,* saying:

> There stands the shadow of a mighty name,
> Like to a tall oak in a fruitful field.

Having discovered this, not for many days did I lie idle in his shadow. But as I gradually began to come to his lectures more rarely, certain among the more forward of his disciples took it amiss, as though I were shewing contempt for so great a master. Thereafter him also secretly exciting against me with vile suggestions, they made me offensive in his sight. But it fell upon a day that after certain controversies of opinion we scholars were disporting ourselves. When, after a certain one had inquired of me with menacing intent what I thought as to the reading of the Holy Scriptures, I, who had as yet studied nothing save physics only, replied that it was indeed most salutary, the study of this lore in which the salvation of the soul is revealed, but that I marvelled greatly that, to them who were literate men, the Scriptures themselves or the glosses upon them should not be sufficient, so that they should require no other instruction. Many of those present, laughing at me, asked whether I was able and presumed to approach this task. I replied that I was ready to try it if they wished. Then, shouting together and laughing all the more: "Certainly," they said, "we agree. Let some one find, therefore, and bring to us here an expositor of some little read Scripture, and let us put what you promise to the proof."

And they all agreed upon the most obscure prophecy of *Ezekiel*. And so, taking up the expositor, I at once invited them to attend my lecture on the morrow, who, pouring counsels into my unwilling ears, said that in so weighty a matter there was nothing to be gained by haste, but that seeing my inexperience I must give longer thought to the examination and strengthening of my exposition. But I indignantly replied that it was not my custom to advance by practice but rather by intelligence; and added that either I abandoned the contest altogether or they, abiding by my judgment, must come to my lecture without delay. And my first lecture indeed few attended, since that to all it seemed ridiculous that I, who hitherto had been almost wholly unacquainted with Holy Writ, should so hastily approach it. To all, however, who did attend, that lecture was so pleasing that they extolled it with singular commendation, and compelled me to furnish further glosses in the style of my first lecture. Which becoming known, those who had not been present began to flock eagerly to my second lecture and my third, and all alike were solicitous at the start of each to take down in writing the glosses which I had begun on the first day.

IV] *Of the persecution of him by his master* Anselm

Wherefore the old man aforesaid, being stirred by vehement envy, and having already been stimulated against me by the persuasion of divers persons, as I have before recounted, began no less to persecute me over the Holy Scriptures than our *William* had aforetime done over philosophy. Now there were at the time in this old man's school two who appeared to predominate over the rest, namely *Alberic* of Rheims and *Lotulph,* a Lombard: who, the more they presumed upon themselves, were the more kindled against me. And so, his mind greatly perturbed by their suggestions, as later it came to light, this old man boldly forbade me to continue further the work of interpretation which I had begun in his place of teaching. Advancing this pretext forsooth, that if perchance I were to write anything in error in my work, being still untrained in that study, it might be imputed to him. This coming to the ears of the scholars, they were moved with the utmost indignation against so manifest a calumny of envy, the like of which had never befallen any man yet. Which, the more manifest it was, the more honourable was it to me, and so by persecution my fame increased.

v] *How, having returned to Paris, he completed the interpretations which he had begun to deliver at Laon*

So, after a few days, returning to Paris, the schools that had long before been intended for me and offered to me, from which I had at first been driven out, I held for some years in quiet, and there at the opening of my course I strove to complete those interpretations of *Ezekiel* which I had begun at Laon. Which indeed were so acceptable to their readers that they believed me to be no less adept in the Holy Scriptures than they had seen me to be in philosophy. Whence in both kinds of study our school vehemently multiplying, what pecuniary gain and what reputation it brought me cannot have failed to reach your ears. But inasmuch as prosperity ever puffs up fools, and worldly tranquillity enervates the vigour of the mind, and easily loosens it by carnal allurements, when now I esteemed myself as reigning alone in the world as a philosopher, nor was afraid of any further disturbance, I began to give rein to my lust, who hitherto had lived in the greatest continence. And the farther I advanced in philosophy or in the Holy Scriptures, the farther I receded by the impurity of my life from philosophers and divines. For it is well known that philosophers, not to say divines, that is to say men intent on the exhortations of Holy Scripture, have excelled principally by the grace of continence. When, therefore, I was labouring wholly in pride and lechery, the remedy for either malady was by divine grace conferred on me, albeit unwilling; and first for lechery, then for pride. For lechery, indeed, by depriving me of those parts with which I practised it; but for the pride which was born in me from my surpassing knowledge of letters, as is said by the Apostle: "Knowledge puffeth up" — by humiliating me by the burning of that book in which most I gloried. The story of both which things I wish you now to learn more accurately from a statement of the facts than by common hearsay, in the order in which they befell me. Since, therefore, I ever abhorred the uncleanness of harlots, and was withheld from the society of noble women by the assiduity of my studies, nor had ever held much conversation with those of the common sort, lewd fortune, as the saying is, caressing me, found a more convenient opportunity whereby she might the more easily dash me down from the pinnacle of this sublimity; so that in my overweening pride, and unmindful of the grace I had received, divine pity might recall me humbled to itself.

VI] *How having fallen in love with* Heloise *he was thereby wounded as well in body as in mind*

Now there was in this city of Paris a certain young maiden by the name of *Heloise,* the niece of a certain Canon who was called *Fulbert,* who, so great was his love for her, was all the more diligent in his zeal to instruct her, so far as was in his power, in the knowledge of letters. Who, while in face she was not inferior to other women, in the abundance of her learning was supreme. For inasmuch as this advantage, namely literary knowledge, is rare in women, so much the more did it commend the girl and had won her the greatest renown throughout the realm. Seeing in her, therefore, all those things which are wont to attract lovers, I thought it suitable to join her with myself in love, and believed that I could effect this most easily. For such renown had I then, and so excelled in grace of youth and form, that I feared no refusal from whatever woman I might deem worthy of my love. All the more easily did I believe that this girl would consent to me in that I knew her both to possess and to delight in the knowledge of letters; even in absence it would be possible for us to reach one another's presence by written intermediaries, and to express many things more boldly in writing than in speech, and so ever to indulge in pleasing discussions.

So, being wholly inflamed with love for this girl, I sought an opportunity whereby I might make her familiar with me in intimate and daily conversation, and so the more easily lead her to consent. With which object in view, I came to terms with the aforesaid uncle of the girl, certain of his friends intervening, that he should take me into his house, which was hard by our school, at whatever price he might ask. Putting forward this pretext, that the management of our household gravely hindered my studies, and that the expense of it was too great a burden on me. Now he was avaricious, and most solicitous with regard to his niece that she should ever progress in the study of letters. For which two reasons I easily secured his consent and obtained what I desired, he being all agape for my money, and believing that his niece would gain something from my teaching. Whereupon earnestly beseeching me, he acceded to my wishes farther than I might presume to hope and served the purpose of my love: committing her wholly to my mastership, that as often as I returned from my school, whether by day or by night, I might devote my leisure to her instruction, and, if I found her idle, vehemently chastise her. In which matter, while marvelling greatly at his simplicity, I was no less stupefied within myself than if he had entrusted a tender lamb to a ravening wolf. For in giving her to me, not only to be taught but to be vehemently chastised, what else was he doing than giving every licence to my desires and providing an opportunity whereby, even if I did not wish, if I could not move her by blandishments I might the more easily bend her by threats and blows. But there were two things which kept him most of all from base suspicions, namely his love for his niece and the fame of my continence in the past.

What more need I say? First in one house we are united, then in one mind. So, under the pretext of discipline, we abandoned ourselves utterly to love, and those secret retreats which love demands, the study of our texts afforded us. And so, our books lying open before us, more words of love rose to our lips than of literature, kisses were more frequent than speech. Oftener went our hands to each other's bosom than to the pages; love turned our eyes more frequently to itself than it directed them to the study of the texts. That we might be the less suspected, blows were given at times, by love, not by anger, affection, not indignation, which surpassed all ointments in their sweetness. What more shall I say? No stage of love was omitted by us in our cupidity, and, if love could elaborate anything new, that we took in addition. The less experienced we were in these joys, the more ardently we persisted in them and the less satiety did they bring us. And the more this pleasure occupied me the less leisure could I find for my philosophy and to attend to my school. Most tedious was it for me to go to the school or to stay there; laborious likewise when I was keeping nightly vigils of love and daily of study. Which also so negligently and tepidly I now performed that I produced nothing from my mind but everything from memory; nor was I anything now save a reciter of things learned in the past, and if I found time to compose a few verses, they were amorous, and not secret hymns of philosophy. Of which songs the greater part are to this day, as thou knowest, repeated and sung in many parts, principally by those to whom a like manner of life appeals.

NOTES

1. William of Champeaux (1070–1121) was a noted teacher and defender of the realist position.

2. A Greek scholar and Neoplatonic philosopher of the third century who wrote commentaries on Aristotle's philosophical works.

3. A Latin grammarian who lived at the beginning of the sixth century and whose works were highly regarded in the Middle Ages.

4. A famous master at the cathedral school of Laon in the late eleventh and early twelfth centuries.

12

The Search for Christian Truth

In the three hundred years between 1000 and 1300 the most distinguished minds of western Europe turned to the interpretation and definition of Christian truth as it had come down to the Middle Ages in the Old and New Testaments, the writings of the church fathers, and the canon law. What was more natural than that theology should be the queen of the sciences in an age of profound and sincere faith and should number among her servants some of the most brilliant men of the High Middle Ages? As long as western Europe's knowledge of Greek and Arabic philosophy was limited to Platonic thought as interpreted by St. Augustine and to a few of the minor treatises of Aristotle on logic, theologians did not need to worry about systems of thought that might contradict Christian truth. But with the introduction during the twelfth and thirteenth centuries of Aristotle's major philosophical works accompanied by Arabic commentary, Christian theologians confronted the problem of relating this new body of thought to Christian doctrine. Perhaps the most distinguished master to tackle this problem was Thomas Aquinas (1226–1274) of the University of Paris. In the short period of twenty years he wrote many works concerned with the whole range of Christian doctrine and philosophical thought. The selection that follows is from his treatise Summa Contra Gentiles (known traditionally by the title "On the Truth of the Christian Faith"), composed between 1259 and 1264. It shows better than any other of his works how the scholastic mind operated and how it was dedicated to the explication of Christian truth. This treatise, the only complete summa (compendium) of Christian doctrine written by Thomas Aquinas, arose from the need to understand better and to assimilate the thought of Aristotle and of such Arabic commentators as Avicenna (d. 1037) and Averroës (d. 1198) and to employ it to explain Christian truth. That the theology of Thomas Aquinas remains the official theology of the Catholic church shows how well he accomplished this task.

Thomas Aquinas, Summa Contra Gentiles ("On the Truth of the Catholic Faith")

I, 13] *Arguments in proof of the existence of God*

1] We have now shown that the effort to demonstrate the existence of God is not a vain one. We shall therefore proceed to set forth the arguments by which both philosophers and Catholic teachers have proved that God exists.

2] We shall first set forth the arguments by which Aristotle proceeds to prove that God exists. The aim of Aristotle is to do this in two ways, beginning with motion.

3] Of these ways the first is as follows. Everything that is moved is moved by another. That some things are in motion — for example, the sun — is evident from sense. Therefore, it is moved by something else that moves it. This mover is itself either moved or not moved. If it is not, we have reached our conclusion — namely, that we must posit some unmoved mover. This we call God. If it is moved, it is moved by another mover. We must, consequently, either proceed to infinity, or we must arrive at some unmoved mover. Now, it is not possible to proceed to infinity. Hence, we must posit some prime unmoved mover.

4] In this proof, there are two propositions that need to be proved, namely, that *everything that is moved is moved by another,* and that *in movers and things moved one cannot proceed to infinity.*

5] The first of these propositions Aristotle proves in three ways. The *first* way is as follows. If something moves itself, it must have within itself the principle of its own motion; otherwise, it is clearly moved by another. Furthermore, it must be primarily moved. This means that it must be moved by reason of itself, and not by reason of a part of itself, as happens when an animal is moved by the motion of its foot. For, in this sense, a whole would not be moved by itself, but a part, and one part would be moved by another. It is also

From ON THE TRUTH OF THE CATHOLIC FAITH. SUMMA CONTRA GEN-TILES (pp. 85–96). *Translated and with an introduction by Anton C. Pegis. Copyright © 1955 by Doubleday & Company, Inc. Reprinted by permission of the publisher.*

necessary that a self-moving being be divisible and have parts, since, as it is proved in the *Physics,* whatever is moved is divisible.

6] On the basis of these suppositions Aristotle argues as follows. That which is held to be moved by itself is primarily moved. Hence, when one of its parts is at rest, the whole is then at rest. For if, while one part was at rest, another part in it were moved, then the whole itself would not be primarily moved; it would be that part in it which is moved while another part is at rest. But nothing that is at rest because something else is at rest is moved by itself; for that being whose rest follows upon the rest of another must have its motion follow upon the motion of another. It is thus not moved by itself. Therefore, that which was posited as being moved by itself is not moved by itself. Consequently, everything that is moved must be moved by another.

7] Nor is it an objection to this argument if one might say that, when something is held to move itself, a part of it cannot be at rest; or, again, if one might say that a part is not subject to rest or motion except accidentally, which is the unfounded argument of Avicenna. For, indeed, the force of Aristotle's argument lies in this: *if* something moves itself primarily and through itself, rather than through its parts, that it is moved cannot depend on another. But the moving of the divisible itself, like its being, depends on its parts; it cannot therefore move itself primarily and through itself. Hence, for the truth of the inferred conclusion it is not necessary to assume as an absolute truth that a part of a being moving itself is at rest. What must rather be true is this conditional proposition: *if the part were at rest, the whole would be at rest.* Now, this proposition would be true even though its antecedent be impossible. In the same way, the following conditional proposition is true: *if man is an ass, he is irrational.*

8] In the *second* way, Aristotle proves the proposition by induction. Whatever is moved by accident is not moved by itself, since it is moved upon the motion of another. So, too, as is evident, what is moved by violence is not moved by itself. Nor are those beings moved by themselves that are moved by their nature as being moved from within; such is the case with animals, which evidently are moved by the soul. Nor, again, is this true of those beings, such as heavy and light bodies, which are moved through nature. For such beings are moved by the generating cause and the cause removing impediments. Now, whatever is moved is moved through itself or by accident. If it is moved through itself, then it is moved either violently or by nature; if by nature, then either through itself, as the animal, or not through itself, as heavy and light bodies. Therefore, everything that is moved is moved by another.

9] In the *third* way, Aristotle proves the proposition as follows. The same thing cannot be at once in act and in potency with respect to the same thing. But everything that is moved is, as such, in potency. For motion is *the act of something that is in potency inasmuch as it is in potency.* That which moves, however, is as such in act, for nothing acts except according as it is in act. Therefore, with respect to the same motion, nothing is both mover and moved. Thus, nothing moves itself.

10] It is to be noted, however, that Plato, who held that every mover is moved, understood the name *motion* in a wider sense than did Aristotle. For Aristotle understood motion strictly, according as it is the act of what exists in potency inasmuch as it is such. So understood, motion belongs only to divisible bodies, as it is proved in the *Physics*. According to Plato, however, that which moves itself is not a body. Plato understood by motion any given operation, so that *to understand* and *to judge* are a kind of motion. Aristotle likewise touches upon this manner of speaking in the *De anima*. Plato accordingly said that the first mover moves himself because he knows himself and wills or loves himself. In a way, this is not opposed to the reasons of Aristotle. There is no difference between reaching a first being that moves himself, as understood by Plato, and reaching a first being that is absolutely unmoved, as understood by Aristotle.

11] The second proposition, namely, *that there is no procession to infinity among movers and things moved,* Aristotle proves in three ways.

12] The *first* is as follows. If among movers and things moved we proceed to infinity, all these infinite beings must be bodies. For whatever is moved is divisible and a body, as is proved in the *Physics*. But every body that moves some thing moved is itself moved while moving it. Therefore, all these infinites are moved together while one of them is moved. But one of them, being finite, is moved in a finite time. Therefore, all those infinites are moved in a finite time. This, however, is impossible. It is, therefore, impossible that among movers and things moved one can proceed to infinity.

13] Furthermore, that it is impossible for the abovementioned infinites to be moved in a finite time Aristotle proves as follows. The mover and the thing moved must exist simultaneously. This Aristotle proves by induction in the various species of motion. But bodies cannot be simultaneous except through continuity or contiguity. Now, since, as has been proved, all the aforementioned movers and things moved are bodies, they must constitute by continuity or contiguity a sort of single mobile. In this way, one infinite is moved in a finite time. This is impossible, as is proved in the *Physics.*

14] The *second* argument proving the same conclusion is the following. In an ordered series of movers and things moved (this is a series in which one is moved by another according to an order), it is necessarily the fact that, when the first mover is removed or ceases to move, no other mover will move or be moved. For the first mover is the cause of motion for all the others. But, if there are movers and things moved following an order to infinity, there will be no first mover, but all would be as intermediate movers. Therefore, none of the others will be able to be moved, and thus nothing in the world will be moved.

15] The *third* proof comes to the same conclusion, except that, by beginning with the superior, it has a reversed order. It is as follows. That which moves as an instrumental cause cannot move unless there be a principal moving cause. But, if we proceed to infinity among movers and things moved, all movers will be as instrumental causes, because they will be moved movers and there will be nothing as a principal mover. Therefore, nothing will be moved.

16] Such, then, is the proof of both propositions assumed by Aristotle in the first demonstrative way by which he proved that a first unmoved mover exists.

17] The second way is this. If every mover is moved, this proposition is true either by itself or by accident. If by accident, then it is not necessary, since what is true by accident is not necessary. It is something possible, therefore, that no mover is moved. But, if a mover is not moved, it does not move: as the adversary says. It is therefore possible that nothing is moved. For, if nothing moves, nothing is moved. This, however, Aristotle considers to be impossible — namely, that at any time there be no motion. Therefore, the first proposition was not possible, since from a false possible, a false impossible does not follow. Hence, this proposition, *every mover is moved by another,* was not true by accident.

18] Again, if two things are accidentally joined in some being, and one of them is found without the other, it is probable that the other can be found without it. For example, if *white* and *musical* are found in Socrates, and in Plato we find *musical* but not *white,* it is probable that in some other being we can find the *white* without the *musical.* Therefore, if mover and thing moved are accidentally joined in some being, and the thing moved be found without the mover in some being, it is probable that the mover is found without that which is moved. Nor can the example of two things, of which one depends on the other, be brought as an objection against this. For the union we are speaking of is not essential, but accidental.

19] But, if the proposition that every mover is moved is true by itself, something impossible or awkward likewise follows. For the mover must be moved either by the same kind of motion as that by which he moves, or by another. If the same, a cause of alteration must itself be altered, and further, a healing cause must itself be healed, and a teacher must himself be taught and this with respect to the same knowledge. Now, this is impossible. A teacher must have science, whereas he who is a learner of necessity does not have it. So that, if the proposition were true, the same thing would be possessed and not possessed by the same being — which is impossible. If, however, the mover is moved by another species of motion, so that (namely) the altering cause is moved according to place, and the cause moving according to place is increased, and so forth, since the genera and species of motion are finite in number, it will follow that we cannot proceed to infinity. There will thus be a first mover, which is not moved by another. Will someone say that there will be a recurrence, so that when all the genera and species of motion have been completed the series will be repeated and return to the first motion? This would involve saying, for example, that a mover according to place would be altered, the altering cause would be increased, and the increasing cause would be moved according to place. Yet this whole view would arrive at the same conclusion as before: whatever moves according to a certain species of motion is itself moved according to the same species of motion, though mediately and not immediately.

20] It remains, therefore, that we must posit *some first mover that is not moved by any exterior moving cause.*

21] Granted this conclusion — namely, that there is a first mover that is not moved by an exterior moving cause — it yet does not follow that this mover is absolutely unmoved. That is why Aristotle goes on to say that the condition of the first mover may be twofold. The first mover can be absolutely unmoved. If so, we have the conclusion we are seeking: there is a first unmoved mover. On the other hand, the first mover can be self-moved. This may be argued, because that which is through itself is prior to what is through another. Hence, among things moved as well, it seems reasonable that the first moved is moved through itself and not by another.

22] But, on this basis, the same conclusion again follows. For it cannot be said that, when a mover moves himself, the whole is moved by the whole. Otherwise, the same difficulties would follow as before: one person would both teach and be taught, and the same would be true among other motions. It would also follow that a being would be both in potency and in act; for a mover is, as such, in act, whereas the thing moved is in potency. Consequently, one part of the self-moved mover is solely moving, and the other part solely moved. We thus reach the same conclusion as before: there exists an unmoved mover.

23] Nor can it be held that both parts of the self-moved mover are moved, so that one is moved by the other, or that one moves both itself and the other, or that the whole moves a part, or that a part moves the whole. All this would involve the return of the aforementioned difficulties: something would both move and be moved according to the same species of motion; something would be at once in potency and in act; and, furthermore, the whole would not be primarily moving itself, it would move through the motion of a part. The conclusion thus stands: one part of a self-moved mover must be unmoved and moving the other part.

24] But there is another point to consider. Among self-moved beings known to us, namely, animals, although the moving part, which is to say the soul, is unmoved through itself, it is yet moved by accident. That is why Aristotle further shows that the moving part of the first self-moving being is not moved either through itself or by accident. For, since self-moving beings known to us, namely, animals, are corruptible, the moving part in them is moved by accident. But corruptible self-moving beings must be reduced to some first self-moving being that is everlasting. Therefore, some self-moving being must have a mover that is moved neither through itself nor by accident.

25] It is further evident that, according to the position of Aristotle, some self-moved being must be everlasting. For if, as Aristotle supposes, motion is everlasting, the generation of self-moving beings (this means beings that are generable and corruptible) must be endless. But the cause of this endlessness cannot be one of the self-moving beings, since it does not always exist. Nor can the cause be all the self-moving beings together, both because they would be infinite and because they would not be simultaneous. There must therefore be some endlessly self-moving being, causing the endlessness of generation among these sublunary self-movers. Thus, the mover of the self-moving being is not moved, either through itself or by accident.

26] Again, we see that among beings that move themselves some initiate a new motion as a result of some motion. This new motion is other than the motion by which an animal moves itself, for example, digested food or altered air. By such a motion the self-moving mover is moved by accident. From this we may infer that no self-moved being is moved everlastingly whose mover is moved either by itself or by accident. But the first self-mover is everlastingly in motion; otherwise, motion could not be everlasting, since every other motion is caused by the motion of the self-moving first mover. The first self-moving being, therefore, is moved by a mover who is himself moved neither through himself nor by accident.

27] Nor is it against this argument that the movers of the lower spheres produce an everlasting motion and yet are said to be moved by accident. For they are said to be moved by accident, not on their own account, but on account of their movable subjects, which follow the motion of the higher sphere.

28] Now, God is not part of any self-moving mover. In his *Metaphysics,* therefore, Aristotle goes on from the mover who is a part of the self-moved mover to seek another mover — God — who is absolutely separate. For, since everything moving itself is moved through appetite, the mover who is part of the self-moving being moves because of the appetite of some appetible object. This object is higher, in the order of motion, than the mover desiring it; for the one desiring is in a manner a moved mover, whereas an appetible object is an absolutely unmoved mover. There must, therefore, be an absolutely unmoved separate first mover. This is God.

29] Two considerations seem to invalidate these arguments. The first consideration is that, as arguments, they presuppose the eternity of motion, which Catholics consider to be false.

30] To this consideration the reply is as follows. The most efficacious way to prove that God exists is on the supposition that the world is eternal. Granted this supposition, that God exists is less manifest. For, if the world and motion have a first beginning, some cause must clearly be posited to account for this origin of the world and of motion. That which comes to be anew must take its origin from some innovating cause; since nothing brings itself from potency to act, or from non-being to being.

31] The second consideration is that the demonstrations given above presuppose that the first moved being, namely, a heavenly body, is self-moved. This means that it is animated, which many do not admit.

32] The reply to this consideration is that, if the prime mover is not held to be self-moved, then it must be moved immediately by something absolutely unmoved. Hence, even Aristotle himself proposed this conclusion as a disjunction: it is necessary either to arrive immediately at an unmoved separate first mover, or to arrive at a self-moved mover from whom, in turn, an unmoved separate first mover is reached.

33] In *Metaphysics* II Aristotle also uses another argument to show that there is no infinite regress in efficient causes and that we must reach one first cause—God. This way is as follows. In all ordered efficient causes, the first is the cause of the intermediate cause, whether one or many, and this is the cause of the last cause. But, when you suppress a cause, you suppress its effect. Therefore, if you suppress the first cause, the intermediate cause cannot be a cause. Now, if there were an infinite regress among efficient causes, no cause would be first. Therefore, all the other causes, which are intermediate, will be suppressed. But this is manifestly false. We must, therefore, posit that there exists a first efficient cause. This is God.

34] Another argument may also be gathered from the words of Aristotle. In *Metaphysics* II he shows that what is most true is also most a being. But in *Metaphysics* IV he shows the existence of something supremely true from the observed fact that of two false things one is more false than the other, which means that one is more true than the other. This comparison is based on the nearness to that which is absolutely and supremely true. From these Aristotelian texts we may further infer that there is something that is supremely being. This we call God.

35] Damascene[1] proposes another argument for the same conclusion taken from the government of the world. Averroës likewise hints at it. The argument runs thus. Contrary and discordant things cannot, always or for the most part, be parts of one order except under someone's government, which enables all and each to tend to a definite end. But in the world we find that things of diverse natures come together under one order, and this not rarely or by chance, but always or for the most part. There must therefore be some being by whose providence the world is governed. This we call God.

NOTE

1. An eminent theologian of the Eastern Church whose writings influenced the scholastic theology of western Europe in the thirteenth century.

13

The Medieval Idea of History

HISTORY as we know it today was seldom written in the Middle Ages. For the most part it was limited to biographies of holy men and to parochial chronicles and annals concerned more with local and daily events than with the wider historical developments of western Christendom. In varying degrees all historical writing also showed how the will of God affected the course of human history. There were exceptions, however, and from the twelfth century on the number of histories that were oriented towards a world view and made some attempt to verify evidence and to evaluate events realistically and objectively began to increase. Two of the best historians of the twelfth century were Otto, bishop of Freising (1111?–1158) and uncle of the emperor Frederick Barbarossa, and William of Tyre (1130?–1185). Otto's work, which covered the history of the world from its creation to the middle of the twelfth century, exemplifies the medieval philosophy of history – the teleological nature of history – and reveals the dependence of Otto upon the grand scheme of divine and human history as drawn in St. Augustine's Civitas Dei ("The City of God"). The history of William, who was archbishop of Tyre (1175–1185) and a native of the Latin Kingdom of Jerusalem, also has a wide perspective. Of the numerous histories of the crusades William's is the most comprehensive and perhaps the most valuable. It records events from the First Crusade to the eve of the fall of Jerusalem in 1187. What is most remarkable about this history is William's conscious effort to sift myth and unreliable evidence from true facts and to produce objective history. That he came close to attaining these goals is evidenced by the value still accorded his work as a source for the crusades.

A Otto, Bishop of Freising, Historia de Duabus Civitatibus ("The History of the Two Cities")

IN pondering long and often in my heart upon the changes and vicissitudes of temporal affairs and their varied and irregular issues, even as I hold that a wise man ought by no means to cleave to the things of time, so I find that it is by the faculty of reason alone that one must escape and find release from them. For it is the part of a wise man not to be whirled about after the manner of a revolving wheel, but through the stability of his powers to be firmly fashioned as a thing foursquare. Accordingly, since things are changeable and can never be at rest, what man in his right mind will deny that the wise man ought, as I have said, to depart from them to that city which stays at rest and abides to all eternity? This is the City of God, the heavenly Jerusalem, for which the children of God sigh while they are set in this land of sojourn, oppressed by the turmoil of the things of time as if they were oppressed by the Babylonian captivity. For, inasmuch as there are two cities — the one of time, the other of eternity; the one of the earth, earthy, the other of heaven, heavenly; the one of the devil, the other of Christ — ecclesiastical writers have declared that the former is Babylon, the latter Jerusalem.

But, whereas many of the Gentiles have written much regarding one of these cities, to hand down to posterity the great exploits of men of old (the many evidences of their merits, as they fancied), they have yet left to us the task of setting forth what, in the judgment of our writers, is rather the tale of human miseries. There are extant in this field the famous works of Pompeius Trogus, Justin, Cornelius [*i.e.,* Tacitus], Varro, Eusebius, Jerome, Orosius, Jordanes,[1] and a great many others of our number,[2] as well as of their array, whom it would take too long to enumerate; in those writings the discerning reader will be able to find not so much histories as pitiful tragedies made up of mortal woes. We believe that this has come to

From C. C. Mierow, THE TWO CITIES. A CHRONICLE OF UNIVERSAL HISTORY TO THE YEAR 1146 A.D. BY OTTO, BISHOP OF FREISING (New York, 1928), pp. 93–97, 215–222. Reprinted by permission of the Columbia University Press.

pass by what is surely a wise and proper dispensation of the Creator, in order that, whereas men in their folly desire to cleave to earthly and transitory things, they may be frightened away from them by their own vicissitudes, if by nothing else, so as to be directed by the wretchedness of this fleeting life from the creature to a knowledge of the Creator. But we, set down as it were at the end of time, do not so much read of the miseries of mortals in the books of the writers named above as find them for ourselves in consequence of the experiences of our own time. For, to pass over other things, the empire of the Romans, which in Daniel is compared to iron on account of its sole lordship — monarchy, the Greeks call it — over the whole world, a world subdued by war, has in consequence of so many fluctuations and changes, particularly in our day, become, instead of the noblest and the foremost, almost the last. So that, in the words of the poet,[3] scarcely

a shadow of its mighty name remains.

For being transferred from the City[4] to the Greeks,[5] from the Greeks to the Franks, from the Franks to the Lombards, from the Lombards again to the German Franks, that empire not only became decrepit and senile through lapse of time, but also, like a once smooth pebble that has been rolled this way and that by the waters, contracted many a stain and developed many a defect. The world's misery is exhibited, therefore, even in the case of the chief power in the world, and Rome's fall foreshadows the dissolution of the whole structure.

But what wonder if human power is changeable, seeing that even mortal wisdom is prone to slip? We read that in Egypt there was so great wisdom that, as Plato states, the Egyptians called the philosophers of the Greeks childish and immature. Moses also, the giver of the law, "with whom Jehovah spake as a man speaketh unto his friend," and whom He filled with wisdom divine, was not ashamed to be instructed in all the wisdom of Egypt. Did not that great patriarch, appointed by God the father of nations, Abraham, a man trained in the learning of the Chaldeans and endowed with wisdom, did he not, when called by God, desert his former manner of life [*i.e.,* go to Egypt] and yet not lay aside his wisdom? And yet Babylon the great, not only renowned for wisdom, but also "the glory of kingdoms, the beauty of the Chaldeans' pride," has become, in the words of the prophecy of Isaiah, without hope of restoration, a shrine of owls, a house of serpents and of ostriches, the lurking-place of creeping things. Egypt too is said to be in large measure uninhabitable and impassable. The careful student of history will find that learning was transferred from Egypt to the Greeks, then to the Romans, and finally to the Gauls and the Spaniards. And so it is to be observed that all human power or learning had its origin in the East, but is coming to an end in the West, that thereby the transitoriness and decay of all things human may be displayed. This, by God's grace, we shall show more fully in what follows.

Since, then, the changeable nature of the world is proved by this and like evidence, I thought it necessary, my dear brother Isingrim,[6] in response to your request, to compose a history whereby through God's favor I might display the miseries of the citizens of Babylon and also the glory of the kingdom of Christ to which the citizens of Jerusalem are to look forward with hope, and of which they are to have a foretaste even in this life. I have undertaken therefore to bring down as far as our own time, according to the ability that God has given me, the record of the conflicts and miseries of the one city, Babylon; and furthermore, not to be silent concerning our hopes regarding that other city, so far as I can gather hints from the Scriptures, but to make mention also of its citizens who are now sojourning in the worldly city. In this work I follow most of all those illustrious lights of the Church, Augustine[7] and Orosius, and have planned to draw from their fountains what is pertinent to my theme and my purpose. The one of these has discoursed most keenly and eloquently on the origin and the progress of the glorious City of God and its ordained limits, setting forth how it has ever spread among the citizens of the world, and showing which of its citizens or princes stood forth preëminent in the various epochs of the princes or citizens of the world. The other,[8] in answer to those who, uttering vain babblings, preferred the former times to Christian times, has composed a very valuable history of the fluctuations and wretched issues of human greatness, the wars and the hazards of wars, and the shifting of thrones, from the foundation of the world down to his own time. Following in their steps I have undertaken to speak of the Two Cities in such a way that we shall not lose the thread of history, that the devout reader may observe what is to be avoided in mundane affairs by reason of the countless miseries wrought by their unstable character, and that the studious and painstaking investigator may find a record of past happenings free from all obscurity.

Nor do I think that I shall be justly criticized if, coming after such great men — men so wise and so eloquent — I shall presume in spite of my ignorance to write, since I have both epitomized those things of which they themselves spoke profusely and at length, and have detailed, in however rude a style, the deeds which have been performed by citizens of the world since their time, whether to the advantage of the Church of God or to its hurt. Nor shall I believe that I ought to be assailed by that verse in which the writer of satire[9] says:

All of us, taught or untaught, are everywhere writers of poems.

For it is not because of indiscretion or frivolity, but out of devotion, which always knows how to excuse ignorance, that I, though I am without proper training, have ventured to undertake so arduous a task. Nor can anyone rightfully accuse me of falsehood in matters which — compared with the customs of the present time — will appear incredible, since down to the days still fresh in our memory I have recorded nothing save what I found in the writings of trustworthy men, and then only a few instances out of many. For I should never hold the view that these men are to be held in contempt if certain of them have preserved in their writings the apostolic simplicity, for, as overshrewd subtlety sometimes kindles error, so a devout rusticity is ever the friend of truth.

As we are about to speak, then, concerning the sorrow-burdened insecurity of the one city and the blessed permanence of the other, let us call upon God, who endures with patience the turbulence and confusion of this world, and by the vision of himself augments and glorifies the joyous peace of that other city, to the end that by His aid we may be able to say the things which are pleasing to Him.

The first book extends to Arbaces and the transfer of the Babylonian sovereignty to the Medes, and the beginning of the Roman power.

The second extends to the civil war of the Romans, fought with Julius and Pompey as leaders, to the death of Cæsar, and to our Lord's nativity.

The third extends to Constantine and the times of the Christian Empire, and the transfer of sovereignty to the Greeks.

The fourth extends to Odovacar and the invasion of the kingdom by the Rugians.

The fifth extends to Charles and the transfer of sovereignty to the Franks, and the division of the kingdom and the empire under his descendants.

The sixth extends to Henry the Fourth and the schism between the kingly power and the priestly power; it includes the anathema pronounced against the emperor, the expulsion of Pope Gregory VII from the City, and his death at Salerno.

The seventh extends to the uprising of the Roman people and the ninth year of King Conrad.

The eighth is concerned with Antichrist and the resurrection of the dead and the end of the Two Cities.

At this point we are constrained to cry out against the wretchedness of life's vicissitudes. For lo! we see at what cost, not only to its enemies but even to its own citizens, the Roman Republic grew. For by alternating changes, after the manner of the sea — which is now uplifted by the increases that replenish it, now lowered by natural loss and waste — the republic of the Romans seemed now exalted to the heavens by oppressing nations and kingdoms with war and by subduing them; now in turn was thought to be going down again into the depths when assailed by those nations and kingdoms or overwhelmed by pestilence and sickness, and — what is more significant even than such matters — after they had arranged everything else well and had set it in fine order, they were miserably disemboweled by falling upon one another in internal civil strife. All these calamities springing out of unstable events and (so to speak) the daily deaths of mortal beings should have had the power to direct men to the true and abiding life of eternity. But as we have said above, when the city of the world was afflicted by these and like misfortunes the rising of the true Light was drawing nigh as though following the darkness of murky night. And so, since after hurrying over the instances of fluctuating disasters that affected the Medes and the Persians, as well as the Greeks and the Romans, we are now approaching the coming of Him who, being truly the peacemaker, pacified all things "whether things upon the earth, or things in the heavens,"[10] even Christ Jesus himself, let us set an end to this second book, inasmuch as we are hastening on to speak of that peace which was secured to the whole world under Augustus at the coming of Christ's nativity.[11]

Not unmindful of my promise, beloved brother, I shall not hesitate to complete the discussion of the Two Cities, already brought down to the times of Caesar Octavianus with such style as I had at my command, particularly since we have now come to Christian times, and by God's grace I shall speak the more willingly as I shall now be able, because of growing faith, to speak more fully of the City of God.[12] For heretofore, though I had at my command much regarding the citizens of the world, I was in position to say but little about the citizens of Christ, because from the time of the first man to Christ almost the whole world (except a few of the Israelitish race), led astray by error, given over to empty superstitions, ensnared by the mocking devices of demons and caught in the toils of the world, is found to have fought under the leadership of the devil, the prince of this world. "But when the fulness of the time came, God sent forth his Son"[13] into the world to lead back into the highway mortal men, who were wandering like the brutes through trackless and devious places. By taking upon himself the form of a man He proferred mortal men a highway; to recall those who were utterly astray from the error of falsehood to the light of reason, He revealed Himself as the truth; to make over anew the perishing He showed Himself as the true life saying, "I am the way, and the truth, and the life,"[14] as though He were saying, "You are wandering astray; come therefore to me who am the way. That you may tread this way undismayed, learn that I am the truth. And if you have no provision for the journey, realize that I am the life." For many seek the way but, not finding the true way, wander about instead of walking in the right path. Again many tread a way which seems the true way, but do not thereby attain life. Of these methinks it was said: "There are ways which seem right unto men, but their ends lead to destruction." But the Saviour, coming into the world, says, "I am the way, the truth, and the life," that is, "Through me alone one walks safely, with me alone one reaches truth, in me alone one continues in true life."

But at the very outset the question may properly be raised why the Saviour of all men was willing to be born at the end of the ages which Paul calls "the fulness of the time"; and why He permitted the whole Gentile world to perish in the sin of unbelief in so many past ages. Who that is circumscribed by the corruptible flesh of mortals would venture to inquire into the cause of this dispensation set away in the most profound and righteous treasures of the judgments of God; who, I say, would venture, seeing that the apostle says, "O the depth of the riches both of the wisdom and the knowledge of God! how unsearchable are his judgments, and his ways past finding out!"[15] and so forth? What then shall we do? If we cannot understand we are not to be silent, are we? In that case who will reply to the defamers, stay the assailants and above all confute those who seek by argument and by the force of words to destroy the faith that is in us? Accordingly we cannot comprehend the secret counsels of God and yet we are frequently obliged to attempt an explanation of them. What? Are we to attempt an explanation of things which we are unable to understand? We can render explanations, human explanations to be sure, though we may still be unable to comprehend God's own explanations. And so it comes to pass that while we speak of theological matters, since we lack the language appropriate to these matters, we who are but men use our own terms and in speaking of the great God employ mortal expressions with the more assurance because we have no doubt that He understands the formulas we devise. For who understands better than He who created? Hence it follows that, although God is called ineffable, He yet desires us to say much in His praise. Therefore, since He is called ineffable, after a certain fashion He is seen to be effable. As Augustine says, this contradiction in terms can better be resolved by silent faith than by wordy disputation. And another has said: "Let what is beyond words be revered through the agency of silence."

So then "If God," as the Apostle says, "endured with much long-suffering vessels of wrath fitted unto destruction,"[16] if, desiring to reveal unto His Church the riches of His goodness, He permitted the city of the world to have long temporal prosperity in the free exercise of its own will, He is not to be blamed either because He abandoned that city to its own devices or because to His chosen people — chastised by contrast with that city of the world — He revealed the riches of His goodness. For on the one hand if He permits men to do what they themselves at all events desire to do, He cannot justly be accused by them; and on the other hand He should be greatly praised and revered by those whom, as He bestows on them His grace without price, He deters from such things as they wish to do to their own hurt and prevents from bringing such intentions to accomplishment. He cannot be said to be acting unjustly if in accordance with justice He does not bestow His grace, even as He must be believed to be acting only in mercy when He imparts it without price to whom He will. And so, if He abandoned so many ages of the past, not by forcing them into sin but by not giving them what was His own — with this purpose, that by the example of those that had gone before He might reveal to future generations what must be avoided by them, that they might render thanks unto their Saviour — if, I say, with this purpose He abandoned them to their own will, both that they might learn what they could do by themselves without Him and that when redeemed they might learn in addition what they possessed by their Saviour's mercy, then as He could not justly be blamed by the former, even so He gave the latter abundant reason whereby He ought rightly to be loved by them.

There is besides a reason why Christ wished to be born at this time rather than at any other, namely in the sixth age[17] and when the world was united under the sway of the Romans and organized as a whole under Augustus Caesar. For inasmuch as he willed to be made flesh in order to atone for the sin of our first parent, who, putting away the delights of paradise, preferred to inhabit the land of the curse at the caprice of his own will, it was most fitting that this be done in the sixth age rather than in any other, because He also created that first man on the sixth day. Nor ought He to have been made flesh in an early age of men. For the men that were descended from these sinful parents, men whose nature, marred by disobedience, made them more inclined and prone to evil, who as yet were making no use of their reasoning powers, and were roaming about rather in the manner of wild, brute beasts — the natural goodness within them being obscured, — these men, I say, had not learned to live companionably with one another, to be moulded by laws, to be adorned with virtues, and to be lighted by the power of reason to the knowledge of the truth. Hence we have most shameful stories and even more shameful deeds, most monstrous recitals and still more monstrous acts, regarding all of which I think I have said enough in what has preceded. Since men were thus devoid of reason, incapable of receiving the truth, unacquainted with justice and with laws, how could they receive, how understand, how comprehend the laws and the most lofty precepts about life that were to be given by Christ? And so the Law was given first that it might be suited to their feeble intellects and might support the infancy of the world not with solid food but with milk. Then as this age gradually grew and made progress — partly through the association of men dwelling together, partly through the putting together of their wisdom for the purpose of establishing laws, and partly through the agency of the wisdom and of the teachings of the philosophers — it was fitting that the Saviour of all should appear in the flesh and establish new laws for the world at the time when, as I have said, the whole world had now bowed before the power of the Romans, and had been moulded by the wisdom of the philosophers, and the minds of men were suited to grasp more lofty precepts about right living.

Now at this point I think I ought to answer the question that I put off above, why the Lord of the universe wished the whole world to be subject to the dominion of one city, the whole world to be moulded by the laws of one city. In the first place He wished it, as I have said, that the minds of men might be more ready to understand, more capable of understanding great matters. Secondly, He wished it that unity of faith might be recommended to them after they had been united in this way, in order that all men, being constrained by their fear of a single city to revere one man, might learn also that they ought to hold to one faith, and through that faith might learn that God must be revered and adored not merely as a celestial being but as the Creator of all. Hence upon His coming a census of the whole world was ordered, doubtless that men might learn that One was come who would enroll all who came to Him as citizens in the Eternal City. Hence at His birth throughout the entire circuit of the universe the world, exhausted by calamities and wearied by its own dissensions, willed to be at peace and to serve the emperor of the Romans rather than to rebel, that understanding might be vouchsafed of the fact that He had come in the flesh who said in mercy to those weighed down and wearied by the weight of earthly burdens, "Come unto me, all ye that labor and are heavy laden, and I will give you rest."[18] For this reason peace, at that time a new thing, was granted to the world in order that the servants of the new king might be able to journey more freely over the whole world and implant health-bringing precepts about right living. It is not therefore to accidental causes, nor to the worship of false gods, but to the true God who forms the light and creates the darkness that, in my judgment, we must ascribe the fact that the commonwealth of the Romans expanded from a poor and lowly estate to such heights and to a great sovereignty under the primacy of one man. But why He bestowed this boon upon that people or that city rather than on others we cannot even discuss; unless perhaps I should say it was done because of the merits of the chief of the apostles who, He foresaw, would have His seat there, upon whom as upon a foundation He also promised that He would build His Church, namely, that the place which was to be the head of the Church universal (on account of the seat of the chief of the apostles) might beforehand attain to sole rule over the Gentiles also, from whom true believers were to be gathered. Most fittingly, therefore, that city was in earlier days the head of the world which was afterwards to be the head of the Church. But if any man is contentious, let him hear that it is "in the power of the potter to make one vessel unto honor and another unto dishonor."[19] Let him hear that it is in the power of the judge to put down whom He will and to lift up whom He will. Finally, if the Lord, who is the judge and arbiter of the world, holding a cup in His hand, first making Babylon drunken humiliated it at last at the hands of the Medes and, when the Medes had been brought low by the Persians, the Persians in turn by the Greeks, and the Greeks finally by the Romans, wished for a time to exalt Rome, which was also in its turn to be put down, if, weighing in balanced scales all human events, He weaves such changes as those, will it be possible for the Creator to be blamed by His creature? And so let us humble ourselves under the mighty hand of the Lord who changes thrones and according to His will has mercy on whom he pleases, and let us, ascribing it to His compassion if we are anything (who of ourselves are nothing), and attributing to His grace what we say (who of ourselves know nothing), pursue the work we have begun.

B   William of Tyre, Historia Rerum in Partibus Transmarinis Gestarum ("History of the Deeds Done Beyond the Sea")

PROLOGUE] William, by the grace of God unworthy minister of the Holy Church at Tyre, to the venerable brethren in Christ to whom the present work may come: Eternal salvation in the Lord

That it is an arduous task, fraught with many risks and perils, to write of the deeds of kings no wise man can doubt. To say nothing of the toil, the never-ending application, and the constant vigilance which works of this nature always demand, a double abyss inevitably yawns before the writer of history. It is only with the greatest difficulty that he avoids one or the other, for, while he is trying to escape Charybdis, he usually falls into the clutches of Scylla, who, surrounded by her dogs, understands equally well how to bring about disaster. For either he will kindle the anger of many persons against him while he is in pursuit of the actual facts of achievements; or, in the hope of rousing less resentment, he will be silent about the course of events, wherein, obviously, he is not without fault. For to pass over the actual truth of events and conceal the facts intentionally is well recognized as contrary to the duty of a historian. But to fail in one's duty is unquestionably a fault, if indeed duty is truly defined as "the fitting conduct of each individual, in accordance with the customs and institutions of his country." On the other hand, to trace out a succession of events without changing them or deviating from the rule of truth is a course which always excites wrath; for, as says the old proverb, "Compliance wins friends; truth, hatred."[1] As a result, historians either fall short of the duty of their profession by showing undue deference, or, while eagerly seeking the truth of a matter, they must needs endure hatred, of which truth herself is the mother. Thus all too commonly, these two courses are wont to be opposed

From E. A. Babcock and A. C. Krey, A HISTORY OF DEEDS DONE BEYOND THE SEA (New York, 1943), I, pp. 53–59. Reprinted by permission of the Columbia University Press.

to one another and to become equally troublesome by the insistent demands which they make.

In the words of our Cicero, "Truth is troublesome, since verily from it springs hatred which is poisonous to friendship; but compliance is even more disastrous, for, by dealing leniently with a friend, it permits him to rush headlong to ruin" — a sentiment which seems to reflect on the man who, in defiance of the obligations of duty, suppresses the real facts for the sake of being obliging.

As for those who, in the desire to flatter, deliberately weave untruths into their record of history, the conduct of such writers is looked upon as so detestable that they ought not to be regarded as belonging to the rank of historians. For, if to conceal the true facts about achievements is wrong and falls far short of a writer's duty, it will certainly be regarded as a much more serious sin to mingle untruth with truth and to hand to a trusting posterity as verity that which is essentially untrue.

In addition to these risks, the writer of history usually meets with an equal or even more formidable difficulty, which he should endeavor to avoid in so far as in him lies. It is, namely, that the lofty dignity of historical events may suffer loss through feeble presentation and lack of eloquence. For the style of his discourse ought to be on the same high plane as are the deeds which he is relating. Nor should the language and spirit of the writer fall below the nobility of his subject.

It is greatly to be feared, therefore, that the grandeur of the theme may be impaired by faulty handling and that deeds which are of intrinsic value and importance in themselves may appear insignificant and trivial through fault in the narration. For, as the distinguished orator[2] remarks in the first *Tusculan Disputation,* "To commit one's thoughts to writing without being able to arrange them well, present them clearly, or attract the reader by any charm is the act of a man who foolishly abuses literature and his own leisure."

In the present work we seem to have fallen into manifold dangers and perplexities. For, at the series of events seemed to require, we have included in this study on which we are now engaged many details about the characters, lives, and personal traits of kings, regardless of whether these facts were commendable or open to criticism. Possibly descendants of these monarchs, while perusing this work, may find this treatment difficult to brook and be angry with the chronicler beyond his just deserts. They will regard him as either mendacious or jealous — both of which charges, as God lives, we have endeavored to avoid as we would a pestilence.

As for the rest, there can be no doubt that we have rashly undertaken a work far beyond our powers, in the accomplishment of which our language is entirely inadequate to the grandeur of the subject. Nevertheless, we have accomplished something. For just as those who are inexperienced in painting and not yet admitted to the secrets of the art are allowed usually merely to trace out the first design of a picture and apply the rough colors, while later the hand of a more skilled artist adds, with nobler colors, the finishing touches of beauty, so we, ever adhering strictly to the truth from which we have in no wise departed, have laid, at the expense of much effort, the foundations upon which a wiser builder by his excellent treatment may erect a more finished structure.

In view of the many dangerous complications and pitfalls attending this task, it would have been far safer if I had remained silent. I ought to have held my peace and forced my pen to rest. But an insistent love of my country urges me on, and for her, if the needs of the time demand, a man of loyal instincts is bound to lay down his life. She spurs me on, I repeat, and with that authority which belongs to her imperiously commands that those things which have been accomplished by her during the course of almost a century be not buried in silence and allowed to fall into undeserved oblivion. On the contrary, she bids me preserve them for the benefit of posterity by the diligent use of my pen.

Accordingly we have obeyed her behest and have put our hand to a task which we can not with honor refuse. We care but little what the criticism of posterity concerning us may be, or what verdict may be given as to our feeble style of writing while dealing with a subject so noble.

We have, forsooth, obeyed. Would that the result might prove to be as effective as the zeal with which it has been done! Would that it might be as worthy of praise as it is devoted! Drawn by the charm of our native soil, disregarding the inadequacy of our powers and the labor involved, not relying on the aid of genius but moved by genuine affection and sincere love, we have entered upon this task.

To these incentives there was added the command of King Amaury I,[3] of illustrious memory and distinguished record in the Lord (may his hallowed soul enjoy rest!). This command, together with many other urgent reasons, induced me to undertake this work. Moreover, at the order of the king, who himself furnished the necessary Arabic documents, we have also written another history. As the principal source for this we have used the work of the venerable patriarch of Alexandria, Seith,[4] son of Patricius. This history begins from the time of the false prophet Muhammad and extends through five hundred and seventy years even to the present year, which is the 1184th of the Incarnation of the Lord.

For the present work, however, we have no written source, either in Greek or Arabic, to guide us. Except in the case of a few events which we ourselves witnessed, we have depended upon tradition alone. We have followed the order of events. It begins with the departure of those brave men and leaders, beloved of God, who, at the call of the Lord, went out from the kingdoms of the West and appropriated with a strong hand the Land of Promise and practically the whole of Syria. Starting from that point, we have continued the history with great fidelity over a period of eighty-four years, to the reign of Baldwin IV,[5] who holds the seventh place in the list of kings, if Lord Godfrey who first ruled there as duke be included. In order that anyone who is interested may be more fully informed about the condition of the oriental lands, we have set down first, briefly and concisely, at what time they lay under the yoke of servitude and how intense were the sufferings endured. We have also described the condition of the faithful, who, in this intermediary period, dwelt among the infidels in this land, and then, what it was that, after so long a period of bondage, roused the princes of the kingdoms of the West to assume the responsibility of a pilgrimage for the purpose of liberating their brethren.

If the reader will consider the many different cares which rest upon us, he will realize that we are greatly wearied by the variety of these demands. First, we have great responsibility in matters relating to the famous metropolis of Tyre, which rests under the protection of God, and over which we have been chosen to preside, not because of any merit of our own, but by the grace of God alone. Secondly, we have charge also of the business of the lord king, in whose sacred palace we hold the dignity of chancellor. Various other pressing matters which arise from time to time also demand our attention. Taking these facts into consideration, the reader will then be more inclined to grant us indulgence if he finds in the present work anything to which he may only too justly take exception. For when one is occupied with many varied interests, it is impossible for the mind to respond with the same vigor and give careful consideration to each subject. It is impossible to devote as much effort to each individual interest, when the attention is divided in this way, as when mental energy is applied wholly to one thing. Under such circumstances one more readily deserves pardon.

The whole work has been divided into twenty-three books and each of these into a certain number of chapters, that the reader may more easily find whatever he seeks in the different parts of the narrative. It is our intention, if life be granted us, to add from time to time to what has already been written those events of our own era which the vicissitudes of the future may bring forth, and to increase the number of books as the amount of subject matter may warrant.

We are convinced, nor are we wrong in the belief, that this work gives plain evidence of our inexperience. By writing it, in our desire to obey the dictates of affection, we have betrayed those defects which might have been concealed if we had remained silent. Yet we prefer to be found lacking in that which puffs up rather than in that which edifies. For many who have come to the wedding feast without the former have been deemed worthy to sit at the table of the king, but those who have been found among the guests without the latter qualification well deserve to hear the words, "How camest thou in hither not having a wedding garment?"[6] May the Lord, who alone is able to avert it, in His gracious mercy prevent this fate befalling us!

We know well, however, that error is ever wont to attend a multitude of words, and that the tongue of a poor mortal easily incurs guilt. In a spirit of brotherly affection, therefore, we invite and exhort our reader in the Lord, that, if he finds a real point to criticize, he seize upon it without hesitation, with true kindness, and, by correcting our sin, win for himself the reward of eternal life.

May he also remember us in his prayers and thereby win favor for us with the Lord, that, wherever in this work we have fallen into error, it may not be imputed to us for death. May the Saviour of the world, out of His abounding goodness and never-failing mercy, graciously pardon us, for we, wretched and unprofitable servitors in His house, are accused beyond measure by our own conscience and with justice dread His tribunal.

THE PROLOGUE IS ENDED

NOTES

Selection a

1. A reference to Roman historians.
2. Christian writers.
3. The Roman poet Lucan.
4. Rome.
5. The Eastern Roman Empire.
6. A monk of the Swabian monastery of Ottenbeuren.
7. The famous St. Augustine, whose work *The City of God* provided the model for Otto's history.
8. Orosius in his *History Against the Pagans.*
9. The Roman poet Horace.
10. Colossians, i. 20.
11. This is the last chapter of Book II, in which Otto provides a transition from his account of pagan history to the beginning of the Christian era.
12. This section of Otto's history is from his prologue to Book III.
13. Galatians, iv. 4.
14. John, xiv. 6.
15. Romans, xi. 33.
16. Romans, ix. 22.
17. Otto follows the seven ages as enumerated by St. Augustine in *The City of God.*
18. Matthew, xi. 28.
19. Romans, ix. 21.

Selection b

1. A quotation from the Roman dramatist Terence.
2. Cicero.
3. King of the crusader state of Jerusalem.
4. Known in Europe by the name Eutychius. He wrote a history of the Arabs from Mohammed to 937.
5. Baldwin IV ruled from 1174 to 1185.
6. Matthew, xxii. 12.

14

The Construction of
Gothic Cathedrals

TANGIBLE evidence of western Europe's recovery after the year 1000 are the magnificent churches that were erected in lands between the Mediterranean and North seas. The austere, rounded, and heavy Romanesque style prevailed in the eleventh and first half of the twelfth century and then succumbed to the Gothic, which remained with modifications the dominant style throughout the rest of the medieval period. Although the term Gothic has come to symbolize the totality of medieval thought and culture, and although the Gothic cathedral still dominates the European panorama, little is known about the construction of these cathedrals or about the men responsible for this work. Following are two of the best descriptions of Gothic building that we possess. The first and most celebrated is by Abbot Suger of St. Denis (d. 1151), who was responsible for constructing in 1144 a choir for his abbey church, thought to be one of the first Gothic structures in Europe. It was not long before the Île de France was dotted with such graceful Gothic cathedrals as Notre-Dame at Paris, Chartres, and Laon. Of greatest interest in Suger's account are the details given on the efforts to secure good architects, skilled craftsmen, and suitable building materials. The second selection, by Gervase of Canterbury (d. 1210), monk of Christ's Church Canterbury, is the best record we have of the construction of a Gothic cathedral and of the architects responsible for the plans. A witness to the fire that destroyed Canterbury Cathedral in 1174, Gervase describes the conflagration and then the reconstruction, which took the next ten years.

A *Suger*, Libellus Alter de Consecratione Ecclesiae Sancti Dionysii (*"The Other Little Book on The Consecration of the Church of St.-Denis"*)

II] When the glorious and famous King of the Franks, Dagobert,[1] notable for his royal magnanimity in the administration of his kingdom and yet no less devoted to the Church of God, had fled to the village of Catulliacum in order to evade the intolerable wrath of his father Clothaire, and when he had learned that the venerable images of the Holy Martyrs who rested there — appearing to him as very beautiful men clad in snow-white garments — requested his service and unhesitatingly promised him their aid with words and deeds, he decreed with admirable affection that a basilica of the Saints be built with regal magnificence. When he had constructed this [basilica] with a marvelous variety of marble columns he enriched it incalculably with treasures of purest gold and silver and hung on its walls, columns and arches tapestries woven of gold and richly adorned with a variety of pearls, so that it might seem to excel the ornaments of all other churches and, blooming with incomparable luster and adorned with every terrestrial beauty, might shine with inestimable splendor. Only one thing was wanting in him: that he did not allow for the size that was necessary. Not that anything was lacking in his devotion or good will; but perhaps there existed thus far, at that time of the Early Church, no [church] either greater or [even] equal in size; or perhaps [he thought that] a smallish one — reflecting the splendor of gleaming gold and gems to the admiring eyes more keenly and delightfully because they were nearer — would glow with greater radiance than if it were built larger.

Through a fortunate circumstance. attending this singular smallness — the number of the faithful growing and frequently gathering to seek the intercession of the Saints — the aforesaid basilica had come to suffer grave inconveniences. Often on feast days, com-

From Erwin Panofsky, ABBOT SUGER ON THE ABBEY CHURCH OF ST.-DENIS AND ITS TREASURES (Princeton, 1946), pp. 87–115. Reprinted by permission of the Princeton University Press.

pletely filled, it disgorged through all its doors the excess of the crowds as they moved in opposite directions, and the outward pressure of the foremost ones not only prevented those attempting to enter from entering but also expelled those who had already entered. At times you could see, a marvel to behold, that the crowded multitude offered so much resistance to those who strove to flock in to worship and kiss the holy relics, the Nail and Crown of the Lord, that no one among the countless thousands of people because of their very density could move a foot; that no one, because of their very congestion, could [do] anything but stand like a marble statue, stay benumbed or, as a last resort, scream. The distress of the women, however, was so great and so intolerable that [you could see] how they, squeezed in by the mass of strong men as in a winepress, exhibited bloodless faces as in imagined death; how they cried out horribly as though in labor; how several of them, miserably trodden underfoot [but then], lifted by the pious assistance of men above the heads of the crowd, marched forward as though clinging to a pavement; and how many others, gasping with their last breath, panted in the cloisters of the brethren to the despair of everyone. Moreover the brethren who were showing the tokens of the Passion of Our Lord to the visitors had to yield to their anger and rioting and many a time, having no place to turn, escaped with the relics through the windows. When I was instructed by the brethren as a schoolboy I used to hear of this; in my youth I deplored it from without; in my mature years I zealously strove to have it corrected. *But when it pleased Him who separated me from my mother's womb, and called me by His grace,*[2] to place insignificant me, although my merits were against it, at the head of the so important administration of this sacred church; then, impelled to a correction of the aforesaid inconvenience only by the ineffable mercy of Almighty God and by the aid of the Holy Martyrs our Patron Saints, we resolved to hasten, with all our soul and all the affection of our mind, to the enlargement of the aforesaid place — we who would never have presumed to set our hand to it, nor even to think of it, had not so great, so necessary, so useful and honorable an occasion demanded it.

Since in the front part, toward the north, at the main entrance with the main doors, the narrow hall was squeezed in on either side by twin towers neither high nor very sturdy but threatening ruin, we began, with the help of God, strenuously to work on this part, having laid very strong material foundations for a straight nave and twin towers, and most strong spiritual ones of which it is said: *For other foundation can no man lay than that is laid, which is Jesus Christ.*[3] Leaning upon God's inestimable counsel and irrefragable aid, we proceeded with this so great and so sumptuous work to such an extent that, while at first, expending little, we lacked much, afterwards, accomplishing much, we lacked nothing at all and even confessed in our abundance: *Our sufficiency is of God.*[4] Through a gift of God a new quarry, yielding very strong stone, was discovered such as in quality and quantity had never been found in these regions. There arrived a skillful crowd of masons, stonecutters, sculptors and other workmen, so that — thus and otherwise — Divinity relieved us of our fears and favored us with Its goodwill by comforting us and by providing us with unexpected [resources]. I used to compare the least to the greatest: Solomon's riches could not have sufficed for his Temple any more than did ours for this work had not the same Author of the same work abundantly supplied His attendants. The identity of the author and the work provides a sufficiency for the worker.

In carrying out such plans my first thought was for the concordance and harmony of the ancient and the new work. By reflection, by inquiry, and by investigation through different regions of remote districts, we endeavored to learn where we might obtain marble columns or columns the equivalent thereof. Since we found none, only one thing was left to us, distressed in mind and spirit: we might obtain them from Rome (for in Rome we had often seen wonderful ones in the Palace of Diocletian and other Baths) by safe ships through the Mediterranean, thence through the English Sea and the tortuous windings of the River Seine, at great expense to our friends and even under convoy of our enemies, the near-by Saracens. For many years, for a long time, we were perplexed, thinking and making inquiries — when suddenly the generous munificence of the Almighty, condescending to our labors, revealed to the astonishment of all and through the merit of the Holy Martyrs, what one would never have thought or imagined: very fine and excellent [columns]. Therefore, the greater acts of grace, contrary to hope and human expectation, Divine mercy had deigned to bestow by [providing] a suitable place where it could not be more agreeable to us, the greater [acts of gratitude] we thought it worth our effort to offer in return for the remedy of so great an anguish. For near Pontoise, a town adjacent to the confines of our territory, there [was found] a wonderful quarry [which] from ancient times had offered a deep chasm (hollowed out, not by nature but by industry) to cutters of millstones for their livelihood. Having produced nothing remarkable thus far, it reserved, we thought, the beginning of so great a usefulness for so great and divine a building — as a first offering, as it were, to God and the Holy Martyrs. Whenever the columns were hauled from the bottom of the slope with knotted ropes, both our own people and the pious neighbors, nobles and common folk alike, would tie their arms, chests, and shoulders to the ropes and, acting as draft animals, drew the columns up; and on the declivity in the middle of the town the diverse craftsmen laid aside the tools of their trade and came out to meet them, offering their own strength against the difficulty of the road, doing homage as much as they could to God and the Holy Martyrs. There occurred a wonderful miracle worthy of telling which we, having heard it ourselves from those present, have decided to set down with pen and ink for the praise of the Almighty and His Saints.

III] On a certain day when, with a downpour of rain, a dark opacity had covered the turbid air, those accustomed to assist in the work while the carts were coming down to the quarry went off because of the violence of the rain. The ox-drivers complained and protested that they had nothing to do and that the laborers were standing around and losing time. Clamoring, they grew so insistent that some weak and disabled persons together with a few boys — seventeen in number and, if I am not mistaken, with a priest present — hastened to the quarry, picked up one of the ropes, fastened it to a column and abandoned another shaft which was lying on the ground; for there was nobody who would undertake to haul this one. Thus, animated by pious zeal, the little flock prayed: "O Saint Denis, if it pleaseth thee, help us by dealing for thyself with this abandoned shaft, for thou canst not blame us if we are unable to do it." Then, bearing on it heavily, they dragged out what a hundred and forty or at least one hundred men had been accustomed to haul from the bottom of the chasm with difficulty — not alone by themselves, for that would have been impossible, but through the will of God and the assistance of the Saints whom they invoked; and they conveyed this material for the church to the cart. Thus it was made known throughout the neighborhood that this work pleased Almighty God exceedingly, since for the praise and glory of His name He had chosen to give His help to those who performed it by this and similar signs.

As a second instance there is related another notable event worthy of remembrance, remarkable to tell and deserving to be set forth with authority. When the work had been finished in great part, when the stories of the old and the new building had been joined, and when we had laid aside the anxiety we had long felt because of those gaping cracks in the old walls, we undertook with new confidence to repair the damages in the great capitals and in the bases that supported the columns. But when we inquired both of our own carpenters and those of Paris where we might find beams we were told, as was in their opinion true, that such could in no wise be found in these regions owing to the lack of woods; they would inevitably have to be brought hither from the district of Auxerre. All concurred with this view and we were much distressed by this because of the magnitude of the task and the long delay of the work; but on a certain night, when I had returned from celebrating Matins, I began to think in bed that I myself should go through all the forests of these parts, look around everywhere and alleviate those delays and troubles if [beams] could be found here. Quickly disposing of other duties and hurrying up in the early morning, we hastened with our carpenters, and with the measurements of the beams, to the forest called Iveline. When we traversed our possession in the Valley of Chevreuse we summoned through our servants the keepers of our own forests as well as men who knew about the other woods, and questioned them under oath whether we could find there, no matter with how much trouble, any timbers of that measure. At this they smiled, or rather would have laughed at us if they had dared; they wondered whether we were quite ignorant of the fact that nothing of the kind could be found in the entire region, especially since Milon, the Castellan of Chevreuse (our vassal, who holds of us one half of the forest in addition to another fief) had left nothing unimpaired or untouched that could be used for building palisades and bulwarks while he was long subjected to wars both by our Lord the King and Amaury de Montfort. We however —

scorning whatever they might say — began, with the courage of our faith as it were, to search through the woods; and toward the first hour we found one timber adequate to the measure. Why say more? By the ninth hour or sooner we had, through the thickets, the depths of the forests and the dense, thorny tangles, marked down twelve timbers (for so many were necessary) to the astonishment of all, especially those on the spot; and when they had been carried to the sacred basilica, we had them placed, with exultation, upon the ceiling of the new structure, to the praise and glory of our Lord Jesus, Who, protecting them from the hands of plunderers, had reserved them for Himself and the Holy Martyrs as He wished to do. Thus in this matter Divine generosity, which has chosen to limit and to grant all things *according to weight and measure,*[5] manifested itself as neither excessive nor defective; for not one more [timber] than was needed could be found.

IV] Thus continually encouraged in so great enterprises by so great and manifest signs, we immediately hastened to the completion of the aforesaid building. Having deliberated in what manner, by what persons, and how truly solemnly the church should be consecrated to Almighty God, and having summoned the excellent man, Hugues, Archbishop of Rouen, and the other venerable Bishops, Eudes of Beauvais [and] Peter of Senlis, we chanted in celebration of this ceremony a polyphonic praise amidst a great throng of diverse ecclesiastical personages and an enormous one of clergy and laity. These [three dignitaries] blessed, in the central nave of the new addition, the first water in a vat standing there; they then went out with the procession through the chapel of St. Eustace [and] across the square which from ancient times is called "Panetière" (because everything is worn down there by buying and selling); they returned through the other bronze door which opens onto the sacred cemetery; and they performed with the greatest devotion — by bestowing the unction of the eternal blessing and the most holy chrism, and by exhibiting the true body and blood of the High Priest Jesus Christ — whatever is fitting for so great and so sacred an edifice. They dedicated the upper chapel, most beautiful and worthy to be the dwelling place of angels, in honor of the Holy Mother of God, the eternal Virgin Mary, of St. Michael the Archangel, of All the Angels, of St. Romanus (who rests in that very place), and of many other saints whose names are inscribed there. The lower chapel on the right [they dedicated] in honor of St. Bartholomew and many other saints; the lower chapel on the left, however, where St. Hippolytus is said to rest, in honor of him and of Sts. Lawrence, Sixtus, Felicissinus, Agapitus, and many others, to the praise and glory of Almighty God. But we, desiring with all our heart to be made, God granting, the participant in so great a blessing as in a fruit of the expended labor, conferred upon these chapels — as though for a dowry, as the custom is, to meet the expense of buying lights — a certain property adjacent to the cemetery, hard by the church of St. Michael, which we had bought from Guillaume de Cornillon for eighty pounds, so that they might have the rent therefrom in perpetuity. Concerning the date of completion, however, this is the established truth as it can be read — oh, may it not be obscured! — in the golden inscription above the gilded doors which we have caused to be made in honor of God and the Saints:

The year was the One Thousand, One Hundred, and Fortieth Year of the Word when [this structure] was consecrated.

After the consecration of the Chapel of St. Romanus and others which, with the help of the Highest Majesty, had been celebrated in the front part [of the church], our devotion — so much invigorated by its own success, and so long and intolerably distressed by that congestion around the Holy of Holies — directed our intentions toward another goal: free from the aforesaid work, and through postponing the completion of the towers in their upper portions, we would strive with all our might to devote labor and expense, as fittingly and nobly as it could reasonably be done, to the enlargement of the church our mother — as an act of gratitude because Divine condescension had reserved so great a work to so small a man who was the successor to the nobility of such great kings and abbots. We communicated this plan to our very devoted brethren, *whose hearts burned for Jesus while He talked with them by the way.*[6] Deliberating under God's inspiration, we choose — in view of that blessing which, by the testimony of venerable writings, Divine action had bestowed upon the ancient consecration of the church by the extension of [Christ's] own hand — to respect the very stones, sacred as they are, as though they were relics; [and] to endeavor to ennoble the new addition, which was to be begun under the pressure of so great a need, with the beauty of length and width. Upon consideration, then, it was decided to remove that vault, unequal to the higher one, which, overhead, closed the apse containing the bodies of our Patron Saints, all the way [down] to the upper surface of the crypt to which it adhered; so that this crypt might offer its top as a pavement to those approaching by either of the two stairs, and might present the chasses of the Saints, adorned with gold and precious gems, to the visitors' glances in a more elevated place. Moreover, it was cunningly provided that — through the upper columns and central arches which were to be placed upon the lower ones built in the crypt — the central nave of the old nave should be equalized, by means of geometrical and arithmetical instruments, with the central nave of the new addition; and, likewise, that the dimensions of the old side-aisles should be equalized with the dimensions of the new side-aisles, except for that elegant and praiseworthy extension, in [the form of] a circular string of chapels, by virtue of which the whole [church] would shine with the wonderful and uninterrupted light of most sacred windows, pervading the interior beauty.

Thus, when, with wise counsel and under the dictation of the Holy Ghost Whose unction instructs us in all things, that which we proposed to carry out had been designed with perspicuous order, we brought together an assembly of illustrious men, both bishops and abbots, and also requested the presence of our Lord, the Most Serene King of the Franks, Louis.[7] On Sunday, the day before the Ides of July, we arranged a procession beautiful by its ornaments and notable by its personages. Carrying before ourselves, in the hands of the bishops and the abbots, the insignia of Our Lord's Passion, viz., the Nail and the Crown of the Lord, also the arm of the aged St. Simeon and the tutelage of other holy relics, we descended with humble devotion to the excavations made ready for the foundations. Then, when the consolation of the Comforter, the Holy Spirit, had been invoked so that He might crown the good beginning of the house of God with a good end, the bishops — having prepared, with their own hands, the mortar with the blessed water from the dedication of the previous fifth day before the Ides of June — laid the first stones, singing a hymn to God and solemnly chanting the *Fundamenta ejus*[8] to the end of the Psalm. The Most Serene King himself stepped down [into the excavation] and with his own hands laid his [stone]. Also we and many others, both abbots and monks, laid their stones. Certain persons also [deposited] gems out of love and reverence for Jesus Christ, chanting: *Lapides preciosi omnes muri tui.*[9] We, however, exhilarated by so great and so festive a laying of so holy a foundation, but anxious for what was still to be done and fearful of the changes of time, the diminution of persons and my own passing away, ordained in a common council of the brethren, at the advice of those present and by the consent of our Lord the King, an annual revenue for completing this work; namely, one hundred and fifty pounds from the treasury, that is, from the offerings at the altars and at the Relics; one hundred [from the offerings] at the Fair, and fifty [from the offerings] at the Feast of Saint Denis. In addition, fifty from the possession called Villaine in the district of Beauce, previously uncultivated but with the help of God and by our labors brought under cultivation and developed to an annual revenue of eighty or a hundred pounds. If, through any mischance, this possession should fall short of its full contribution, our other [possessions in] Beauce, the revenue of which we had doubled or trebled, would supply the balance. And we decreed that these two hundred pounds, in addition to anything which will be brought to the collection box through the devotion of the faithful or might be offered specifically for the two structures, be applied to the continuation of these works until, without any question, these edifices, the front part as well as the upper choir, will be entirely and honorably completed throughout, including their towers.

v] For three years we pressed the completion of the work at great expense, with a numerous crowd of workmen, summer and winter, lest God have just cause to complain of us: *Thine eyes did see my substance yet being unperfect;*[10] we made good progress with His own cooperation and, in the likeness of the things Divine, there was established to *the joy of the whole earth mount Zion, on the sides of the north, the city of the Great King,*[11] in the *midst* of which *God will not be moved,*[12] but will not disdain, *moved* by the entreaties of the sinners, to be placated and propitiated by the sweet-smelling burnt offerings of the penitent. The *midst* of the edifice, however, was suddenly raised aloft by columns representing the number of the Twelve Apostles and, secondarily, by as many columns in the side-aisles signifying the number of the [minor] Prophets, according to the Apostle who buildeth spiritually. *Now therefore ye are no more strangers and foreigners*, says he, *but fellow citizens with the saints and of the household of God; and are built upon the foundation of the apostles and prophets, Jesus Christ Himself being the chief cornerstone* which joins one wall to the other; *in Whom all the building* — whether spiritual or material — *groweth unto one holy temple in the Lord. In Whom we, too,* are taught *to be builded together for an habitation of God through the* Holy *Spirit*[13] by ourselves in a spiritual way, the more loftily and fitly we strive to build in a material way.

Meanwhile — chiefly solicitous for the translation of our Patron Saints the most Holy Martyrs and also of the other saints who, scattered about the church, were worshiped in the different chapels — we felt devoutly moved to embellish their most sacred chasses, especially those of the Patrons; and selecting [a place] to which they might be transferred [so as to present themselves] to the visitors' glances in more glorious and conspicuous manner, we endeavored, God helping, to build [a tomb] very illustrious both by the exquisite industry of the goldsmiths' art and by a wealth of gold and precious stones. We made preparations to fortify it all round, outwardly noble for ornament by virtue of these and similar [precious materials], yet inwardly not ignoble for safety by virtue of a masonry of very strong stones; and on the exterior — lest the place be disfigured by the substance of unconcealed stones — to adorn it (yet not [so handsomely] as would be proper) with gilded panels of cast copper. For the generosity of so great Fathers, experienced by ourselves and all, demands that we, most miserable men who feel as well as need their tutelage, should deem it worth our effort to cover the most sacred ashes of those whose venerable spirits, radiant as the sun, attend upon Almighty God with the most precious material we possibly can: with refined gold and a profusion of hyacinths, emeralds and other precious stones. One thing, however, we did choose to have done resplendently: we would erect in front of the most honored bodies of the Saints what had never been there before — an altar for the sacrificial worship of God, where popes and persons of high rank might worthily offer the propitiatory Hosts, acceptable to God, with the intercession of those who offered themselves to God as a fragrant burnt offering. While we, overcome by timidity, had planned to set up in front of

this [altar] a panel golden but modest, the Holy Martyrs themselves handed to us such a wealth of gold and most precious gems —
unexpected and hardly to be found among kings — as though they
were telling us with their own lips: "Whether thou wantst it or
not, we want it of the best"; so that we would neither have dared,
nor have been able to, make it other than admirable and very
precious in workmanship as well as material. For not only did the
very pontiffs — who wear them especially on account of the dignity
of their office — consent, if they were present, to assign their pontifical rings, set with a wonderful variety of precious stones, to this
panel; they even, if they were absent in lands overseas, sent them
of their own accord, incited by the love of the Holy Martyrs. Also the
illustrious King himself, offering of his own accord emeralds, pellu-
cid and distinguished by markings — Count Thibaut, hyacinths and
rubies — peers and princes, precious pearls of diverse colors and
properties: [all these] invited us to complete the work in glorious
fashion. In addition, so many [gems and pearls] were brought to us
for sale from nearly all the parts of the world (and, by the grace of
God, we were also offered wherewith to buy them) that we should
have been unable to let them go without great shame and offense
to the Saints. Here and elsewhere we could find by experience: let
there be a good work in the will — then, with the aid of God, will
it be in perfection. Thus, should anyone presume to take away with
rash temerity, or knowingly to diminish, this ornament presented
by the devotion of such great men to such great Protectors: may
he deserve the wrath of our Lord Denis and to be pierced by the
sword of the Holy Ghost.

Nor do we think it proper to be silent in regard to the following
fact: when the work on the new addition with its capitals and upper
arches was being carried forward to the peak of its height, but the
main arches — standing by themselves — were not yet held together,
as it were, by the bulk of the vaults, there suddenly arose a
terrible and almost unbearable storm with an obfuscation of clouds,
an inundation of rain, and a most violent rush of wind. So mighty
did this [storm] become that it blew down, not only well-built
houses but even stone towers and wooden bulwarks. At this time,
on a certain day (the anniversary of the glorious King Dagobert),
when the venerable Bishop of Chartres, Geoffroy, was solemnly
celebrating at the main altar a conventual Mass for the former's

soul, such a force of contrary gales hurled itself against the aforesaid arches, not supported by any scaffolding nor resting on any
props, that they threatened baneful ruin at any moment, miserably trembling and, as it were, swaying hither and thither. The
Bishop, alarmed by the strong vibration of these [arches] and the
roofing, frequently extended his blessing hand in the direction of
that part and urgently held out toward it, while making the sign
of the cross, the arm of the aged St. Simeon; so that he escaped
disaster, manifestly not through his own strength of mind but
by the grace of God and the merit of the Saints. Thus [the tem-
pest], while it brought calamitous ruin in many places to buildings
thought to be firm, was unable to damage these isolated and newly
made arches, tottering in mid-air, because it was repulsed by the
power of God.

There followed another memorable event which happened, not
by accident (as is believed of such matters by those agreeing with
that doctrine according to which

> *Chance wanders aimlessly,*
> *Brings and brings back events; and Accident*
> *rules all that is mortal),*[14]

but by Divine Generosity Which abundantly provides for those who
place their hope in It in all things great and small, and administers
what It knows to be beneficial. On a certain day we conferred with
our friends, servants and stewards about the provisions for the
court [to be held on the occasion] of the imminent consecration, because we anticipated it would be very great; and, considering the
difficulty of the times (for in June almost all victuals were scarce),
we had fairly well provided for all other things. Only one thing
worried us grievously: because of a plague among the sheep born
in that year we would have to search for mutton in the district
of Orléans and toward Burgundy. I had reluctantly ordered to
give 1,000 shillings, or whatever was necessary, to those who would
go there for this purpose, lest they should take too long in returning inasmuch as they had started so late. But on the following
morning, when I, according to custom, hurried from our little
chamber to the celebration of Holy Mass, a Premonstratensian
monk suddenly drew me back to my room in spite of my protests.
When I — a little irritated because he detained me from so great

a task — had answered him without too much civility, he said: "We have heard, Lord Father, that you need mutton for the impending celebration of your consecration; therefore, sent by our brethren, I bring to your Paternal Grace a very great flock of rams so that you may keep what you like and send us back what you do not like." When we had heard this we requested him to wait for us until after Mass, and after Mass we informed our brethren in his presence of what he had offered to us. They ascribed this to Divine Generosity because It had unexpectedly furnished, through the pious brethren's bringing it hither, the only thing which we were lacking and should have found tiresome to search for.

VI] Now the laborious consummation of the work and our own suspended devotion, which had been panting for this a long time, demanded the consecration of the new church. And since we fervently wished this consecration as well as the translation of our Patron Saints to be a most solemn event — as an act of gratitude, as it were, and as a most welcome fruit of our labors — we fixed, upon deliberation and with the gracious consent of his Royal Majesty Louis the Most Serene King of the Franks[15] (for he ardently wished to see the Holy Martyrs, his protectors), the date of the ceremony for the second Sunday in June, that is to say the third day before the Ides, the day of the Apostle Barnabas.

We sent invitations by many messengers, also by couriers and envoys, through almost all the districts of Gaul and urgently requested the archbishops and bishops, in the name of the Saints and as a debt to their apostolate, to be present at so great a solemnity. Numerous and different ones of these [we welcomed] joyfully to this celebration; more joyfully we would have welcomed all of them had that been possible. Our Lord King Louis himself and his spouse Queen Eleanor, as well as his mother, and the peers of the realm arrived on the third day. Of the diverse counts and nobles from many regions and dominions, of the ordinary troops of knights and soldiers there is no count. But of the archbishops and bishops who were present the names are placed on record as follows: Samson, Archbishop of Reims; Hugues, Archbishop of Rouen; Guy, Archbishop of Sens; Theobald, Archbishop of Canterbury; Geoffroy, Bishop of Chartres; Jocelin, Bishop of Soissons; Simon, Bishop of Noyon; Elias, Bishop of Orléans; Eudes, Bishop of Beauvais; Hugues, Bishop of Auxerre; Alvise, Bishop of Arras; Guy, Bishop of Châlons;

Algare, Bishop of Coutances; Rotrou, Bishop of Evreux; Milon, Bishop of Térouanne; Manasseh, Bishop of Meaux; Peter, Bishop of Senlis. Since all of these had come to so noble a ceremony and so great a spectacle in state, in their capacity of higher dignitaries of their church, their outward apparel and attire indicated the inward intention of their mind and body. We, however, were not so much [intent upon] external matters (for these we had already ordained to be provided in affluence without argument), but on the preceding Saturday took the bodies of the saints out of their chapels and, according to custom, placed them most honorably in draped tents at the exit of the [monks'] choir. Devoutly looking forward to so great a joy, we prepared the sacramental implements for the consecration and made arrangements by which the eager and so sacred procession of so many persons might smoothly wend its way throughout the church, within and without. Then, when we had humbly asked the glorious and most humble Louis, King of the Franks, to keep away, through his peers and nobles, the impeding crowd from the procession itself, he answered, more humbly by far, that he would gladly do this in person as well as through his retinue.

Spending the whole preceding night in reading the office of Matins in praise of God, we devoutly implored our Lord Jesus Christ Who was made the Propitiator for our sins that, for His own honor and for love of His Saints, He might deign mercifully to visit the holy place and to participate in the holy ceremonies, not only potentially but also in person. In the early morning, then, the archbishops and bishops came with the archdeacons, abbots and other honorable persons from their respective guest-quarters to the church, arranged themselves in episcopal manner, and very solemnly, very venerably assumed, for the consecration with the [holy] water, their places near the vat, [namely,] in the upper choir between the tombs of the Martyrs and the altar of the Saviour. You might have seen — and those present did see not without great devotion — how so great a chorus of such great pontiffs, decorous in white vestments, splendidly arrayed in pontifical miters and precious orphreys embellished by circular ornaments, held the crosiers in their hands, walked round and round the vessel and invoked the name of God by way of exorcism; how so glorious and admirable men celebrated the wedding of the Eternal Bridegroom so piously that the King and the attending nobility believed themselves to behold a chorus celestial rather than terrestrial, a ceremony divine rather than human. The populace milled around outside with the drive of its intolerable magnitude; and when the aforesaid chorus sprinkled the holy water onto the exterior, competently aspersing the walls of the church with the aspergillum, the King himself and his officials kept back the tumultuous impact and protected those returning to the doors with canes and sticks.

B   *Gervase of Canterbury*, Tractatus de Combustione et Reparatione Doroborniensis Ecclesiae (*"Tract on the Burning and Repair of the Church of Canterbury"*)

1] *The Conflagration*

IN the year of grace one thousand one hundred and seventy-four, by the just but occult judgment of God, the church of Christ at Canterbury was consumed by fire, in the forty-fourth year from its dedication,[1] that glorious choir, to wit, which had been so magnificently completed by the care and industry of Prior Conrad.

Now the manner of the burning and repair was as follows. [A.D. 1174. Sep. 5 between 3 and 4 P.M.] In the aforesaid year, on the nones of September, at about the ninth hour, and during an extraordinarily violent south wind, a fire broke out before the gate of the church, and outside the walls of the monastery, by which three cottages were half destroyed. From thence, while the citizens were assembling and subduing the fire, cinders and sparks carried aloft by the high wind, were deposited upon the church, and being driven by the fury of the wind between the joints of the lead, remained there amongst the half rotten planks, and shortly glowing with increasing heat, set fire to the rotten rafters; from these the fire was communicated to the larger beams and their braces, no one yet

From R. *Willis*, THE ARCHITECTURAL HISTORY OF CANTERBURY CATHE-DRAL (London, 1845), pp. 32–62.

perceiving or helping. For the well-painted ceiling below, and the sheet-lead covering above, concealed between them the fire that had arisen within.

Meantime the three cottages, whence the mischief had arisen, being destroyed, and the popular excitement having subsided, everybody went home again, while the neglected church was consuming with internal fire unknown to all. But beams and braces burning, the flames rose to the slopes of the roof; and the sheets of lead yielded to the increasing heat and began to melt. Thus the raging wind, finding a freer entrance, increased the fury of the fire; and the flames beginning to shew themselves, a cry arose in the church-yard: "See! see! the church is on fire."

Then the people and the monks assemble in haste, they draw water, they brandish their hatchets, they run up the stairs, full of eagerness to save the church, already, alas! beyond their help. But when they reach the roof and perceive the black smoke and scorching flames that pervade it throughout, they abandon the attempt in despair, and thinking only of their own safety, make all haste to descend.

And now that the fire had loosened the beams from the pegs that bound them together, the half-burnt timbers fell into the choir below upon the seats of the monks; the seats, consisting of a great mass of wood-work, caught fire, and thus the mischief grew worse and worse. And it was marvellous, though sad, to behold how that glorious choir itself fed and assisted the fire that was destroying it. For the flames multiplied by this mass of timber, and extending upwards full fifteen cubits,[2] scorched and burnt the walls, and more especially injured the columns of the church.

And now the people ran to the ornaments of the church, and began to tear down the pallia and curtains, some that they might save, but some to steal them. The reliquary chests were thrown down from the high beam and thus broken, and their contents scattered; but the monks collected them and carefully preserved them from the fire. Some there were, who, inflamed with a wicked and diabolical cupidity, feared not to appropriate to themselves the things of the church, which they had saved from the fire.

In this manner the house of God, hitherto delightful as a paradise of pleasures, was now made a despicable heap of ashes, reduced to a dreary wilderness, and laid open to all the injuries of the weather.

The people were astonished that the Almighty should suffer such things, and maddened with excess of grief and perplexity, they tore their hair and beat the walls and pavement of the church with their heads and hands, blaspheming the Lord and His saints, the patrons of the church; and many, both of laity and monks, would rather have laid down their lives than that the church should have so miserably perished.

For not only was the choir consumed in the fire, but also the infirmary, with the chapel of St. Mary, and several other offices in the court; moreover many ornaments and goods of the church were reduced to ashes.

2] *The Operations of the first year*

Bethink thee now what mighty grief oppressed the hearts of the sons of the Church under this great tribulation; I verily believe the afflictions of Canterbury were no less than those of Jerusalem of old, and their wailings were as the lamentations of Jeremiah; neither can mind conceive, or words express, or writing teach, their grief and anguish. Truly that they might alleviate their miseries with a little consolation, they put together as well as they could, an altar and station in the nave of the church, where they might wail and howl, rather than sing, the diurnal and nocturnal services. Meanwhile the patron saints of the church, St. Dunstan and St. Elfege, had their resting-place in that wilderness. Lest, therefore, they should suffer even the slightest injury from the rains and storms, the monks, weeping and lamenting with incredible grief and anguish, opened the tombs of the saints and extricated them in their coffins from the choir, but with the greatest difficulty and labour, as if the saints themselves resisted the change.

They disposed them as decently as they could at the altar of the Holy Cross in the nave. Thus, like as the children of Israel were ejected from the land of promise, yea, even from a paradise of delight, that it might be like people, like priest, and that the stones of the sanctuary might be poured out at the corners of the streets; so the brethren remained in grief and sorrow for five years in the nave of the church, separated from the people only by a low wall.

Meantime the brotherhood sought counsel as to how and in what manner the burnt church might be repaired, but without success; for the columns of the church, commonly termed the *pillars,* were exceedingly weakened by the heat of the fire, and were scaling in pieces and hardly able to stand, so that they frightened even the wisest out of their wits.

French and English artificers were therefore summoned, but even these differed in opinion. On the one hand, some undertook to repair the aforesaid columns without mischief to the walls above. On the other hand, there were some who asserted that the whole church must be pulled down if the monks wished to exist in safety. This opinion, true as it was, excruciated the monks with grief, and no wonder, for how could they hope that so great a work should be completed in their days by any human ingenuity.

However, amongst the other workmen there had come a certain William of Sens, a man active and ready, and as a workman most skilful both in wood and stone. Him, therefore, they retained, on account of his lively genius and good reputation, and dismissed the others. And to him, and to the providence of God was the execution of the work committed.

And he, residing many days with the monks and carefully surveying the burnt walls in their upper and lower parts, within and without, did yet for some time conceal what he found necessary to be done, lest the truth should kill them in their present state of pusillanimity.

But he went on preparing all things that were needful for the work, either of himself or by the agency of others. And when he found that the monks began to be somewhat comforted, he ventured to confess that the pillars rent with the fire and all that they supported must be destroyed if the monks wished to have a safe and excellent building. At length they agreed, being convinced by reason and wishing to have the work as good as he promised, and above all things to live in security; thus they consented patiently, if not willingly, to the destruction of the choir.

And now he addressed himself to the procuring of stone from beyond sea. He constructed ingenious machines for loading and unloading ships, and for drawing cement and stones. He delivered molds for shaping the stones to the sculptors who were assembled, and diligently prepared other things of the same kind. The choir thus condemned to destruction was pulled down, and nothing else was done in this year.

And now the description, as concise as I could make it, of the church which we are going to pull down, has brought us to the tomb of the martyr, which was at the end of the church; let therefore the church and the description come to an end together; for although this description has already extended itself to a greater length than was proposed, yet many things have been carefully omitted for the sake of brevity. Who could write all the turnings, and windings, and appendages of such and so great a church as this was? Leaving out, therefore, all that is not absolutely necessary, let us boldly prepare for the destruction of this old work and the marvellous building of the new, and let us see what our master William has been doing in the meanwhile.

5] *Operations of the first five years*

Sep. 6, 1174, to Sep. 5, 1175] The Master began, as I stated long ago, to prepare all things necessary for the new work, and to destroy the old. In this way the first year was taken up. In the following year, that is, after the feast of St. Bertin (Sep. 5, 1175), before the winter, he erected four pillars, that is, two on each side, and A.D. 1176] after the winter two more were placed, so that on each side were three in order, upon which and upon the exterior wall of the aisles he framed seemly arches and a vault, that is, three *claves*[3] on each side. I put *clavis* for the whole *ciborium*[4] because the *clavis* placed in the middle locks up and binds together the parts which converge to it from every side. With these works the second year was occupied.

A.D. 1176–77] In the third year he placed two pillars on each side, the two extreme ones of which he decorated with marble columns placed around them, and because at that place the choir and crosses were to meet, he constituted these principal pillars. To which, having added the key-stones and vault, he intermingled the lower triforium from the great tower to the aforesaid pillars, that is, as far as the cross, with many marble columns. Over which he adjusted another triforium of other materials, and also the upper windows. And in the next place, three *claves* of the great vault, from the tower, namely, as far as the crosses. All which things appeared to us and to all who saw them, incomparable and most worthy of praise. And at so glorious a beginning we rejoiced and conceived good hopes of the end, and provided for the acceleration of the work with diligence and spirit. Thus was the third year occupied and the beginning of the fourth.

A.D. 1178] In the summer of which, commencing from the cross, he erected ten pillars, that is, on each side five. Of which the two first were ornamented with marble columns to correspond with the other two principal ones. Upon these ten he placed the arches and vaults. And having, in the next place, completed on both sides the triforia and upper windows, he was, at the beginning of the fifth year, in the act of preparing with machines for the turning of the great vault, when suddenly the beams broke under his feet, and he fell to the ground, stones and timbers accompanying his fall, from the height of the capitals of the upper vault, that is to say, of fifty feet. Thus sorely bruised by the blows from the beams and stones, he was rendered helpless alike to himself and for the work, but no other person than himself was in the least injured. Against the master only was this vengeance of God or spite of the devil directed.

The master, thus hurt, remained in his bed for some time under medical care in expectation of recovering, but was deceived in this hope, for his health amended not. Nevertheless, as the winter approached, and it was necessary to finish the upper vault, he gave charge of the work to a certain ingenious and industrious monk, who was the overseer of the masons; an appointment whence much envy and malice arose, because it made this young man appear more skilful than richer and more powerful ones. But the master reclining in bed commanded all things that should be done in order. And thus was completed the ciborium between the four principal pillars. In the key-stone of this ciborium the choir and crosses seem as it were to meet. Two ciboria on each side were formed before the winter; when heavy rains beginning stopped the work. In these operations the fourth year was occupied and the beginning of the fifth. But on the eighth day from the said fourth year, on the idus of September, there happened an eclipse of the sun at about the sixth hour, and before the master's accident.

And the master, perceiving that he derived no benefit from the physicians, gave up the work, and crossing the sea, returned to his home in France. And another succeeded him in the charge of the works; William by name, English by nation, small in body, but in workmanship of many kinds acute and honest. [A.D. 1179] He in the summer of the fifth year finished the cross on each side, that is, the south and the north, and turned the ciborium which is above the great Altar, which the rains of the previous year had hindered, although all was prepared. Moreover, he laid the foundation for the enlargement of the church at the eastern part, because a chapel of St. Thomas[5] was to be built there.

For this was the place assigned to him; namely, the chapel of the Holy Trinity, where he celebrated his first mass, where he was wont to prostrate himself with tears and prayers, under whose crypt for so many years he was buried, where God for his merits had performed so many miracles, where poor and rich, kings and princes, had worshipped him, and whence the sound of his praises had gone forth into all lands.

The master William began, on account of these foundations, to dig in the cemetery of the monks, from whence he was compelled to disturb the bones of many holy monks. These were carefully collected and deposited in a large trench, in that corner which is between the chapel and the south side of the infirmary house. Having, therefore, formed a most substantial foundation for the exterior wall with stone and cement, he erected the wall of the crypt as high as the bases of the windows.

Thus was the fifth year employed and the beginning of the sixth.

6] *The entry into the new Choir*

A.D. 1180] In the beginning of the sixth year from the fire, and at the time when the works were resumed, the monks were seized with a violent longing to prepare the choir, so that they might enter it at the coming Easter. And the master, perceiving their desires, set himself manfully to work, to satisfy the wishes of the convent. He constructed, with all diligence, the wall which encloses the choir and presbytery. He erected the three altars of the presbytery. He carefully prepared a resting-place for St. Dunstan and St. Elfege. A wooden wall to keep out the weather was set up transversely between the penultimate pillars[6] at the eastern part, and had three glass windows in it.

The choir, thus hardly completed even with the greatest labour and diligence, the monks were resolved to enter on Easter Eve with the new fire.[7] As all that was required could not be fully performed on the Saturday because of the solemnities of that sacred day, it became necessary that our holy fathers and patrons, St. Dunstan and St. Elfege, the co-exiles of the monks, should be transferred to the new choir beforehand. Prior Alan, therefore, taking with him nine of the brethren of the church in whom he could trust, went by night to the tombs of the saints, that he might not be incommoded by a crowd, and having locked the doors of the church, he commanded the stone-work that enclosed them to be taken down.

The monks and servants of the church, therefore, in obedience to the Prior's commands, took the structure to pieces, opened the stone coffins of the saints, and bore their relics to the *vestiarium*. Then, having removed the cloths in which they had been wrapped, and which were half consumed from age and rottenness, they covered them with other and more handsome palls, and bound them with linen bands. They bore the saints, thus prepared, to their altars, and deposited them in wooden chests, covered within and without with lead; which chests, thus lead-covered, and strongly bound with iron, were enclosed in stone-work that was consolidated with melted lead. Queen Ediva also, who had been placed under the altar of the holy cross after the fire, was similarly conveyed to the vestiarium.

Wednesday night, Ap. 16] These things were done on the night preceding the fifth feria before the holy Easter; that is, on the sixteenth calend of May. On the morrow, however, when this translation of the saints became known to the whole convent, they were exceedingly astonished and indignant that it should have been done without their consent, for they had intended that the translation of the fathers should have been performed with great and devout solemnity.

They cited the prior and those who were with him, before the venerable Archbishop Richard, to answer for the slight thus presumptuously cast upon themselves and the holy patrons of the church, and endeavoured to compel the prior and his assistants to renounce their offices. But by the intervention of the archbishop and other men of authority, and after due apology and repentance, the convent was appeased; and harmony being thus restored, the service of Holy Saturday was performed in the chapter-house, because the station of the monks and the altar which had been in the nave of the church, were removed to prepare for the solemnities of the following Easter Sunday. About the sixth hour the archbishop in cope and mitre, and the convent in albs, according to the custom of the church, went in procession to the new fire, and having consecrated it, proceeded towards the new choir with the appointed hymn. At the door of the church which opens to the martyrium of St. Thomas, the archbishop reverently received from a monk the pix,[8] with the Eucharist, which was usually suspended over the great Altar. This he carried to the great Altar of the new choir. Thus our Lord went before us into Galilee, that is, in our transmigration to the new church. The remainder of the offices that appertain to the day were devoutly celebrated. And then the pontiff, standing at the Altar and vested with the infula, began the Te Deum laudamus; and the bells ringing, the convent took up the song with great joy, and shedding sweet tears, they praised God with voice and heart for all His benefits.

The convent was ejected by the fire from the choir, even as Adam from paradise, in the year of the Word 1174, in the month of September, on the fifth day of the month, and about the ninth hour. They remained in the nave of the church five years, seven months, and thirteen days. And returned into the new choir in the year of grace 1180, in the month of April, on the nineteenth day of the month, at about the ninth hour of Easter Eve.

7] *Remaining operations of the sixth year*

A.D. 1180] Our craftsman had erected outside the choir four altars, where the bodies of the holy archbishops were deposited, as they were of old, and as we have above described. At the altar of St. Martin; Living, and Wilfrid. At the altar of St. Stephen; Athelard, and Cuthbert. In the south cross at the altar of St. John; Elfric, and Ethelgar. At the altar of St. Gregory; Bregwin, and Plegemund. But Queen Ediva, who before the fire reposed under a gilded *feretrum*[9] in nearly the middle of the south cross, was now deposited at the altar of St. Martin, under the *feretrum* of Living.

Moreover, in the same summer, that is of the sixth year, the outer wall round the chapel of St. Thomas, begun before the winter, was elevated as far as the turning of the vault. But the master had begun a tower at the eastern part outside the circuit of the wall as it were, the lower vault of which was completed before the winter.

The chapel of the Holy Trinity above mentioned was then levelled to the ground; this had hitherto remained untouched out of reverence to St. Thomas, who was buried in the crypt. But the saints who reposed in the upper part of the chapel were translated elsewhere, and lest the memory of what was then done should be lost, I will record somewhat thereof. On the eighth idus of July the altar of the Holy Trinity was broken up, and from its materials the altar of St. John the Apostle was made; I mention this lest the history of the holy stone should be lost upon which St. Thomas celebrated his first mass, and many times after performed the divine offices. The stone structure which was behind this altar was taken to pieces. Here, as before said, St. Odo and St. Wilfrid reposed for a long period. These saints were raised in their leaden coffins (*capsis plumbeis*) and carried into the choir. St. Odo, in his coffin, was placed under the feretrum of St. Dunstan, and St. Wilfrid under the feretrum of St. Elfege.

Archbishop Lanfranc was found enclosed in a very heavy sheet of lead, in which, from the day of his first burial up to that day, he had rested untouched, in mitre and pall, for sixty-nine years and some months. He was carried to the vestiarium in his leaden covering, and there deposited until the community should decide what should be done with so great a Father. When they opened the tomb of Archbishop Theodbald, which was built of marble slabs, and came to his sarcophagus, the monks who were present expecting to find his body reduced to dust, brought wine and water to wash his bones. But when the lid of the sarcophagus was raised, he was found entire and rigid, and still subsisting in bones and nerves, skin and flesh, but somewhat attenuated. The bystanders marvelled at this sight, and placing him upon a bier (*tabulam gestatoriam*), they carried him as they had done Lanfranc, to the vestiarium, to await the decision of the convent. But the rumour began to spread among the people, and already, for this unwonted incorruption, many called him St. Theodbald. He was exhibited to some who desired to see him, and they helped to spread the tale among the rest.

He was thus raised from his sepulchre in the nineteenth year from his death, his body being incorrupted, and his silk vestments entire. And by the decision of the convent was buried in a leaden coffin (*in arca plumbea*) before the altar of St. Mary, in the nave of the church, which place he had wished for while living. The marble tomb was put together over him, as it was before. But Lanfranc having remained, as before said, untouched for sixty-nine years, his very bones were consumed with rottenness, and nearly all reduced to powder. The length of time, the damp vestments, the natural frigidity of the lead, and above all, the frailty of the human structure, had conspired to produce this corruption. But the larger bones, with the remaining dust, were collected in a leaden coffer (*in capsa plumbea*) and deposited at the altar of St. Martin. The two archbishops who lay to the right and left of St. Thomas in the crypt were taken up, and placed for the time in their leaden coffins (*capsis*) under the altar of St. Mary, in the crypt.

The translation of these Fathers having been thus effected, the chapel, together with its crypt, was destroyed to the very ground; only that the translation of St. Thomas was reserved until the completion of his chapel. For it was fitting and manifest that such a translation should be most solemn and public. In the mean time, therefore, a wooden chapel, sufficiently decent for the place and occasion, was prepared around and above his tomb. Outside of this a foundation was laid of stones and cement, upon which eight pillars of the new crypt, with their capitals, were completed. The master also carefully opened an entrance from the old to the new crypt. And thus the sixth year was employed, and part of the seventh. But before I follow the works of this seventh year, it may not be amiss to recapitulate some of the previous ones which have either been omitted from negligence or purposely for the sake of brevity.

8] *Explanations*

It has been above stated, that after the fire nearly all the old portions of the choir were destroyed and changed into somewhat new and of a more noble fashion. The differences between the two works may now be enumerated. The pillars of the old and new work are alike in form and thickness but different in length. For the new pillars were elongated by almost twelve feet. In the old capitals the work was plain, in the new ones exquisite in sculpture. There the circuit of the choir had twenty-two pillars, here are twenty-eight. There the arches and every thing else was plain, or sculptured with an axe and not with a chisel. But here almost throughout is appropriate sculpture. No marble columns were there, but here are innumerable ones. There, in the circuit around the choir, the vaults were plain, but here they are arch-ribbed and have keystones. There a wall set upon pillars divided the crosses from the choir, but here the crosses are separated from the choir by no such partition, and converge together in one keystone, which is placed in the middle of the great vault which rests on the four principal pillars. There, there was a ceiling of wood decorated with excellent painting, but here is a vault beautifully constructed of stone and light tufa. There, was a single triforium, but here are two in the choir and a third in the aisle of the church. All which will be better understood from inspection than by any description.

This must be made known, however, that the new work is higher than the old by so much as the upper windows of the body of the choir, as well as of its aisles, are raised above the marble tabling.

And as in future ages it may be doubtful why the breadth which was given to the choir next the tower should be so much contracted at the head of the church, it may not be useless to explain the causes thereof. One reason is, that the two towers of St. Anselm and of St. Andrew, placed in the circuit on each side of the old church, would not allow the breadth of the choir to proceed in the direct line. Another reason is, that it was agreed upon and necessary that the chapel of St. Thomas should be erected at the head of the church, where the chapel of the Holy Trinity stood, and this was much narrower than the choir.

The master, therefore, not choosing to pull down the said towers, and being unable to move them entire, set out the breadth of the choir in a straight line, as far as the beginning of the towers. Then, receding slightly on either side from the towers, and preserving as much as he could the breadth of the passage outside the choir on account of the processions which were there frequently passing, he gradually and obliquely drew in his work, so that from opposite the altar, it might begin to contract, and from thence, at the third pillar, might be so narrowed as to coincide with the breadth of the chapel, which was named of the Holy Trinity. Beyond these, four pillars were set on the sides at the same distance as the last, but of a different form; and beyond these other four were arranged in a circle, and upon these the superposed work (of each side) was brought together and terminated. This is the arrangement of the pillars.

The outer wall, which extends from the aforesaid towers, first proceeds in a straight line, is then bent into a curve, and thus in the round tower the wall on each side comes together in one, and is there ended. All of which may be more clearly and pleasantly seen by the eyes than taught in writing. But this much was said that the differences between the old and new work might be made manifest.

9] *Operations of the seventh, eighth, and tenth years*

A.D. 1181] Now let us carefully examine what were the works of our mason in this seventh year from the fire, which, in short, included the completion of the new and handsome crypt,[10] and above the crypt the exterior walls of the aisles up to their marble capitals. The windows, however, the master was neither willing nor able to turn, on account of the approaching rains. Neither did he erect the interior pillars. Thus was the seventh year finished, and the eighth begun. A.D. 1182] In this eighth year the master erected eight interior pillars and turned the arches and the vault with the windows in the circuit. He also raised the tower up to the bases of the highest windows under the vault. [A.D. 1183] In the ninth year no work was done for want of funds. [A.D. 1184] In the tenth year the upper windows of the tower, together with the vault, were finished. Upon the pillars was placed a lower and an upper triforium, with windows and the great vault. Also was made the upper roof where the cross stands aloft, and the roof of the aisles as far as the laying of the lead. The tower was covered in, and many other things done this year. In which year Baldwin bishop of Worcester was elected to the rule of the church of Canterbury on the eighteenth kalend of January, and was enthroned there on the feast of St. Dunstan next after. . . .

Here endeth Gervase his history of the burning and repair of the Church of Canterbury

NOTES

Selection a

1. Dagobert, the last strong Merovingian king, ruled from 623 to 639.
2. Galatians, i. 15.
3. I Corinthians, iii. 11.
4. II Corinthians, iii. 5.
5. See Book of Wisdom, xi. 21.
6. Luke, xxiv. 32.

7. King Louis VII (1137–1180).

8. Psalms, lxxxvi. This phrase reads: The foundations thereof [are in the holy mountains] (from Douai version of the Bible).

9. From the *Roman Breviary, Commune Dedicationis Ecclesiae.* This phrase reads: All thy walls are precious stones.

10. Psalms, cxxxviii. 16.

11. Psalms, xlvii. 3.

12. Psalms, xlv. 6.

13. Ephesians, ii. 19–22.

14. Lucan, *Pharsalia,* II. 13.

15. Louis VII, king of France (1137–1180).

Selection b

1. This would be 1130.

2. About 25 feet.

3. The *claves* are the bosses of a ribbed vault.

4. The *ciborium* is the canopy of the high altar and is here compared to a compartment of a vault because it also is supported by four pillars.

5. A reference to St. Thomas Becket.

6. The ninth row of pillars.

7. A reference to lighting of the Easter candle, which was lighted on Easter eve and allowed to burn until Ascension Day.

8. The vessel in which the Host is reserved.

9. A bier or shrine for the bones of a saint.

10. The crypt of St. Thomas's chapel.

15

Two Medieval Kings

THE fortune of the medieval state depended almost solely upon the central figure — the ruler. If he was a valiant and successful warrior who protected his subjects, established peace and security within his realm, and respected the church, he was hailed by chronicler and biographer as a "good" king. Rulers who did not meet these medieval standards were judged to be "bad" kings. Although a king's reputation rested somewhat upon biographers whose judgments were based upon a variety of considerations, including whether or not the biographer was a cleric or a layman, generally the effective rulers of the Middle Ages appear in a favorable light in the records. Two of the most powerful and respected kings of medieval Europe were Henry II of England (1154–1189) and St. Louis (Louis IX) of France (1226–1270). The best characterization of Henry II comes from a prominent cleric and contemporary, Gerald of Wales (d. 1220). If one remembers that Henry II forged the great Angevin Empire, renovated English legal and political institutions, sired an unruly brood of sons, played a key role in continental affairs, and fought a desperate encounter with Thomas Becket, archbishop of Canterbury, he will realize that Gerald's description is a masterpiece in the delineation of Henry's physical and mental traits. The best-known biography of a medieval king is that of St. Louis by the king's loyal companion Jean de Joinville (1234–1317), who in his eighty-fifth year dictated his memoirs on the beloved king. Even though an intimate of the king and a companion on the ill-fated crusade to Egypt in 1248, Joinville regarded his king objectively and criticized certain traits and policies. Joinville has given us one of our few close pictures of a medieval king, perhaps the greatest king of the Middle Ages.

A   *Gerald of Wales,* Expugnatio Hibernica (*"The Conquest of Ireland"*)

XLV]   *A description of Henry II, King of England*

IT were not amiss in this place to draw the portrait of the king, that so his person as well as his character may be familiar to posterity; and those who in future ages shall hear and read of his great achievements, may be able to picture him to themselves as he was. For the history on which I am employed must not suffer so noble an ornament of our times to pass away with only a slight notice. But herein we crave pardon for speaking the exact truth, for without it, history not only loses all authority, but does not even merit the name. It is the business of art to copy nature, and the painter is not to be trusted who exaggerates graces and conceals blemishes.

No man indeed is born without faults, but he is best who has the least; and the wise will think that nothing which concerns mankind is devoid of interest. There is no certainty in worldly matters, and no perfect happiness; good is mixed with evil, and virtue with vice. Wherefore, if things spoken in commendation of a man's disposition or conduct are pleasant to the ear, it should not be taken amiss if his faults are told. It was the remark of a philosopher, that princes ought to be treated with deference, and not exasperated by severe things being said of them; and a comic writer tells us that smooth words make friends, but the language of truth makes enemies; so that it is a dangerous matter to say anything against one who has the power of revenging himself; and it is still more perilous, and more arduous than profitable, to describe freely and in many words a prince who, by a single word, can consign you to ruin. It would surely be a pleasing task, but I confess that it is one beyond my powers, to tell the truth respecting a prince in everything without in any way offending him. But to the purpose.

Henry II, king of England, had a reddish complexion, rather dark, and a large round head. His eyes were grey, bloodshot, and flashed in anger. He had a fiery countenance, his voice was tremulous, and his

From Thomas Wright, THE HISTORICAL WORKS OF GIRALDUS CAMBRENSIS (London, 1905), pp. 249–253.

neck a little bent forward; but his chest was broad, and his arms were muscular. His body was fleshy, and he had an enormous paunch, rather by the fault of nature than from gross feeding. For his diet was temperate, and indeed in all things, considering he was a prince, he was moderate, and even parsimonious. In order to reduce and cure, as far as possible, this natural tendency and defect, he waged a continual war, so to speak, with his own belly by taking immoderate exercise. For in time of war, in which he was almost always engaged, he took little rest, even during the intervals of business and action. Times of peace were no seasons of repose and indulgence to him, for he was immoderately fond of the chase, and devoted himself to it with excessive ardour. At the first dawn of day he would mount a fleet horse, and indefatigably spend the day in riding through the woods, penetrating the depths of forests, and crossing the ridges of hills. On his return home in the evening he was seldom seen to sit down, either before he took his supper or after; for, notwithstanding his own great fatigue, he would weary all his court by being con-stantly on his legs. But it is one of the most useful rules in life, not to have too much of any one thing, and even medicine is not in itself perfect and always to be used; even so it befel this king. For he had frequent swellings in his legs and feet, increased much by his violent exercise on horseback, which added to his other complaints, and if they did not bring on serious disorders, at least hastened that which is the source of all, old age. In stature he may be reckoned among men of moderate height, which was not the case with either of his sons; the two eldest being somewhat above the middle height, and the two youngest somewhat below.

When his mind was undisturbed, and he was not in an angry mood, he spoke with great eloquence, and, what was remarkable in those days, he was well learned. He was also affable, flexible, and facetious, and, however he smothered his inward feelings, second to no one in courtesy. Withal, he was so clement a prince, that when he had subdued his enemies, he was overcome himself by his pity for them. Resolute in war, and provident in peace, he so much feared the doubtful fortune of the former, that, as the comic poet writes, he tried all courses before he resorted to arms. Those whom he lost in battle he lamented with more than a prince's sorrow, hav-ing a more humane feeling for the soldiers who had fallen than for the survivors; and bewailing the dead more than he cared for the living. In troublesome times no man was more courteous, and when all things were safe, no man more harsh. Severe to the unruly, but clement to the humble; hard towards his own household, but liberal to strangers; profuse abroad, but sparing at home; those whom he once hated, he would scarcely ever love, and from those he loved, he seldom withdrew his regard. He was inordinately fond of hawking and hunting, whether his falcons stooped on their prey, or his sagacious hounds, quick of scent and swift of foot, pursued the chase. Would to God he had been as zealous in his devotions as he was in his sports.

It is said that after the grievous dissensions between him and his sons, raised by their mother, he had no respect for the obligations of the most solemn treaties. True it is that from a certain natural inconstancy he often broke his word, preferring rather, when driven to straits, to forfeit his promise than depart from his purpose. In all his doings he was provident and circumspect, and on this account he was sometimes slack in the administration of justice, and, to his people's great cost, his decisions on all proceedings were dilatory. Both God and right demand that justice should be administered gratuitously, yet all things were set to sale and brought great wealth both to the clergy and laity; but their end was like Gehazi's gains.

He was a great maker of peace, and kept it himself; a liberal alms-giver, and an especial benefactor to the Holy Land. He loved the humble, curbed the nobility, and trod down the proud; filling the hungry with good things, and sending the rich empty away; exalting the meek, and putting down the mighty from their seat. He ventured on many detestable usurpations in things belonging to God, and through a zeal for justice (but not according to knowledge), he joined the rights of the church to those of the crown, and therein confused them, in order to centre all in himself. Although he was the son of the church, and received his crown from her hands, he either dissembled or forgot the sacramental unction. He could scarcely spare an hour to hear mass, and then he was more occupied in counsels and conversation about affairs of state than in his devotions. The revenues of the churches during their avoidance, he drew into his own treasury, laying hands on that which belonged to Christ; and as he was always in fresh troubles and engaged in mighty wars, he expended all the money he could get, and lavished upon unrighteous soldiers what was due to the priests. In his great prudence he devised many plans, which, however, did not all turn out according to his expectations; but no great mishap ever occurred, which did not originate in some trifling circumstance.

He was the kindest of fathers to his legitimate children during their childhood and youth, but as they advanced in years looked on them with an evil eye, treating them worse than a step-father; and although he had such distinguished and illustrious sons, whether it was that he would not have them prosper too fast, or whether they were ill-deserving, he could never bear to think of them as his successors. And as human prosperity can neither be permanent nor perfect, such was the exquisite malice of fortune against this king, that where he should have received comfort he met with opposition; where security, danger; where peace, turmoil; where support, ingratitude; where quiet and tranquility, disquiet and disturbance. Whether it happened from unhappy marriages, or for the punishment of the father's sins, there was never any good agreement either of the father with his sons, or of the sons with their parent, or between themselves.

At length, all pretenders to the government and disturbers of the peace being put down, and the brothers, his sons, and all others, both at home and abroad, being reconciled, all things succeeded according to his will. Would to God that he had, even late, acknowledged this crowning proof of the divine mercy by works worthy of repentance. I had almost forgotten to mention that his memory was so good, that, notwithstanding the multitudes who continually surrounded him, he never failed of recognizing any one he had ever seen before, nor did he forget any thing important which he had ever heard. He was also master of nearly the whole course of history, and well versed in almost all matters of experience. To conclude in few words: if this king had been finally chosen of God, and had turned himself to obey his commands, such were his natural endowments that he would have been, beyond all comparison, the noblest of all the princes of the earth in his times. But enough: let what I have written, briefly and imperfectly indeed, but not altogether foreign to my subject, content the reader. Having somewhat cleared the way for other writers to follow out so noble a passage of history, we will now return to our Ireland, from which we have digressed.

B *Jean de Joinville*, Histoire de Saint Louis ("*The History of Saint Louis*")

Beginning of the First Book — principal virtues of St. Lewis

IN the name of God Almighty, I, John, Lord of Joinville, seneschal of Champagne, dictate the life of our holy King Lewis; that which I saw and heard by the space of six years that I was in his company on pilgrimage oversea, and that which I saw and heard after we returned. And before I tell you of his great deeds, and of his prowess, I will tell you what I saw and heard of his good teachings and of his holy words, so that these may be found here set in order for the edifying of those who shall hear thereof.

This holy man loved God with all his heart, and followed Him in His acts; and this appeared in that, as God died for the love He bore His people, so did the king put his body in peril, and that several times, for the love he bore to his people; and such peril he might well have avoided, as you shall be told hereafter.

The great love that he bore to his people appeared in what he said during a very sore sickness that he had at Fontainebleau, unto my Lord Lewis, his eldest son. "Fair son," he said, "I pray thee to make thyself beloved of the people of thy kingdom; for truly I would rather that a Scot should come out of Scotland and govern the people of the kingdom well and equitably than that thou shouldest govern it ill in the sight of all men." The holy king so loved truth, that, as you shall hear hereafter, he would never consent to lie to the Saracens as to any covenant that he had made with them.

Of his mouth he was so sober, that on no day of my life did I ever hear him order special meats, as many rich men are wont to do; but he ate patiently whatever his cooks had made ready, and was set before him. In his words he was temperate; for on no day of my life did I ever hear him speak evil of any one; nor did I ever hear him name the Devil — which name is very commonly spoken throughout the kingdom, whereby God, as I believe, is not well pleased.

From Frank Marzials, MEMOIRS OF THE CRUSADES BY VILLEHARDOUIN AND DE JOINVILLE (London, 1908), pp. 139–143, 145–146, 148–150, 307–309, 316–318. Reprinted by permission of E. P. Dutton and Co.

He put water into his wine by measure, according as he saw that the strength of the wine would suffer it. At Cyprus he asked me why I put no water into my wine; and I said this was by order of the physicians, who told me I had a large head and a cold stomach, so that I could not get drunk. And he answered that they deceived me; for if I did not learn to put water into my wine in my youth, and wished to do so in my old age, gout and diseases of the stomach would take hold upon me, and I should never be in health; and if I drank pure wine in my old age, I should get drunk every night, and that it was too foul a thing for a brave man to get drunk.

He asked me if I wished to be honoured in this world, and to go into paradise at my death? And I said "Yes." And he said: "Keep yourself then from knowingly doing or saying anything which, if the whole world heard thereof, you would be ashamed to acknowledge, saying 'I did this,' or 'I said that.' " He told me to beware not to contradict or impugn anything that was said before me — unless indeed silence would be a sin or to my own hurt — because hard words often move to quarrelling, wherein men by the thousand have found death.

He said that men ought to clothe and arm their bodies in such wise that men of worth and age would never say, this man has done too much, nor young men say, this man has done too little. And I repeated this saying to the father of the king that now is, when speaking of the embroidered coats of arms that are made nowadays; and I told him that never, during our voyage oversea, had I seen embroidered coats, either belonging to the king or to any one else. And the king that now is told me that he had such suits, with arms embroidered, as had cost him eight hundred pounds *parisis*.[1] And I told him he would have employed the money to better purpose if he had given it to God, and had had his suits made of good taffeta (satin) ornamented with his arms, as his father had done.

St. Lewis's horror of sin — his love for the poor

He called me once to him and said: "Because of the subtle mind that is in you I dare not speak to you of the things relating to God; so I have summoned these two monks that are here, as I want to ask you a question." Now the question was this: "Seneschal," said he, "what manner of thing is God?" And I said: "Sire, it is so good a thing that there cannot be better." "Of a truth," said he, "you have answered well; for the answer that you have given is written in this book that I hold in my hand."

"Now I ask you," said he, "which you would the better like, either to be a leper, or to have committed a mortal sin?" And I, who never lied to him, made answer that I would rather have committed thirty mortal sins than be a leper. And when the monks had departed, he called me to him alone, and made me sit at his feet, and said, "How came you to say that to me yesterday?" And I told him that I said it again. And he answered, "You spoke hastily and as a fool. For you should know that there is no leprosy so hideous as the being in mortal sin, inasmuch as the soul that is in mortal sin is like unto the Devil; wherefore no leprosy can be so hideous. And sooth it is that, when a man dies, he is healed of the leprosy in his body; but when a man who has committed mortal sin dies, he cannot know of a certainty that he has, during his lifetime, repented in such sort that God has forgiven him; wherefore he must stand in great fear lest that leprosy of sin should last as long as God is in paradise. So I pray you," said he, "as strongly as I can, for the love of God, and for the love of me, so to set your heart that you prefer any evil that can happen to the body, whether it be leprosy, or any other sickness, rather than that mortal sin should enter into your soul."

He asked me if I washed the feet of the poor on Holy Thursday. "Sire," I said, "it would make me sick! The feet of these villains will I not wash." "In truth," said he, "that was ill said; for you should never disdain what God did for our teaching. So I pray you, for the love of God first, and then for the love of me, that you accustom yourself to wash the feet of the poor."

Regard of St. Lewis for worth and uprightness

He so loved all manner of people who had faith in God and loved Him, that he gave the constableship of France to my Lord Giles Le Brun, who was not of the kingdom of France, because men held him in so great repute for his faith and for love to God. And verily I believe that his good repute was well deserved.

He caused Master Robert of Sorbon[2] to eat at his table, because of the great repute in which he was held as a man of uprightness and worth. One day it chanced that Master Robert was eating at my side, and we were talking to one another. The king took us up, and said: "Speak out, for your companions think you are speaking ill of them. If you talk at table of things that can give us pleasure, speak out, and, if not, hold your peace."

When the king would be mirthful he would say to me: "Seneschal, tell me the reasons why a man of uprightness and worth (prud'-homme) is better than a friar?" Then would begin a discussion between me and Master Robert. When we had disputed for a long while, the king would give sentence and speak thus: "Master Robert, willingly would I bear the title of upright and worthy (prud'-homme) provided I were such in reality — and all the rest you might have. For uprightness and worth are such great things and such good things that even to name them fills the mouth pleasantly."

On the contrary, he said it was an evil thing to take other people's goods. "For," he said, "to restore is a thing so grievous, that even in the speaking the word restore scratches the throat by reason of the *rs* that are in it, and these *rs* are like so many rakes with which the Devil would draw to himself those who wish to 'restore' what they have taken from others. And very subtly does the Devil do this; for he works on great usurers and great robbers in such sort that they give to God what they ought to 'restore' to men."

He told me to warn King Thibaut, from him, to beware of the house of the Preachers of Provins, which he was building, lest he should encumber his soul on account of the great sums he was spending thereon. "For wise men," said he, "should, while they live, deal with their possessions as executors ought to do. Now the first thing a good executor does is to satisfy all the claims upon the dead, and pay back to others what is due to them, and it is only after having done this that he should spend in alms what remains of the dead man's possessions."

What St. Lewis thought about faith

The holy king endeavoured with all his power — as you shall here be told — to make me believe firmly in the Christian law, which God has given us. He said that we ought to believe so firmly the articles of faith that neither from fear of death, nor for any mischief that might happen to the body, should we be willing to go against them in word or deed. And he said that the Enemy is so subtle that, when people are dying, he labours all he can to make them die doubting as to some points of the faith. For he knows that he can in no wise deprive a man of the good works he has done; and he knows also that the man is lost to him if he dies in the faith.

Wherefore we should so guard and defend ourselves from this snare, as to say to the Enemy, when he sends such a temptation: "Away!" Yes, "Away!" must one say to the Enemy. "Thou shalt not tempt me so that I cease to believe firmly all the articles of the faith. Even if thou didst cause all my members to be cut off, yet would I live and die in the faith." And whosoever acts thus, overcomes the Enemy with the very club and sword that the Enemy desired to murder him withal.

He said that the Christian faith and creed were things in which we ought to believe firmly, even though we might not be certain of them except by hearsay. On this point he asked me what was my father's name? And I told him his name was Simon. And he asked how I knew it. And I said I thought I was certain of it, and believed it firmly, because my mother had borne witness thereto. Then he said, "So ought you to believe all the articles of the faith, to which the Apostles have borne witness, as also you chant of a Sunday in the Creed."

The devotions of St. Lewis — how he did justice in his land

The rule of his land was so arranged that every day he heard the hours sung, and a *Requiem* mass without song; and then, if it was convenient, the mass of the day, or of the saint, with song. Every day he rested in his bed after having eaten, and when he had slept and rested, he said, privily in his chamber — he and one of his chaplains together — the office for the dead; and after he heard vespers. At night he heard complines.

A gray-friar (Franciscan) came to him at the castle of Hyères, there where we disembarked; and said in his sermon, for the king's instruction, that he had read the Bible, and the books pertaining to heathen princes, and that he had never found, either among believers or misbelievers, that a kingdom had been lost, or had changed lords, save there had first been failure of justice. "Therefore let the king, who is going into France, take good heed," said he, "that he do justice well and speedily among his people, so that our Lord suffer his kingdom to remain in peace all the days of his life." It is said that the right worthy man who thus instructed the king, lies buried at Marseilles, where our Lord, for his sake, performs many a fine miracle. He would never consent to remain with the king, however much the king might urge it, for more than a single day.

The king forgat not the teaching of the friar, but ruled his land very loyally and godly, as you shall hear. He had so arranged that my Lord of Nesle, and the good Count of Soissons, and all of us who were about him, should go, after we had heard our masses, and hear the pleadings at the gate which is now called the gate of Requests.

And when he came back from church, he would send for us and sit at the foot of his bed, and make us all sit round him, and ask if there were any whose cases could not be settled save by himself in person. And we named the litigants; and he would then send for such and ask: "Why do you not accept what our people offer?" And they would make reply, "Sire, because they offer us very little." Then would he say, "You would do well to accept what is proposed, as our people desire." And the saintly man endeavoured thus, with all his power, to bring them into a straight path and a reasonable.

Ofttimes it happened that he would go, after his mass, and seat himself in the wood of Vincennes, and lean against an oak, and make us sit round him. And all those who had any cause in hand came and spoke to him, without hindrance of usher, or of any other person. Then would he ask, out of his own mouth, "Is there any one who has a cause in hand?" And those who had a cause in hand stood up. Then would he say, "Keep silence all, and you shall be heard in turn, one after the other." Then he would call my Lord Peter of Fontaines and my Lord Geoffry of Villette, and say to one of them, "Settle me this cause."

And when he saw that there was anything to amend in the words of those who spoke on his behalf, or in the words of those who spoke on behalf of any other person, he would himself, out of his own mouth, amend what they had said. Sometimes have I seen him, in summer, go to do justice among his people in the garden of Paris, clothed in a tunic of camlet, a surcoat of tartan without sleeves, and a mantle of black taffeta about his neck, his hair well combed, no cap, and a hat of white peacock's feathers upon his head. And he would cause a carpet to be laid down, so that we might sit round him, and all the people who had any cause to bring before him stood around. And then would he have their causes settled, as I have told you afore he was wont to do in the wood of Vincennes.

St. Lewis's love of peace

Now it happened that the saintly king laboured so effectually that the King of England,[3] his wife, and his children, came to France to treat of a peace between them and him. To this peace his council were strongly opposed, and they spoke to him thus: "Sire, we marvel greatly that you are minded to give to the King of England a great portion of the land which you and your predecessors have won from him, and which he has forfeited by misfeasance. Now it seems to us that if you believe you have no right to the land, you are not making full restitution unless you restore all the conquests that you and your predecessors have made; while if you believe that you have a right to the land, it seems to us that whatever you restore is restored to your loss."

To this the saintly king replied after the following manner: "Lords, I am convinced that the King of England's predecessors were rightfully dispossessed of all the conquered land that I hold; and the land that I am giving him I do not give as a thing that I am bound to give either to himself or to his heirs; but I give it so that there may be love between my children and his, who are cousins-german. And meseems that what I give him is given to good purpose, since he has not hitherto been by liegeman, but will now have to do me homage."

No man in the world laboured more to maintain peace among his subjects, and specially among the great men who were neighbours, and the princes of the realm; as, for instance, between the Count of Chalon, uncle of the Lord of Joinville, and his son the Count of Burgundy, who were at war when we came back from overseas. And in order to make peace between the father and the son he sent men of his council, at his own charges, into Burgundy; and by his efforts peace was established between the father and the son.

There was at that time war between King Thibaut the Second, of Champagne, and Count John of Chalon, and the Count of Burgundy, his son, regarding the abbey of Luxeuil. To appease this war my lord the king sent Gervais of Escraines, who was then master of the meats in France; and by his efforts he reconciled them.

After this war, which the king appeased, arose another war between the Count Thibaut of Bar and Count Henry of Luxemburg, who had the sister of Count Thibaut to wife. And so it happened that they fought together near Prény, and Count Thibaut of Bar made Count Henry of Luxemburg prisoner, and took the castle of Ligny, which belonged to the Count of Luxemburg in right of his wife. In order to appease this war the king sent, at his own charges, my Lord Peter the chamberlain, the man in the world in whom he had greatest faith; and the king laboured so effectually that they were reconciled.

As to the foreigners whom the king had reconciled, there were some of his council who said he would have done better to let them fight; for if he suffered them to impoverish themselves, they would attack him less readily than if they were rich. And to this the king made answer, and said that they spoke unwisely. "For if the neighbouring princes saw that I let them fight together, they might consult and say: 'It is from malice that he lets us fight together thus.' And so, perchance, out of hatred, they would come and fall upon me, which might be greatly to my loss, to say nothing of the enmity of God that I should incur, who has said: 'Blessed are the peacemakers.'"

Whence it also came that the people of Burgundy and Lorraine, whom he had pacified, loved and obeyed him so well that I have seen them come and plead their suits before him at his courts of Rheims, Paris and Orleans.

Love of St. Lewis for the poor — of his alms and pious foundations

From the time of his childhood, the king had pity on the poor and suffering; and the custom was that, wherever the king went, six score poor persons were always fed every day, in his house, with bread and wine, and meat or fish. In Lent and Advent the number of the poor was increased; and ofttimes it happened that the king served them, and set their food before them, and carved the meat before them, and gave them money with his own hand at their departing.

Particularly at the great vigils, before the solemn festivals, he served the poor in all matters as aforesaid, before he himself either ate or drank. Besides all this he had, every day, to dine or sup near him, old and broken men, and caused them to be fed with the same meats of which he himself partook; and when they had eaten they took away a certain sum of money.

Besides all this the king gave, day by day, large and great alms to the poor religiouses, to the poor in hospitals, to the poor sick, and to poor communities, also to poor gentlemen and ladies, and girls, and to fallen women, and to poor widows, and to women who were lying in, and to poor workmen, who through age or sickness could no longer work at their crafts; so that hardly would it be possible to number his alms. Therefore may it well be said that he was more fortunate than Titus, the Emperor of Rome, of whom old writings tell that he was sad and discomforted for any day on which he had not been able to confer some benefit.

From the first that he came to his kingdom and knew where he stood he began to erect churches, and many religious houses, among which the abbey of Royaumont bears the palm for honour and magnificence. He caused many almshouses to be erected: the alms-house of Paris, that of Pontoise, that of Compiègne and of Vernon, and assigned to them large rents. He founded the abbey of St. Matthew at Rouen, where he set women of the order of the Preaching Brothers; and he founded that of Longchamp, where he set women of the order of the Minorist Brothers, and assigned to them large rents for their livelihood.

And he allowed his mother to found the abbey of the Lis near Melun-sur-Seine, and the abbey near Pontoise, which is called Maubuisson, and there assigned to them large rents and possessions. And he caused to be built the House of the Blind, near Paris, for the reception of the poor blind of the city; and caused a chapel to be built for them, so that they might hear the service of God. And the good king caused the house of the Carthusians, which is called Vauvert, to be built outside Paris, and assigned sufficient rents to the monks who there served our Saviour.

Pretty soon after he caused another house to be built outside Paris, on the way to St. Denis, and it was called the house of the *Filles-Dieu;* and he caused to be placed there a great multitude of women who, through poverty, had lapsed into the sin of incontinence; and he gave them, for their maintenance, four hundred *livres* a year. And in many places of his kingdom he instituted houses for *béguines*,[4] and gave them rents for their livelihood, and commanded that any should be received therein who were minded to live in chastity.

There were some of his familiars who murmured at his giving such large alms, and because he expended so much; and he would say: "I like better that the great and excessive expenditure which I incur should be incurred in alms-giving for the love of God, than in pomp and splendour and for the vainglory of this world." Yet, notwithstanding that the king spent so largely in almsgiving, he did not forbear to incur daily great expenditure in his household. Largely and liberally did the king behave to the parliaments and assemblies of his barons and knights; and he caused his court to be served courteously, and largely, and without stint, and in more liberal fashion than aforetime in the court of his predecessors.

NOTES

Selection b

1. Money of Paris, a common French currency.
2. The chaplain of St. Louis who endowed a residence for poor students at the University of Paris and from whom the Sorbonne derived its name.
3. Henry III.
4. Women who lived by a rule and did charitable acts but did not take religious vows.

16

Medieval Restrictions on Royal Authority

By the twelfth and thirteenth centuries, when it became possible for men to examine the sources and proper limitations of political authority, they naturally centered their discussions on the king and invariably considered his authority from the viewpoint of feudal custom. But whether political theory was written in terms of feudal or natural law there was common agreement that the king, despite his extraordinary powers, must govern his realm in accordance with law, be responsive to the will of his subjects, protect the church, and fulfill the obligations understood to be in the contract made between king and subjects upon his coronation. The king who did not fulfill these obligations was regarded as having broken his contract and disregarded the law. He thus became a tyrant whom his subjects should remove, even by force if necessary. The three selections that follow illustrate the common theme of medieval political thought. John of Salisbury (1110–1180), relying heavily upon Biblical authority, took the extreme position, arguing that subjects were justified in killing a tyrant. Henry de Bracton (d. 1268), famous English jurist of the common law and author of the first comprehensive text on English law, emphasized the reciprocal nature of the feudal contract and developed an eloquent plea for the supremacy of the law over the ruler. Lastly, in the writing of Thomas Aquinas (1226–1274), there appears a reasoned justification for monarchy as the best form of government and a discussion of the circumstances under which the ruler may be removed from office.

A John of Salisbury, Policraticus ("The Statesman's Book")

III, 15] ... To kill a tyrant is not only licit but fair and just. For he who has taken up the sword deserves to die by the sword. But this is understood to refer to him who by his own audacity usurps the sword, not to him who receives from God the authority to use it. Surely he who receives authority from God preserves the laws and is a friend of justice and right. But he who usurps authority tramples on rights and submits the laws to his will. Therefore deservedly rights are armed against him who disarms the laws, and the public power rages against him who attempts to weaken the public hand. And although the crimes of *lèse-majesté* are many, there is none graver than this, which is exercised against the very body of justice. Therefore tyranny is not only a public crime, but, if this is possible, more than a public crime. For if the crime of *lèse-majesté* admits all men as prosecutors, how much more the crime committed against the laws which ought to have empire over emperors themselves! Certainly he who does not pursue the public enemy and take vengeance on him injures himself and the whole body of the earthly commonwealth.

VIII, 17] The tyrant, as the philosophers have painted him, is one who oppresses the people by violent domination, as the prince is one who rules them by laws. ... The prince fights for the laws and the liberty of the people; the tyrant thinks he has accomplished nothing until he has done away with the laws and reduced the people to slavery. The prince is a kind of image of Divinity and the tyrant is the image of the strength of the Enemy, of the wickedness of Lucifer, inasmuch as he imitates him who aspired to set his throne at the north and to be like the Most High, save for His goodness. ... The prince, image of the Deity, ought to be loved, honoured, and cherished; the tyrant, image of the Evil One, ought usually even to be killed. The origin of the tyrant is iniquity, and from the poisoned root grows and flourishes an evil and poisonous tree, which ought to be cut down by any axe. ...

18] Yet I do not deny that tyrants are ministers of God, Who by

From Ewart Lewis, MEDIEVAL POLITICAL IDEAS (New York, 1954), I, 276–278. By permission of Alfred A. Knopf, Inc.

His just judgment has willed them to exist in both primacies, that of souls and that of bodies, that the wicked may be punished through them, and the good corrected and disciplined. For the sins of the people cause a hypocrite to reign [Job 34:30] and, as the Book of Kings testifies, the faults of priests brought tyrants on the people of God. For the early fathers and the patriarchs followed nature, the best guide of life. Then came leaders, beginning with Moses, who kept the law, and judges who ruled the people by the authority of the law; and we read that there were priests. Yet in the rage of the Lord kings were given: some good, but others evil. For Samuel was old, and since his sons did not walk in his ways but pursued avarice and vice, the people, who perhaps had deserved that such priests should be in authority over them, extorted a king for themselves from God, Whom they had despised. Therefore Saul was elected, but with the predicted right of a king: that is, that he would take their sons and make them charioteers, and their daughters to become his bakers and his cooks, and their fields and farms to be distributed to his servants at his pleasure, and that he would oppress all the people with the yoke of slavery. Yet he was called the Lord's anointed; although he practised tyranny he did not lose the honour of a king. For God struck fear into all, that they should reverence him as minister of the Lord, Whose image, in a way, he bore. I shall even add that the tyrants of the gentiles, who have been condemned to death from eternity, are ministers of God and are called the Lord's anointed. . . . For all power is good, because it comes from Him from Whom alone are all things and only good things. Yet sometimes it is not good, but evil to the user or to him who suffers it, although in the broadest view it is good, since it is caused by Him who uses our ills to good purpose. For even as in a picture a dusky black colour or something else is considered unlovely in itself and yet adds beauty to the picture as a whole, so certain things which are perceived to be ugly and evil in themselves appear good and beautiful when they are related to the whole, since He whose every work is exceeding good adapts all things to Himself. Therefore the power even of the tyrant is good, yet nothing is worse than tyranny.

20] The Books of Kings and of Chronicles are a famous history in which . . . it is shown how Israel suffered under tyrants from the beginning, and that Judah, except for David, Josiah, and Hezekiah, had none but wicked kings. . . . And I shall easily be persuaded that

that stiff-necked and hard-hearted people who always resisted the Holy Spirit . . . and provoked God . . . to wrath had deserved tyrants for princes. For penitence blots out, excludes, and destroys the tyrants whom sins require, introduce, and raise to power. And indeed, before their kings, as the story of the judges tells, the children of Israel often served under tyrants, being afflicted at many and various times by divine dispensation; and often, crying to God, they were delivered. For when the time of that dispensation was finished it was permitted to them to cast off the yoke from their necks by the slaughter of the tyrants; and no blame rests on any one of those by whose courage a penitent and humbled people was set free, but he is rather remembered as the minister of God by the happy memory of posterity. . . . [This proposition is illustrated by the story of Ehud in Judges 3:14–24, of Jael in Judges 4:17–26, and of Judith in the Apocryphal book of that name.] The histories teach, however, that no one should attempt the slaying of a tyrant to whom he is bound by the obligation of fealty or an oath. . . . And, although I see that it is sometimes used by unbelievers, I do not read that any licence of poison has been granted by any right. . . . And indeed this is the most useful and safe way of destroying tyrants: that those who are oppressed should flee humbly to the protection of God's mercy, raising pure hands to the Lord in pious prayer, that they may turn aside the scourge with which they are afflicted. For the sins of the wicked are the strength of tyrants. . . .

21] The end of tyrants is confusion, leading to destruction, indeed, if they persist in wickedness; to forgiveness if they reform. For fire awaits the scourge itself when the Father has used it for the correction of His sons. . . . Moreover, wickedness is always punished by God; but sometimes He uses His own weapon and sometimes that of a man for the punishing of the unrighteous.

B Henry de Bracton, De Legibus et Consuetudinibus Regni Angliae ("Concerning the Laws and Customs of England")

What the sword signifies

There are other powerful ones under the king, who are called barons. . . . There are also others who are called vavassors. . . . Also, the knights are under the king. . . . There are also under the king freemen and serfs and those subject to his power, and indeed everyone is under him, and he himself is under no one save God alone.

The king has no peer

Moreover, the king has no peer in his kingdom, because thus he would lose his headship, since an equal has no command over his equal. Again, and all the more strongly, he ought not to have a superior, nor to have anyone more powerful, because thus he would be inferior to his own subjects, and inferiors cannot be equal to the more powerful. Moreover, the king ought not to be under man, but under God and under the law, because the law makes the king. Therefore let the king attribute to the law what the law has attributed to him, namely, domination and power. For there is no king where will rules and not law. And that he ought to be under the law, since he is the vicar of God, appears evidently through his likeness to Jesus Christ, Whose place he occupies on earth. Because the true mercy of God, when many ways were available to Him for the recovery of the human race, ineffably chose the most preferable way, by which He would use not the force of power but the reason of justice for the destruction of the devil's work. And thus He wished to be under the law, that He might redeem those who were under the law. For He did not wish to use force, but judgment. Likewise

From Ewart Lewis, MEDIEVAL POLITICAL IDEAS (New York, 1954), I, 279–284. By permission of Alfred A. Knopf, Inc.

also the blessed bearer of God, the Virgin Mary, Mother of the Lord, who by a singular privilege was above the law, yet to show an example of humility did not refuse to be subject to legal institutes. Thus, therefore, the king, that his power may not remain unbridled. Therefore, there ought not to be anyone greater than he in his own kingdom in the administration of law; however, he ought to be the least, or as if he were the least, if he seeks to obtain judgment. But if judgment is sought from him, since no writ runs against him himself, there will be place for a supplication that he may correct his act and amend it, and if he does not do so it suffices for his punishment that he await the vengeance of God. Let no one, indeed, presume to dispute his deeds, much less to oppose his acts.

That the judges ought not to dispute about or judge royal charters

Neither the judges nor private persons can or ought to dispute about royal charters and the deeds of kings; nor, if some doubt arise in regard to them, can they interpret it. Also, in doubtful or obscure matters, or if any expression may contain two meanings, the interpretation and wish of the lord king ought to be awaited, since interpretation belongs to him whose it is to establish. And even if it is altogether false because of an erasure or because the seal affixed is forged, it is better and safer that the judgment proceed in the presence of the king himself. [Likewise, no one can judge the deed or charter of the king so that the king's act is made void. But someone will be able to say that the king might have done justly and well, and if, by the same reasoning, he has done this, that it is ill done; and will be able to impose upon him the obligation of amending the injustice, lest the king and his justiciars fall into the judgment of the living God on account of the injustice. The king has a superior, namely, God. Likewise the law, through which he was made king. Likewise his court, namely, the counts and barons, because the counts are called, as it were, the partners of the king, and he who has a partner has a master. And therefore, if the king be without a bridle, that is, without law, they ought to put a bridle on him, unless they themselves are, with the king, without a bridle.]

Of franchises, and who can grant them, and what things belong to the king

Now, moreover, we should discuss franchises: who can grant them, and to whom, and how they are transferred, and how they are possessed or virtually possessed, and how they are retained by use. Who can grant them? The lord king himself, it should be known, who has ordinary jurisdiction and dignity and power over all men who are in his kingdom. For he has in his hand all the rights which belong to the crown, and the secular power, and the material sword which pertains to the governance of the realm. He also has justice and judgment, which belong to jurisdiction, that by his jurisdiction he may as minister and vicar of God assign to each what is his. He also has those things that belong to peace, that the people entrusted to him may be quiet and tranquil in peace and that no one may strike or wound or maltreat another, that no one may take away or carry off the goods of another by violence and robbery, and that no one may maim or slay any man. He also has the coercive power, that he may punish and coerce wrongdoers. He also has it in his power that he may himself in his own person observe and make his subjects observe the laws and statutes and assizes which have been provided and approved and sworn in his kingdom. For it is of no avail to establish rights unless there be someone to protect the rights. Therefore the king has rights and jurisdictions of this sort in his hand. He also has, before all others in his kingdom, privileges belonging to him by virtue of the law of peoples in the things which ought by natural law to belong to the finder, as, for instance, treasure trove, wrecks, the great fish, sturgeon, and castaways, which are said to be the property of no one. He also has in his hand by virtue of the law of peoples those things which by the law of nature ought to be common, as, for instance, wild beasts and wild birds, which ought to be common by natural law, through apprehension and capture and hunting. Likewise through the occupation and apprehension of the property of another, as when something is cast away or considered to have been abandoned. But the administration of justice and peace, and those things which are annexed to justice and peace, belong to no one save only the crown and the royal dignity, nor can they be separated from the crown, for they make the crown what it is. For the crown is to make justice and judgment, and to maintain peace, and without these things the crown can not consist nor hold. Moreover, rights or jurisdictions of this sort cannot be transferred to persons or tenements, nor possessed by a private person, nor can the use or execution of right, unless this were given from above, even as jurisdiction cannot be delegated in such a way that ordinary jurisdiction does not remain with the king himself. Those things which are called privileges of the crown, however, although they belong to the crown, can be separated from the crown and transferred to private persons. . . .

Of the organization of the jurisdictions of the kingdom. . . .

We should examine, in regard to those things which belong to the kingdom, who first and principally ought to and can judge them. And it should be known that the king himself and none other can and ought to judge, if alone he is adequate to this, since he is considered bound to this by virtue of his oath. For in his coronation, the oath having been presented, he ought in the name of Jesus Christ to promise these three things to the people subjected to him:

Of the oath which the king ought to make in his coronation

First, that he will command and, so far as he can, see to it that for the church of God and all the Christian people a true peace may be preserved throughout his time. Secondly, that he will forbid plunderings and all iniquities in all ranks. Thirdly, that in all his judgments he will prescribe equity and mercy, that the clement and merciful God may impart His mercy to him, and that through his justice all men may enjoy a firm peace.

For what the king was created, and of his ordinary jurisdiction

Moreover, the king was created and chosen for this: that he should make justice for all, and that in him the Lord should sit, and that he himself should decide his judgments, and that he should sustain and defend what he has justly judged, because if there were no one to make justice peace could easily be wiped out, and it would be vain to establish laws and to do justice if there were no one to protect the laws. Moreover, since the king is vicar of God on earth, he ought to separate right from unright, fair from unfair, that all those who are subjected to him may live honestly and that no one may injure another, and to each may be rendered by a just award what is his own. But he ought to surpass all his subjects in power. Moreover, he ought to have no peer, still less a superior, especially in the administration of justice, that it may truly be said of him, "Our great lord, and his great virtue," etc. Although in the receiving of justice he may be compared to the least person of his kingdom, although he excels all in power, yet since the heart of a king ought to be in the hand of God, lest his power be unbridled let him put on the bridle of temperance and the reins of moderation, lest if it be unbridled he be drawn towards injustice. For the king, since he is minister and vicar of God, can do nothing on earth save only that which is according to law, nor is this contrary to the saying that "what pleases the prince has the force of law," since there follows after "law" "since by the *lex regia* which was made concerning his rule, [etc.]" [*Digest,* 1, 4, 1]: that is, not what is rashly presumed to be the king's will but what has been duly defined with the counsel of his magnates, the king warranting its authority after deliberation and discussion upon it [*Codex,* 1, 14, 8]. Therefore his power is of right and not of unright, and since he is the author of right there ought not to be born occasion of unrights thence whence rights are born; and he who by virtue of his office must prohibit unright to others ought not to commit it himself in his own person. Therefore the king ought to exercise the power of right as God's vicar and minister on earth because that power is from God above; but the power of unright is from the Devil and not from God, and the king will be the minister of that one of the two whose works he does. Therefore, when he does justice he is the vicar of the Eternal King, but he is the Devil's minister when he falls into injustice. For a king (*rex*) is so called from ruling (*regendo*) well and not from reigning, because when he rules well he is a king, but he is a tyrant when he oppresses with violent domination the people entrusted to him. Therefore, let him temper his power by law, which is the bridle of power, that he may live according to the laws, since a human law has stated that laws bind the lawgiver himself, and elsewhere in the same source, "It is a saying worthy of the majesty of rulers that the prince profess himself bound by the laws" [*Codex*, 1, 14, 4]. Again, nothing is so proper to empire as to live by the laws, and "it is greater than empire to submit the principate to the laws," and deservedly he ought to give back to the law what the law has given to him, for the law makes him king. Again, since it is not always fitting that a king be armed with arms, but with laws, let the king learn wisdom and maintain justice, and God will grant it to him, and when he has found it he will be blessed if he has kept it, since in the speech of the sensible there is honour and glory, and in the tongue of the imprudent there lurks his overthrow; and the principate of the wise man is firm, and the sapient king will judge his people. . . .

C Thomas Aquinas, De Regimine Principum ("Concerning the Government of Princes")

II] WE must inquire whether it is more expedient for a province or city to be ruled by many or by one. Moreover, we can consider this by considering what the end of government is. For the objective of a ruler should be to procure the welfare of that which he undertakes to rule. The objective of a pilot should be to preserve his ship from the perils of the sea and bring it, unharmed, to the harbour of safety. Now the good and welfare of an associated multitude is the preservation of its unity, which is called peace, without which the utility of social life perishes — nay more, the discordant multitude becomes a burden to itself. This, therefore, is the special function of the ruler: to procure the unity of peace. . . . Now it is manifest that what is itself one can more effectively bring about unity than can a plurality, even as the most effective cause of heat is what is itself hot. Therefore, the government of one man is more useful than the government of many. Further, it is manifest that a plurality of men disagreeing about everything would not preserve the unity of a multitude at all. For there has to be a certain union among the many if they are to be able to rule at all, even as many helmsmen, unless they agree in some way, cannot bring a ship to one harbour;

From *Ewart Lewis*, MEDIEVAL POLITICAL IDEAS (New York, 1954), I, 284–287. By permission of Alfred A. Knopf, Inc.

now a plurality is said to be united as it approximates unity. Therefore, one man rules better than a plurality, because of approximation to unity. And again, things are at their best when they most resemble nature; for in each individual case nature does what is best; now the common natural rule is by one; for among the many parts of the body there is one, namely, the heart, which moves all the others, and among the parts of the soul one force, namely, reason, presides as ruler. And the bees have one king, and in the whole universe there is one God, Maker and Ruler of all. This is rational, for all multiplicity is derived from unity. Wherefore, if those things that are produced by art imitate those that follow nature, and since a work of art is better in proportion as it copies what is natural, it is necessarily best for the human multitude to be ruled by one man. This is also apparent from experience. For the provinces or cities that are not ruled by one man suffer dissensions and vacillate without peace. Thus the lamentation seems to be fulfilled that the Lord made through His prophet, saying: "Many shepherds have destroyed My vineyard." On the contrary, however, provinces and cities that are ruled by one king enjoy peace, flourish in justice, and rejoice in an abundance of riches. Whence the Lord promised through His prophets, as a great gift to His people, that He would give them one head, and one prince would be in the midst of them.

vi] Therefore, because the government of one man, which is the best, is to be preferred, and because it may happen that this is changed into tyranny, which is the worst, . . . diligent care should be used to provide a king for the multitude in such a way that they will not fall under a tyrant. First, from among those eligible to this office there must be chosen for the kingship a man of such character that he is not likely to lapse into tyranny. . . . Next, the government of the kingdom should be so arranged that the opportunity of tyranny is withdrawn from the king when he is instituted. And at the same time his power should be tempered, so that he cannot easily lapse into tyranny. The things to be done will be considered later.

But now we should consider how the situation could be met if the king should turn to tyranny. And, indeed, if the tyranny is not excessive, it would be more expedient to endure a lax tyranny for a time rather than to bring about many dangers graver than the tyranny itself by opposing it. For it may happen that those who oppose the tyrant cannot prevail, and the tyrant, provoked by their opposition, grows more cruel. But if some one is able to prevail against the tyrant, this very fact often leads to the most serious dissensions in the people, either in the course of the rebellion or when, after the tyrant is overthrown, the multitude breaks into factions over the ordination of the government. It also sometimes happens that when the multitude expels a tyrant with the help of a certain leader, he in turn seizes tyrannical power and in the fear of sharing the fate of his predecessor he may oppress his subjects with even heavier servitude. . . .

If the tyranny is extreme beyond endurance, some people have thought that it is appropriate to the virtue of brave men to kill the tyrant and to expose themselves to the risk of death for the liberation of the multitude; and there is an instance of this in the Old Testament. For a certain Ehud killed Eglon, king of Moab, with a dagger thrust into his side, because he was oppressing the people of God with heavy servitude; and he became a judge of the people [Judges 3]. But this does not agree with the teaching of the apostles. For Peter teaches us to be reverently subject "not only to good and moderate rulers, but also to the harsh" [I Peter 2:18]. . . . Moreover, if people should attempt the death of rulers, even of tyrants, by private presumption, it would be dangerous to the multitude and to its rulers. For evil men expose themselves to risks of this sort more often than the good, and the dominion of kings, no less than of tyrants, is generally burdensome to evildoers. . . . Therefore, such presumption would be more likely to result in the loss to the multitude of a good king than in the beneficial abolition of a tyrant.

Thus it seems that action against a tyrant should not be taken by the private presumption of individuals but rather by public authority. First, if the multitude has the right to provide itself with a king, it can justly depose its king or restrain his power if he tyrannically abuses his royal authority. And in this case the multitude should not be considered to act disloyally in deposing a tyrant, since if he does not bear himself faithfully in the government of the multitude, as the office of king requires, his subjects are no longer bound by their contract with him. . . . If, however, some superior has the right to provide the multitude with a king, they should look to him for a remedy against the evildoing of the tyrant. . . . But if no human aid at all can be obtained against the tyrant, recourse must be had to God, King of all, Who gives aid in time of tribulation. . . .

17

Magna Carta

ALTHOUGH the Middle Ages have traditionally been associated with political instability, feudal anarchy, and particularism, the political institutions and thought of the western world owe much of their success and appeal to certain medieval political developments and traditions. It must be remembered that the success of feudalism depended upon the contract entailing mutual obligations of lord and vassal. Either party could be punished for not fulfilling these obligations. The ultimate penalty for a king could be renouncement by his vassals of feudal obligation to him, which amounted to deposition. Such action, however, was not fruitful or constructive unless the malcontents presented their grievances and made provision for their remedy and support in the future. This entailed a spirit of unity and cooperation that is found earliest and most constantly in England. Despite the power and efficiency of the Norman-Angevin kings, government under John (1199–1216) became so arbitrary and unpopular that the English barons renounced their feudal ties to John, revolted, and forced his consent to the famous Magna Carta of June 15, 1215. Fundamentally a feudal document attempting to redress grievances of the barons, Magna Carta did not, as is popularly believed, benefit the majority of English subjects. Because its clauses dealt, however, with fundamental issues affecting king and subject, they eventually came to be used as precedents for the development of constitutional devices that limited the king. Magna Carta was therefore the first successful attempt to restrict the powers of a medieval king, an event which sparked a series of developments culminating in the civil and political privileges of our western democratic governments.

Magna Carta

JOHN, by the grace of God, king of England, lord of Ireland, duke of Normandy and Aquitaine, count of Anjou, to the archbishops, bishops, abbots, earls, barons, justiciars, foresters, sheriffs,

From E. P. Cheyney, TRANSLATIONS AND REPRINTS FROM THE ORIGINAL SOURCES OF EUROPEAN HISTORY: ENGLISH MEDIAEVAL INSTITUTIONS (Philadelphia, 1900), I, no. 6, 6–17.

reeves, servants, and all bailiffs and his faithful people greeting. Know that by the suggestion of God and for the good of our soul and those of all our predecessors and of our heirs, to the honor of God and the exaltation of holy church, and the improvement of our kingdom, by the advice of our venerable fathers Stephen, archbishop of Canterbury, primate of all England and cardinal of the holy Roman church, Henry, archbishop of Dublin, William of London, Peter of Winchester, Jocelyn of Bath and Glastonbury, Hugh of Lincoln, Walter of Worcester, William of Coventry, and Benedict of Rochester, bishops; of Master Pandulf, subdeacon and member of the household of the lord Pope, of Brother Aymeric, master of the Knights of the Temple in England; and of the noblemen William Marshall, earl of Pembroke, William, earl of Salisbury, William, earl of Warren, William, earl of Arundel, Alan of Galloway, constable of Scotland, Warren Fitz-Gerald, Peter Fitz-Herbert, Hubert de Burgh, steward of Poitou, Hugh de Nevil, Matthew Fitz-Herbert, Thomas Bassett, Alan Bassett, Philip d'Albini, Robert de Roppelay, John Marshall, John Fitz-Hugh, and others of our faithful.

1] In the first place we have granted to God, and by this our present charter confirmed, for us and our heirs forever, that the English church shall be free, and shall hold its rights entire and its liberties uninjured; and we will that it thus be observed; which is shown by this, that the freedom of elections, which is considered to be most important and especially necessary to the English church, we, of our pure and spontaneous will, granted, and by our charter confirmed, before the contest between us and our barons had arisen; and obtained a confirmation of it by the lord Pope Innocent III; which we will observe and which we will shall be observed in good faith by our heirs forever.

We have granted moreover to all free men of our kingdom for us and our heirs forever all the liberties written below, to be had and holden by themselves and their heirs from us and our heirs.

2] If any of our earls or barons, or others holding from us in chief by military service shall have died, and when he has died his heir shall be of full age and owe relief, he shall have his inheritance by the ancient relief; that is to say, the heir or heirs of an earl for the whole barony of an earl a hundred pounds; the heir or heirs of a baron for a whole barony a hundred pounds; the heir or heirs of a knight, for a whole knight's fee, a hundred shillings at most; and who owes less let him give less according to the ancient custom of fiefs.

3] If moreover the heir of any one of such shall be under age, and shall be in wardship, when he comes of age he shall have his inheritance without relief and without a fine.

4] The custodian of the land of such a minor heir shall not take from the land of the heir any except reasonable products, reasonable customary payments, and reasonable services, and this without destruction or waste of men or of property; and if we shall have committed the custody of the land of any such a one to the sheriff or to any other who is to be responsible to us for its proceeds, and that man shall have caused destruction or waste from his custody we will recover damages from him, and the land shall be committed to two legal and discreet men of that fief, who shall be responsible for its proceeds to us or to him to whom we have assigned them; and if we shall have given or sold to any one the custody of any such land, and he has caused destruction or waste there, he shall lose that custody, and it shall be handed over to two legal and discreet men of that fief who shall be in like manner responsible to us as is said above.

5] The custodian moreover, so long as he shall have the custody of the land, must keep up the houses, parks, warrens, fish ponds, mills, and other things pertaining to the land, from the proceeds of the land itself; and he must return to the heir, when he has come to full age, all his land, furnished with ploughs and implements of husbandry according as the time of wainage requires and as the proceeds of the land are able reasonably to sustain.

6] Heirs shall be married without disparity, so nevertheless that before the marriage is contracted, it shall be announced to the relatives by blood of the heir himself.

7] A widow, after the death of her husband, shall have her marriage portion and her inheritance immediately and without obstruction, nor shall she give anything for her dowry or for her marriage portion, or for her inheritance which inheritance her husband and she held on the day of the death of her husband; and she may remain in the house of her husband for forty days after his death, within which time her dowry shall be assigned to her.

8] No widow shall be compelled to marry so long as she prefers to live without a husband, provided she gives security that she will not marry without our consent, if she holds from us, or without the consent of her lord from whom she holds, if she holds from another.

9] Neither we nor our bailiffs will seize any land or rent, for any debt, so long as the chattels of the debtor are sufficient for the payment of the debt; nor shall the pledges of a debtor be distrained so long as the principal debtor himself has enough for the payment of the debt; and if the principal debtor fails in the payment of the debt, not having the wherewithal to pay it, the pledges shall be responsible for the debt; and if they wish, they shall have the lands and the rents of the debtor until they shall have been satisfied for the debt which they have before paid for him, unless the principal debtor shall have shown himself to be quit in that respect towards those pledges.

10] If any one has taken anything from the Jews, by way of a loan, more or less, and dies before that debt is paid, the debt shall not draw interest so long as the heir is under age, from whomsoever he holds; and if that debt falls into our hands, we will take nothing except the chattel contained in the agreement.

11] And if any one dies leaving a debt owing to the Jews, his wife shall have her dowry, and shall pay nothing of that debt; and if there remain minor children of the dead man, necessaries shall be provided for them corresponding to the holding of the dead man; and from the remainder shall be paid the debt, the service of the lords being retained. In the same way debts are to be treated which are owed to others than the Jews.

12] No scutage or aid shall be imposed in our kingdom except by the common council of our kingdom, except for the ransoming of our body, for the making of our oldest son a knight, and for once marrying our oldest daughter, and for these purposes it shall be only a reasonable aid; in the same way it shall be done concerning the aids of the city of London.

13] And the city of London shall have all its ancient liberties and free customs, as well by land as by water. Moreover, we will and grant that all other cities and boroughs and villages and ports shall have all their liberties and free customs.

14] And for holding a common council of the kingdom concerning the assessment of an aid otherwise than in the three cases mentioned above, or concerning the assessment of a scutage we shall cause to be summoned the archbishops, bishops, abbots, earls, and greater barons by our letters under seal; and besides we shall cause to be summoned generally, by our sheriffs and bailiffs all those who hold from us in chief, for a certain day, that is at the end of forty days at least, and for a certain place; and in all the letters of that summons, we will express the cause of the summons, and when the summons has thus been given the business shall proceed on the appointed day, on the advice of those who shall be present, even if not all of those who were summoned have come.

15] We will not grant to any one, moreover, that he shall take an aid from his free men, except for ransoming his body, for making his oldest son a knight, and for once marrying his oldest daughter; and for these purposes only a reasonable aid shall be taken.

16] No one shall be compelled to perform any greater service for a knight's fee, or for any other free tenement than is owed from it.

17] The common pleas shall not follow our court, but shall be held in some certain place.

18] The recognitions of *novel disseisin, mort d'ancestor,* and *darrein presentment* shall be held only in their own counties and in this manner: we, or if we are outside of the kingdom our principal justiciar, will send two justiciars through each county four times a year, who with four knights of each county, elected by the county, shall hold in the county and on the day and in the place of the county court, the aforesaid assizes of the county.

19] And if the aforesaid assizes cannot be held within the day of the county court, a sufficient number of knights and free-holders shall remain from those who were present at the county court on that day to give the judgments, according as the business is more or less.

20] A free man shall not be fined for a small offence, except in proportion to the measure of the offence; and for a great offence he shall be fined in proportion to the magnitude of the offence, saving his freehold; and a merchant in the same way, saving his merchandise; and the villain shall be fined in the same way, saving his wainage, if he shall be at our mercy; and none of the above fines shall be imposed except by the oaths of honest men of the neighborhood.

21] Earls and barons shall only be fined by their peers, and only in proportion to their offence.

22] A clergyman shall be fined, like those before mentioned, only in proportion to his lay holding, and not according to the extent of his ecclesiastical benefice.

23] No manor or man shall be compelled to make bridges over the rivers except those which ought to do it of old and rightfully.

24] No sheriff, constable, coroners, or other bailiffs of ours shall hold pleas of our crown.

25] All counties, hundreds, wapentakes, and trithings[1] shall be at the ancient rents and without any increase, excepting our demesne manors.

26] If any person holding a lay fief from us shall die, and our sheriff or bailiff shall show our letters-patent of our summons concerning a debt which the deceased owed to us, it shall be lawful for our sheriff or bailiff to attach and levy on the chattels of the deceased found on his lay fief, to the value of that debt, in the view of legal men, so nevertheless that nothing be removed thence until the clear debt to us shall be paid; and the remainder shall be left to the executors for the fulfilment of the will of the deceased; and if nothing is owed to us by him, all the chattels shall go to the deceased, saving to his wife and children their reasonable shares.

27] If any free man dies intestate, his chattels shall be distributed by the hands of his near relatives and friends, under the oversight of the church, saving to each one the debts which the deceased owed to him.

28] No constable or other bailiff of ours shall take anyone's grain or other chattels, without immediately paying for them in money, unless he is able to obtain a postponement at the good-will of the seller.

29] No constable shall require any knight to give money in place of his ward of a castle if he is willing to furnish that ward in his own person or through another honest man, if he himself is not able to do it for a reasonable cause; and if we shall lead or send him into the army he shall be free from ward in proportion to the amount of time by which he has been in the army through us.

30] No sheriff or bailiff of ours or any one else shall take horses or wagons of any free man for carrying purposes except on the permission of that free man.

31] Neither we nor our bailiffs will take the wood of another man for castles, or for anything else which we are doing, except by the permission of him to whom the wood belongs.

32] We will not hold the lands of those convicted of a felony for more than a year and a day, after which the lands shall be returned to the lords of the fiefs.

33] All the fish-weirs in the Thames and the Medway, and throughout all England shall be done away with, except those on the coast.

34] The writ which is called *praecipe* shall not be given for the future to anyone concerning any tenement by which a free man can lose his court.

35] There shall be one measure of wine throughout our whole kingdom, and one measure of ale, and one measure of grain, that is the London quarter, and one width of dyed cloth and of russets and of halbergets, that is two ells within the selvages; of weights, moreover it shall be as of measures.

36] Nothing shall henceforth be given or taken for a writ of inquisition concerning life or limbs, but it shall be given freely and not denied.

37] If anyone holds from us by fee farm or by soccage or by burgage, and from another he holds land by military service, we will not have the guardianship of the heir or of his land which is of the fief of another, on account of that fee farm, or soccage, or burgage; nor will we have the custody of that fee farm, or soccage, or burgage, unless that fee farm itself owes military service. We will not have the guardianship of the heir or of the land of anyone, which he holds from another by military service on account of any petty serjeanty which he holds from us by the service of paying to us knives or arrows, or things of that kind.

38] No bailiff for the future shall place any one to his law on his simple affirmation, without credible witnesses brought for this purpose.

39] No free man shall be taken or imprisoned or dispossessed, or outlawed, or banished, or in any way destroyed, nor will we go upon him, nor send upon him, except by the legal judgment of his peers or by the law of the land.

40] To no one will we sell, to no one will we deny, or delay right or justice.

41] All merchants shall be safe and secure in going out from England and coming into England and in remaining and going through England, as well by land as by water, for buying and selling, free from all evil tolls, by the ancient and rightful customs, except in time of war, and if they are of a land at war with us; and if such are found in our land at the beginning of war, they shall be attached without injury to their bodies or goods, until it shall be known from us or from our principal justiciar in what way the merchants of our land are treated who shall be then found in the country which is at war with us; and if ours are safe there, the others shall be safe in our land.

42] It is allowed henceforth to anyone to go out from our kingdom, and to return, safely and securely, by land and by water, saving their fidelity to us, except in time of war for some short time, for the common good of the kingdom; excepting persons imprisoned and outlawed according to the law of the realm, and people of a land at war with us, and merchants, of whom it shall be done as is before said.

43] If anyone holds from any escheat, as from the honor of Wallingford, or Nottingham, or Boulogne, or Lancaster, or from other escheats which are in our hands and are baronies, and he dies, his heir shall not give any other relief, nor do to us any other service than he would do to the baron, if that barony was in the hands of the baron; and we will hold it in the same way as the baron held it.

44] Men who dwell outside the forest shall not henceforth come before our justiciars of the forest, on common summons, unless they are in a plea of, or pledges for any person or persons who are arrested on account of the forest.

45] We will not make justiciars, constables, sheriffs or bailiffs except of such as know the law of the realm and are well inclined to observe it.

46] All barons who have founded abbeys for which they have charters of kings of England, or ancient tenure, shall have their custody when they have become vacant, as they ought to have.

47] All forests which have been afforested in our time shall be disafforested immediately; and so it shall be concerning river banks which in our time have been fenced in.

48] All the bad customs concerning forests and warrens and concerning foresters and warreners, sheriffs and their servants, river banks and their guardians shall be inquired into immediately in each county by twelve sworn knights of the same county, who shall be elected by the honest men of the same county, and within forty days after the inquisition has been made, they shall be entirely destroyed by them, never to be restored, provided that we be first informed of it, or our justiciar, if we are not in England.

49] We will give back immediately all hostages and charters which have been liberated to us by Englishmen as security for peace or for faithful service.

50] We will remove absolutely from their bailiwicks the relatives of Gerard de Athyes, so that for the future they shall have no bailiwick in England; Engelard de Cygony, Andrew, Peter and Gyon de Chancelles, Gyon de Cygony, Geoffrey de Martin and his brothers, Philip Mark and his brothers, and Geoffrey his nephew and their whole retinue.

51] And immediately after the re-establishment of peace we will remove from the kingdom all foreign-born soldiers, cross-bow men, servants, and mercenaries who have come with horses and arms for the injury of the realm.

52] If anyone shall have been dispossessed or removed by us without legal judgment of his peers, from his lands, castles, franchises, or his right we will restore them to him immediately; and if contention arises about this, then it shall be done according to the judgment of the twenty-five barons, of whom mention is made below concerning the security of the peace. Concerning all those things, however, from which anyone has been removed or of which he has been deprived without legal judgment of his peers by King Henry our father, or by King Richard our brother, which we have in our hand, or which others hold, and which it is our duty to guarantee, we shall have respite till the usual term of crusaders; excepting those things about which the suit has been begun or the inquisition made by our writ before our assumption of the cross; when, however, we shall return from our journey or if by chance we desist from the journey, we will immediately show full justice in regard to them.

53] We shall, moreover, have the same respite and in the same manner about showing justice in regard to the forests which are to be disafforested or to remain forests, which Henry our father or Richard our brother made into forests; and concerning the custody of lands which are in the fief of another, custody of which we have until now had on account of a fief which anyone has held from us by military service; and concerning the abbeys which have been founded in fiefs of others than ourselves, in which the lord of the fee has asserted for himself a right; and when we return or if we should desist from our journey we will immediately show full justice to those complaining in regard to them.

54] No one shall be seized nor imprisoned on the appeal of a woman concerning the death of anyone except her husband.

55] All fines which have been imposed unjustly and against the law of the land, and all penalties imposed unjustly and against the law of the land are altogether excused, or will be on the judgment of the twenty-five barons of whom mention is made below in connection with the security of the peace, or on the judgment of the majority of them, along with the aforesaid Stephen, archbishop of Canterbury, if he is able to be present, and others whom he may wish to call for this purpose along with him. And if he should not be able to be present, nevertheless the business shall go on without him, provided that if any one or more of the aforesaid twenty-five barons are in a similar suit they should be removed as far as this particular judgment goes, and others who shall be chosen and put upon oath, by the remainder of the twenty-five shall be substituted for them for this purpose.

56] If we have dispossessed or removed any Welshmen from their lands, or franchises, or other things, without legal judgment of their peers, in England, or in Wales, they shall be immediately returned to them; and if a dispute shall have arisen over this, then it shall be settled in the borderland by judgment of their peers, concerning holdings of England according to the law of England, concerning holdings of Wales according to the law of Wales, and concerning holdings of the borderland according to the law of the borderland. The Welsh shall do the same to us and ours.

57] Concerning all those things, however, from which any one of the Welsh shall have been removed or dispossessed without legal judgment of his peers, by King Henry our father, or King Richard our brother, which we hold in our hands, or which others hold, and we are bound to warrant to them, we shall have respite till the usual period of crusaders, those being excepted about which suit was begun or inquisition made by our command before our assumption of the cross. When, however, we shall return or if by chance we shall desist from our journey, we will show full justice to them immediately, according to the laws of the Welsh and the aforesaid parts.

58] We will give back the son of Lewellyn immediately, and all the hostages from Wales and the charters which had been liberated to us as a security for peace.

59] We will act toward Alexander, king of the Scots, concerning the return of his sisters and his hostages, and concerning his franchises and his right, according to the manner in which we shall act toward our other barons of England, unless it ought to be otherwise by the charters which we hold from William his father, formerly king of the Scots, and this shall be by the judgment of his peers in our court.

60] Moreover, all those customs and franchises mentioned above which we have conceded in our kingdom, and which are to be fulfilled, as far as pertains to us, in respect to our men; all men of our kingdom as well clergy as laymen, shall observe as far as pertains to them, in respect to their men.

61] Since, moreover, for the sake of God, and for the improvement of our kingdom, and for the better quieting of the hostility sprung up lately between us and our barons, we have made all these concessions; wishing them to enjoy these in a complete and firm stability forever, we make and concede to them the security described below; that is to say, that they shall elect twenty-five barons of the kingdom, whom they will, who ought with all their power to observe, hold, and cause to be observed, the peace and liberties which we have conceded to them, and by this our present charter confirmed to them; in this manner, that if we or our justiciar, or our bailiffs, or any one of our servants shall have done wrong in any way toward any one, or shall have transgressed any of the articles of peace or security; and the wrong shall have been shown to four barons of the aforesaid twenty-five barons, let those four barons come to us or to our justiciar, if we are out of the kingdom, laying before us the transgression, and let them ask that we cause that transgression to be corrected without delay. And if we shall not have corrected the transgression or, if we shall be out of the kingdom, if our justiciar shall not have corrected it within a period of forty days, counting from the time in which it has been shown to us or to our justiciar, if we are out of the kingdom; the aforesaid four barons shall refer the matter to the remainder of the twenty-five barons, and let these twenty-five barons with the whole community of the country distress and injure us in every way they can; that is to say by the seizure of our castles, lands, possessions, and in such other ways as they can until it shall have been corrected according to their judgment, saving our person and that of our queen, and those of our children; and when the correction has been made, let them devote themselves to us as they did before. And let whoever in the country wishes take an oath that in all the above-mentioned measures he will obey the orders of the aforesaid twenty-five barons, and that he will injure us as far as he is able with them, and we give permission to swear publicly and freely to each one who wishes to swear, and no one will we ever forbid to swear. All those, moreover, in the country who of themselves and their own will are unwilling to take an oath to the twenty-five barons as to distressing and injuring us along with them, we will compel to take the oath by our mandate, as before said. And if any one of the twenty-five barons shall have died or departed from the land or shall in any other way be prevented from taking the above-mentioned action, let the remainder of the aforesaid twenty-five barons choose another in his place, according to their judgment, who shall take an oath in the same way as the others. In all those things, moreover, which are committed to those five and twenty barons to carry out, if perhaps the twenty-five are present, and some disagreement arises among them about something, or if any of them when they have been summoned are not willing or are not able to be present, let that be considered valid and firm which the greater part of those who are present arrange or command, just as if the whole twenty-five had agreed in this; and let the aforesaid twenty-five swear that they will observe faithfully all the things which are said above, and with all their ability cause them to be observed. And we will obtain nothing from anyone, either by ourselves or by another by which any of these concessions and liberties shall be revoked or diminished; and if any such thing shall have been obtained, let it be invalid and void, and we will never use it by ourselves or by another.

62] And all ill-will, grudges, and anger sprung up between us and our men, clergy and laymen, from the time of the dispute, we have fully renounced and pardoned to all. Moreover, all transgressions committed on account of this dispute, from Easter in the sixteenth year of our reign till the restoration of peace, we have fully remitted to all, clergy and laymen, and as far as pertains to us, fully pardoned. And moreover we have caused to be made for them testimonial letters-patent of lord Stephen, archbishop of Canterbury, lord Henry, archbishop of Dublin, and of the aforesaid bishops and of master Pandulf, in respect to that security and the concessions named above.

63] Wherefore we will and firmly command that the Church of England shall be free, and that the men in our kingdom shall have and hold all the aforesaid liberties, rights and concessions, well and peacefully, freely and quietly, fully and completely, for themselves and their heirs, from us and our heirs, in all things and places, forever, as before said. It has been sworn, moreover, as well on our part as on the part of the barons, that all these things spoken of above shall be observed in good faith and without any evil intent. Witness the above named and many others. Given by our hand in the meadow which is called Runnymede, between Windsor and Staines, on the fifteenth day of June, in the seventeenth year of our reign.

NOTE

1. Local administrative districts.